To:
Mrs. macdonald.
    When glancing
through this book,
remember the class
            of
            1982
    Best Wishes!

AMERICAN PLAYS AND PLAYWRIGHTS
OF THE CONTEMPORARY THEATRE

Also by ALLAN LEWIS

The Contemporary Theatre

AMERICAN PLAYS AND PLAYWRIGHTS OF THE CONTEMPORARY THEATRE

by

ALLAN LEWIS

CROWN PUBLISHERS, INC.   NEW YORK

For Lanny

ACKNOWLEDGMENTS

Much of the material in this book is an outgrowth of lectures given at The New School for Social Research.

To a demanding audience, eager to know how the theatre can serve in shaping the future of society, this writer is indebted. Acknowledgments also should be made to the New School itself, which permitted whatever experiment in teaching the author preferred; to a wife and daughter who tolerated a critic in the house; to Ira Sollar, who generously supplied the funds for secretarial assistance; to Kay Pinney, who read the manuscript; and to Herbert Michelman, an understanding and patient editor.

CONTENTS

INTRODUCTION — "*The Purpose of Playing . . .*"

That is why we must have a theatre; for above all, the theatre places man in the centre of the world. We must have a point of adventurous stillness, the quiet eye of the storm, from which to witness the age-old revelation of a man challenging God in the working out of his fate.
ARTHUR MILLER

For this writing of plays is a great matter, forming as it does the minds and affections of men in such sort that whatsoever they see done in show on the stage, they will presently be doing in earnest in the world.
GEORGE BERNARD SHAW, The Dark Lady of the Sonnets

A BOOK ON THE AMERICAN THEATRE today becomes of necessity a critical analysis of plays and playwrights. Performance and production, though close in time and memorable on occasion, are the least enduring of the theatre arts, and become significant only as they reveal new interpretations or develop a language which establishes communion with the audience.

Important plays are cultural milestones holding within them the hopes, dreams, struggles, victories, and ceaseless inquietude of man's conflict with himself and the external world. The actual physical production in the theatre remains as memory. The script survives, and therefore receives major emphasis, but it is a single element in an aggregate of architecture, design, acting, direction. Unlike sculpture and painting, and more like music, the theatre is an art which endures only as it, like Dionysus, is repeatedly brought back to life. The script is the link to history at a particular level of consciousness, and is available for study, but the power of the theatre is its living impact on audiences.

This book is not an anthology or a comment on all plays presented between 1957 and 1964. Rather, it is an effort to judge the theatre today as part of a continuing experience, with roots in the past; to witness our heritage unfolding in contemporary terms and in relation to a changing historical situation, to observe what trends reach out to the future, and to serve as a guide to the often confusing and complex diversity of the theatre today.

The basic problem facing man is that of survival. A nuclear age compels decisions, the most dramatic decisions of all history. Either man gives way to despair and denial and passively awaits annihilation, in which event the theatre or criticism of it is unnecessary, or he acts in the belief that man who created the present overwhelming dilemma can also create the will to conquer it.

The dichotomy between pessimism and hope—between lamenting at the abyss of the grave and hailing a future with unprecedented possibilities—has sharpened. It is our conviction that the tide has turned toward responsibility and commitment, toward an aroused conscience which prefers the search for values to research for destruction. "Our choice," Arnold Toynbee has said, "is going to be, not between a whole world and a shredded-up world, but between one world and no world."

Man, having accepted fire from Prometheus, is forced to conquer fire itself, beginning with the fire in his heart. The struggle in the arts is a parallel of man's predicament. The function of the artist is to set inaccessible goals, to strive for the impossible, and to allow humanity to catch up later. Though the theatre of this decade may have been preoccupied with the trivial and the personal, there are strong indications that absorption with the self has grown too threadbare for continued use.

The theatre is ever of the age which nourishes it, and whatever weaknesses exist may be the fault of the age itself. The supreme achievement of the theatre lies in the fusion of form and meaning. The first is the playwright's mastery of technique; the second, the extent of his imagination and insight. Though many today retreat to form rather than meaning, the union, when achieved in script and performance, is the reward for enduring the work of lesser men. But this fusion is a delicate balance and represents the ceaseless struggle of the artist to bring order to chaos. Here he joins with the scientist, but whereas the scientist reduces life to law, the playwright clings to its mystery. The scientist codifies the unknown; the artist articulates the ever-unknowable. The scientist augments technological power; the artist is concerned with its effect on man.

Both theme and form are an outgrowth of history, resultants of sensitivity to the insistence of the living moment from which no artist can escape. The playwright, combining style and vision, shapes the uncertain present and offers to others his creation. In doing so, he also breaches the estrangement of the artist from his fellowman, and shares with him a concentrated, occasionally lyric, and, at rare moments, universal expression of experience.

The United States has assumed world leadership. The theatre is its cultural image, and the survey of that theatre is an attempt to understand our culture in the making.

The playwright expresses in metaphorical terms the goals of man, and, as in all the arts, is endlessly in pursuit of freedom—freedom from arbitrary values, freedom to go beyond convention, freedom from submission to technology, freedom of the imagination and the will, freedom to live with science, and freedom to be in conflict with one's self. The extent to which the American theatre of today has shed light on this pursuit is the underlying concern of this book.

1

EUGENE O'NEILL — *The Tragic Homecoming*

And that is as clearly as I wish an audience to comprehend it. It is Mystery—the mystery that one man or woman can feel but not understand as the meaning of any event or accident in any life on earth and it is this Mystery I want to realize in the theater.

Letter to A. H. Quinn

". . . I no longer fear death! . . . I advise you, my brothers, fear not Caesars! . . . Caesar is your fear of man! I counsel you, laugh away your Caesars!"

Lazarus Laughed

AT THE TIME of his death in 1953, the reputation of Eugene O'Neill was in decline. The towering achievement of *Mourning Becomes Electra* twenty years earlier had seemingly exhausted the creative energies of America's most distinguished playwright. No wonder, indeed. In ten years he had written nine plays, including *The Great God Brown, Strange Interlude, Marco Millions,* and *Lazarus Laughed.*

Mourning Becomes Electra, a play in fourteen acts which lasts a half-hour more than the marathon *Strange Interlude,* was the final triumph for O'Neill on the New York stage in his own lifetime. The critics were unanimously jubilant. Brooks Atkinson considered it "magnificently wrought in style and structure"; John

15

Mason Brown called it "an achievement which restores the theater
to its high estate"; Joseph Wood Krutch went so far as to say: "It
may turn out to be the only permanent contribution yet made by
the twentieth century to dramatic literature." A restless pursuit
for "a tragic expression in terms of transfigured modern values and
symbols" had emerged as a modern retelling of the trilogy of
Aeschylus.

After long preoccupation with Strindberg, and the tortured
anguish of discovering God in a material world, O'Neill turned to
ancient Greek drama for a model through which to transform
"the most ignoble debased lives" into the grandeur and transfiguring nobility of tragedy. He spent years in a careful study of the
Oresteia. His characters closely parallel those of Aeschylus: Orin
—Orestes, Ezra Mannon—Agamemnon, Christine—Clytemnestra,
Aegisthus—Adam; but the blind forces of destruction become
Puritan suppression and psychoneurotic frustrations.

Greek heroes violate social law and are doomed until harmony
is restored. O'Neill explores the dark recesses of the inner self. In
both cases, man is pitted against unknowable and mysterious elements beyond control; but with the Greeks, order, though delicately balanced, is preserved. The blood sacrifice purges social ills
and checks the ravages of passion with the temporary reign of
reason. With O'Neill, chaos and disorder continue, as does creation. The Greeks found consolation in the intervention of the gods
and the persistence of justice. For O'Neill, in an accelerated age,
meaning is bewilderingly elusive, a resultant of vectors endlessly
shifting. Psychological terms are used, not as comforting explanations, but as modern terms for ancient human drives. The American Civil War replaces the Trojan War as the battleground from
which heroes return filled with the same insatiable lust that per-
verts the attainment of happiness.

O'Neill is always disturbed by the failure to find peace and
forgetfulness, which slip away as drives for personal gain corrode
human love. Trapped by a hostile reality, man turns to mystic
release, the welcoming of death, or escape to an idyllic retreat.
Brant, one of the hunted, pursued and devoured by two women,
says with hopeless yearning,

"... the Blessed Isles—maybe we can still find happiness and forget!
I can see them now—so close—and a million miles away! The warm

earth in the moonlight, the trade winds rustling the coco palms, the surf on the barrier reef . . . Aye! There's peace and forgetfulness for us there—if we can ever find those islands now!"

All the themes of O'Neill's later plays are combined in this massive trilogy, which is divided into *Homecoming, The Hunted,* and *The Haunted.* The loved one who becomes the perverted trinity of mother-wife-mistress, repeated in *A Moon for the Misbegotten* and *More Stately Mansions,* echoes in Orin's searching words to Lavinia,

"I mean the change in your soul, too . . . I've watched it ever since we sailed for the East. Little by little, it grew like Mother's soul— as if you were stealing hers—as if her death had set you free—to become her!"

The torture of the Strindberg love-guilt complex that invites insanity, compounded in O'Neill with incestuous desire, is expressed in Orin's violent words to his sister as she pulls away in revulsion, "I love you now with all the guilt in me—the guilt we share! Perhaps I love you too much, Vinny!" The need for home, the haven after fruitless journeyings, is Lavinia's unfulfilled dream as she drowns out the pistol shot of Orin's suicide with,

"Oh, won't it be wonderful, Peter, once we're married and have a home with garden and trees! . . . I love everything that grows simply —up toward the sun—everything that's straight and strong! I hate what's warped and twists and eats into itself and dies for a lifetime in shadow . . . . I can't bear waiting—waiting and waiting and waiting!"

French playwrights more frequently use classical legends to depict modern conflicts. A public schooled in Greek mythology welcomes contemporary interpretations. For American audiences, O'Neill wisely chose identifiable characters. In comparing Giraudoux's *Electra* and O'Neill's treatment of the same theme, John Gassner wrote:

Giraudoux faces the Greeks one moment and the rest of mankind the next moment. But in neither case can we forget that a scholar-gentleman is holding the stage and arranging the lecture for us, whereas in O'Neill's case we may feel the Mannons themselves are forcing the issue blindly and insistently.

Honor and world acclaim followed the world premiere, but O'Neill was spent. He retreated to the spectral shadows of Tao House with Carlotta Monterey. His only comedy, *Ah, Wilderness!*, appeared two years later, and finally, in 1934, after all his defiance, he returned to the bosom of the Catholic Church in *Days Without End*—nostalgia and repentance for the tired Viking. The mystic was haunted by his own guilt. Ill and spiritually exhausted, a Tyrone estranged from the world, he kept silent while a depression ravaged a nation and a second world war was in the making. The quest was over. Then, after thirteen years of absence from the stage, O'Neill returned with a thundering whimper. *The Iceman Cometh*, the last of his plays to be presented before his death, took him back to where he had begun his first one-act plays, the sordid ugliness of a waterfront saloon. True, there was little reason to expect that the long retreat and contemplation would result in any earthshaking revelation.

O'Neill's soul-searching had resulted in an impasse—the absence of a positive faith and the futility of any clearly defined philosophy. He had discovered that all conviction was transient; that no absolutes existed, save emptiness and death; and that man could only go on, seeking and never finding. But in the wilderness of his despair, O'Neill challenged the will of the gods. He wrote:

The playwright today must dig at the roots of the sickness of today as he feels it—the death of the old God and the failure of science and materialism to give any satisfying new one. . . .

With *The Iceman Cometh*, he abandoned his battle with the giants and sought peace in self-sustaining illusions. Even the restless Titan was subdued. To use his own words, the playwright who "simply scribbles around the surface of things . . . has no more status than a parlor entertainer." America's most disturbing dramatist had come through with a watered-down version of *The Wild Duck*. Ibsen reacted to a world in which the relativity of knowledge and the impermanence of truth were successively bolstered by new scientific discoveries. Gregers Werle is a mockery of Ibsen himself, who had presumed in his earlier plays to lay down the rigid path to Truth. Social upheavals and personal experience had shown that Truth can destroy, as well as Lies, and the two become interchangeable under different pressures. But O'Neill, almost reluctantly, affirmed that only with self-deception could man go on. Our "pipe-dreams," though false, are preferable to fact. Destroying illusions destroys man. The dream nurtures a residue of hope, especially when one is not sober.

Gorky, in *The Lower Depths,* has Luka, an itinerant peasant, the Christ figure, rekindle hope and then disappear. The ragged derelicts whose lives he has touched sink deeper into despair, but from out of their hovel, from below life itself, rises the powerful cry of Satin, affirming the glory of man. O'Neill ends on total negativism. Each of his lost outcasts lives with a secret guilt that paralyzes the will to act, and turns to drink for solace and forgetfulness. Hickey, the hardware salesman, who has watered their lies with free whiskey, unexpectedly taunts them to reveal their secrets and achieve freedom through rediscovery of reality. He grimly discloses that his free will and definite action have resulted in his murdering his wife for her intolerable goodness, but all he has gained is a longing for death. He leaves with the police officers, saying, "I want to go to the chair," and adds, "Do you suppose I give a damn about life now? Why, you bonehead, I haven't got a single damned lying hope or pipe-dream left."

Hickey, the hero, has no choice but to welcome death, but O'Neill does not end at this point. Larry, the one tramp who has a philosophic awareness of Hickey's ambivalence, says to Parritt, his young companion, "May the chair bring him peace at last, the poor tortured bastard!" Parritt, however, is envious of the peace Hickey will find. He says, "He's lucky. It's all decided for him. I wish it were decided for me." Parritt suffers from obsession with the freedom dreams his mother had fed him about the proletarian revolution. Larry, inadvertently, consents to the young man's suicide. Parritt, as he goes off, says, "It's the only possible way I can ever get free from her."

For a postwar world, exhausted with the reality of crushing fascism and desperately in need of regenerating faith, O'Neill's return to self-deception and release through death is like telling the victims of Hiroshima to trust in the aimless ignorance of the gods. Robert, the dreamer, in O'Neill's first Broadway play, *Be-*

yond the Horizon, in 1920, betrayed by love and broken by the hard, dull life of a New England farm, exultantly awaited his death as the moment of freedom. In *The Iceman Cometh,* O'Neill was back where he had started. Jimmie the Priest's saloon of the one-act plays had now become Harry Hope's West Side bar, and the "horizon far away and as alluring as ever" had become the grave. The Iceman is a grimmer symbol of death than the bridegroom, more akin to the gravedigger of Samuel Beckett, who "down in the hole, lingeringly . . . puts on the forceps."

O'Neill had failed to keep abreast of a changing world, now in a more intense crisis of decision. Like Ella in *All God's Chillun,* he preferred the bliss of innocence where "we can play marbles" and pretend. The hard realism of the twenties and the shattering dramatic expressionism of the thirties were reduced to the shreds of a tattered romanticism. The father he had rejected, claimed the son of Monte Cristo.

A year after *The Iceman Cometh, A Moon for the Misbegotten* was tried out by the Theatre Guild in the Midwest and failed to reach Broadway. O'Neill's star had set. The double failure was an opportunity for the critics, who had always been embarrassed by O'Neill's abrasive defiance of the traditional intellectual pursuit of meaning, to pull him down to size. Eric Bentley wrote a curious eulogy in which he claimed that though he tried to love O'Neill, it was like trying to hug a bear.

Ten years later, the tide turned. It all began with the revival in 1956 of *The Iceman Cometh* in an off-Broadway theatre, the Circle in the Square, directed by José Quintero and starring Jason Robards, Jr. A brilliant production in the round elicited critical enthusiasm and renewed interest in O'Neill's work. *Moon for the Misbegotten* was picked out of discard and brought to Broadway. Two posthumous plays, *Long Day's Journey into Night* and *A Touch of the Poet,* quickly followed, and were hailed as the finest works of two successive seasons. Revivals of his old plays won new audiences. The Phoenix Theatre presented *The Great God Brown,* not seen in New York for two decades, and the Circle in the Square added an excellent production of *Desire Under the Elms,* with George C. Scott in the role originally played by Walter Huston. So inflated did the O'Neill boom become that he had the questionable distinction of having two musical plays based on his original works, *New Girl in Town* (*Anna Christie*) in 1957, and

Take Me Along (*Ah, Wilderness!*) in 1959. *More Stately Mansions* was flown to Stockholm by Dr. Karl Gierow and given its world premiere at the Swedish Royal Theatre, in accordance with the desires of Carlotta O'Neill. *Hughie,* a long one-act monologue, was likewise produced in Sweden and later shown in other European cities.

José Quintero's reversal of the earlier judgments on *The Iceman Cometh* won the warm endorsement of O'Neill's widow, who retained full production rights. She named him as the director for the Actors Studio revival of *Strange Interlude* and the Lincoln Center production of *Marco Millions.* Unfortunately, he was not as successful in these later efforts. His approach was too theatrical and his interpretation over-romantic, but for O'Neill it was a resounding revindication. The phoenix risen had flown to greater heights than ever before. No other playwright had held sway for five decades and withstood so ably the test of time. All others walked in his shadow.

A re-examination of the plays offered in the past few years indicates his variety of techniques, his restless search for new materials, his unswerving dedication to the pursuit of truth, and his inordinate sensitivity to the American scene. He pulled the theatre with him and, alone, stands with the great masters of the European drama.

Desire Under the Elms is one of the first plays of O'Neill's early realistic period. Its structure is that of the well-made play of crisis and increasing tension, but when first presented on the American stage it shocked with its hard language, brutal violence, and psychological truth. The Los Angeles company was hauled off to jail on charges of lewdness and immorality. Today, we accept sex and violence with greater tolerance, little realizing that five decades ago the American theatre, dominated by an entrenched Puritanism, restricted any honest discussion of human relations. The turn of the century preferred action melodramas, matinee idols, Victorian prudery, abstemious language, and the perpetuation of favorable myths.

Beyond the Horizon in 1920, brought out cautiously from the Provincetown Playhouse for special performances and then a long run at the Morosco Theatre, marked the coming of age of the American theatre. As in *Desire Under the Elms,* the background is the New England farm, the characters caught in a web of frustration, of hope in hopelessness, as they fight for emotional freedom in the stifling atmosphere of imposed restraints. Robert, the dreamer, who should be wandering beyond the horizon, is trapped by the unrelenting land and the dishonesty of love. Andrew, the brother who goes off to sea, belongs on the farm. Romance is no longer glorious, but a game played for security. Ibsen and Strindberg had been planted on American soil. *Desire Under the Elms* carries the same theme to more violent conclusions. Father turns against son, and wife against husband, as the lust for property uproots human love and whirls in fury to blind destructiveness. The age-old conflict of passion against reason, the disturbance of the order-establishing mores when impulses go unchecked, finds new intensity on the rocky soil, so fertile for the Puritan denial of life.

O'Neill never abandoned this central theme. He rebelled against American cultural development, which placed material values above spiritual goals. He saw beauty, art, and all human relations corrupted by the insane pursuit of gold. In his final years, as the culmination of his career, he planned a massive cycle of plays tracing the fortunes of an American family, in which not social revolution nor political unrest would overthrow those in power, but their own worship of possessions. This projected series was to consist of eleven plays with the overall title *A Tale of Possessors Self-Dispossessed.*

In *Desire Under the Elms,* this theme is revealed in a bestial family struggle. Newfound symbols weave around the realistic core. The enormous elms "brood oppressively over the house. They are like exhausted women resting their sagging breasts and hands and hair on its roof." Lust, seduction, murder, theft, hysteria, occur under their enormous shadows. When the child born of an adulterous affair between son and stepmother is killed on stage, the scene rises to unbearable horror, unprecedented on the American stage. Zola had called for "life in the raw," and Tolstoy, in *The Power of Darkness,* had Nikita, the idiot peasant, crush a new-born babe with his heavy farm boots. Yet these modern scenes are no more shocking than Medea's bloody murder of her young sons, than Gloucester's eyes ripped from their sockets. With O'Neill, the infanticide is related to the drive for love, which, crushed too long, rises to destroy life itself and overwhelms remorse. In the final scene, when Eben tells Abbie he loves her, she pulls him wildly to her breast and cries out ecstatically, "I'd fergive ye all the sins in hell fur sayin' that!" Cabot, the gaunt old farmer, stares at them vindictively, like an angry God of wrath, and says,

"Ye'd ought t' be both hung on the same limb an' left thar t' swing in the breeze an' rot—a warnin' t' old fools like me t' b'ar their lonesomeness alone—an' fur young fools like ye t' hobble their lust . . . It's a-goin' t' be lonesomer now than ever it war afore—an' I'm gittin' old, Lord—ripe on the bough . . . Waal—what d'ye want? God's lonesome, hain't He? hain't He? God's hard an' lonesome!"

The Puritan has found his consolation.

In these early years, O'Neill was so prolific that in one season, 1924, seven of his plays were being presented, as though, singlehanded, he wanted to move the American theatre forward. In all of them, characters act to determine their own destiny. Their lives and situations are related to environment and social forces. *Anna Christie*, more conventional in structure and melodramatic in content, deals with a sick, down-to-earth, man-hating prostitute, not the idealized fallen woman with a heart of gold. The play is more significant for its further broadside against Puritan morality and its unusual characters—the inarticulate Swedish tug captain, the brawling Irish seaman, and, above all, the sea, which redeems the contrived plot by becoming the symbol of interchangeable good and evil. Yet what a history this one play has had! With Pauline Lord in the original production it won the Pulitzer Prize, Blanche Sweet played it as a silent motion picture, Greta Garbo used it for her first speaking role on the screen, and, finally, it achieved the pinnacle of Broadway acclaim by being made into a musical, *New Girl in Town*.

The Great God Brown belongs to O'Neill's second period, beginning with 1926, when he explored experimentally for a dramatic articulation of the problems of modern man. He broke all technical conventions, violated all the rules, used masks, asides, expressionistic fantasy, wrote a play with an intermission for dinner and plays which even today are unproducible.

With *The Great God Brown*, O'Neill turned to masks to explore the hidden nuances of the human personality. Masks are as old as the theatre, but O'Neill used them as a psychological device for exhibiting the different selves of a single person. He once wrote that the "new psychological insight into human cause and effect" was but "an exercise in unmasking." The Italian *teatro del grottesco,* particularly in the work of Luigi Chiarelli, had used masks to portray the face one turns to the world and the true self that remains hidden. O'Neill was deeply involved in "conveying a sense of the tragic mystery drama of Life revealed through the lives in this play," and spoke in one of his letters of "the background pattern of conflicting tides in the soul of man," which should not throw out of proportion the recognizable human being, but which should be "mystically within and behind them." His explanation is even more confusing than the text of the play.

Dion Anthony, a combination of Dionysus and Saint Anthony, the god of revelry and wine merged with the Christian ascetic, is the sensitive poet, the creative force, the architect, who is O'Neill himself, "a stranger walking alone . . . dark, spiritual, poetic, passionately supersensitive, helplessly unprotected," with a childlike religious faith in life. Unable to communicate with parents, friends, or loved ones, he struggles to understand the enigma of life. Billy Brown, the successful businessman, longs to possess the self that is Dion's. He envies Dion his talent, fame, his creative joy, and the love of Margaret, which are all beyond his own reach. Yet Dion, his inner self too sensitive for revelation, appears masked even to Margaret, his wife. Only to Cybel, Mother Earth, comfort to all men, the Dionysian priestess, can he disclose his failure. Brown kills Dion, takes his mask, lives his life, but cannot *be* Dion, for he has assumed, as O'Neill wrote, not Dion's Pan-like genius for love and creation, but Dion's Pan-mask "slowly transformed by his struggle with reality into Mephistopheles." The mask has an existence of its own; the abstraction becomes a reality. In the final scene, Cybel places Dion's mask on a stand, and Margaret kneels beside it and kisses it, recognizing her lost husband. O'Neill was groping for a means to visualize the unseen, but was unable to translate it into understandable symbols. The obscurity was compounded.

At times, the dream fantasy does break into illuminating metaphors. When Brown tears Dion's architectural plan to pieces, he says,

"A little paste . . . and all will be well! . . . A little dab of pasty resignation here and there and even broken hearts may be repaired . . . Man is born broken . . . He lives by mending . . . The grace of God . . . is glue."

Extraordinary is the final scene when Brown, fleeing from the police, dies in Cybel's arms. He has returned to the womb for rebirth and acceptance by the Earth-mother. The dialogue rises to glowing images; then, as is so frequently the case with O'Neill, slips back to maudlin commonplaces. Margaret kneels at the mask of Dion, mingling her grief with the cry that he will "sleep under my heart forever." Cybel turns to the audience and with "profound pain" utters one of O'Neill's more poetic passages—

"Always, love and conception and birth and pain again—spring bearing the intolerable chalice of life again! . . . bearing the glorious blazing crown of life again,"

a paean to pagan sensuousness and Catholic mysticism, O'Neill's search for the fusion of the Apollonian and the Dionysian. But the scene plummets to the absurd when the police captain enters and says, "Well, what's his name?" and Cybel answers, "Man!" If that isn't enough, the captain adds, "How d'yuh spell it?"

Such liberties have exasperated critics. O'Neill's intensity could not avoid pretentious posturing and clumsy incoherence, but *The Great God Brown* is a remarkable play of daring inventiveness and dramatic courage, in which, because O'Neill forced the issue, waves of meaning are released that are increasingly stimulating.

From Brown's final lines,

"Out of Earth's transfigured birth pain the laughter of Man returns to bless and play again in innumerable dancing gales of flame upon the knees of God!"

comes *Lazarus Laughed*, the most amazing play in the English language. It was produced at the Pasadena Playhouse, but has not as yet been seen in New York. Always concerned with the problem of death, O'Neill used Lazarus, resurrected from the tomb, as the symbol of death-defeated, with pagan laughter rising from a joy of life. Caesar is defied, for he holds no power over men if death holds no fears. Multiple choruses chant in balanced rhythms of laughter as Lazarus grows younger and more beautiful with man's ultimate triumph. As literature, it is overwhelming; as drama, almost impossible to produce.

Marco Millions, which the Lincoln Center chose to revive, is a better play than the unfavorable reaction of the critics would suggest. The production was marred by José Quintero's concern with technical staging. Admittedly, the characters are immediately established and vary very slightly as the play unfolds. O'Neill never intended it as a psychological drama of character change. He hammers away—often over-repetitiously, it is true— at a central theme, that Western man in the pursuit of material gains has crushed all sensitivity to beauty. *Marco Millions* is an extravaganza, a spectacle that is close to ballet. To condemn it for simplicity of characterization is to ignore O'Neill's interplay of symbols in mounting intensities. Marco is the pursuit of money. Any youthful yearning for poetry is quickly extinguished. He is likable, self-confident, swaggering, the salesman with only "an acquisitive instinct." He sees nothing but potential profit in everything, including marriage. He no longer can respond to love. Kukachin is grace and elegance, delicacy and spirit. The contrast between East and West is recorded with a wealth of incident. Marco is a detailed study of a man who is all materialism. He turns the explosives for fireworks into instruments of destruction, and then says with contemporary relevance,

> "War is a waste of money . . . why war, I ask myself? How are you going to end it? There's only one workable way, and that's to conquer everyone else in the world, so they'll never dare fight you again!"

The play is essentially satire and spectacle.

Strange Interlude, which was the first production of the Actors Studio Theatre, was a more impressive production when first played by the Theatre Guild in 1928. O'Neill used asides to replace masks. In the original production, as an actor spoke his inner thoughts, all others on stage froze into a tableau to indicate a suspension of life. The recent production avoided the asides and ran all the speeches together, confusing the audience, making the play a straight realistic recital, and eliminating its most theatrical effect. With present-day popular understanding of psychology, the asides are a needless device and more a tour de force than an insight into the human heart, but without the asides the impact is lost. The play of Nina and her men is a nine-act *Hedda Gabler* with an intermission for dinner, a triple triangle of involved psychological interpretations which are no longer convincing. It is

the most complicated study of an unfulfilled woman with an over-
powering drive for life, frustrated by her father and the death of
her hero-lover. The long case study until her own son, the reborn
Gordon, flies off with his wife, is sufficiently weak for O'Neill to
add his usual excursions into philosophical obscurity. Nina says,

> "The Sons of the Father have all been failures! Failing they died
> for us, they flew away to other lives, they could not stay with us,
> they could not give us happiness!"

And then adds,

> "Our lives are merely strange dark interludes in the electrical dis-
> play of God the Father."

Not even Lynn Fontanne or Geraldine Page could relate these
words to events. They are an admission that the anxieties and
longings are more verbal than actual. Yet, as so often with O'Neill,
the total recital accumulates power. Few in the audience do not
return after dinner.

Had O'Neill never been heard from again, his work would
have been of sufficient magnitude, but the long retirement had
not been inactive. Of *A Tale of Possessors Self-Dispossessed* two
plays are available, and several he and Carlotta burned. Wracked
with physical pain and a fatal disease, he never abandoned his
writing and the pursuit of new meanings. But the debate with
God and the abstract condemnation of a relentlessly cruel universe were abandoned for a return to realism and the family, the
core of human relations, and the daily test of the individual.
These are the dark plays of O'Neill, full of pain and sorrow. All
are autobiographical, a treatise on love and death and the search
for self. One that was burned was entitled *And Give Me Death*.
Work on the large cycle of plays was interrupted for *Long Day's
Journey into Night* and *A Moon for the Misbegotten*, which do not
belong to the Harford family series, but to the Tyrones. But
whether Harfords or Tyrones, O'Neill himself is the central character. From *Beyond the Horizon* to *Long Day's Journey into
Night* is a long voyage of a sensitive explorer to find order in the
distant night of nothingness. These final plays differ in their increased knowledge of human motives and the newfound faith in

love as a creative force, best revealed by the moving dedication he wrote to Carlotta:

For Carlotta, on our 12th Wedding Anniversary . . .

Dearest: I give you the original script of this play of old sorrow, written in tears and blood. A sadly inappropriate gift, it would seem, for a day celebrating happiness. But you will understand. I mean it as a tribute to your love and tenderness which gave me the faith in love that enabled me to face my dead at last and write this play—write it with deep pity and understanding and forgiveness for *all* the four haunted Tyrones.

These twelve years, Beloved One, have been a Journey into Light—into love. You know my gratitude. And my love!

Gene

The haunted Tyrones are the members of O'Neill's own family with the names slightly changed. The father, a matinee idol, resents catering to popular taste and not having perfected his art. The mother is addicted to drugs as a result of opium administered by an incompetent doctor at the time her younger son was born. Tyrone, Sr., out of ingrained penury, refused to engage a more expensive doctor. James, the elder son, is a drunk and a wastrel. Edmund is ill with tuberculosis, as was O'Neill, and needs medical attention. All are morally sick, escaping into themselves, uncomfortable with love yet needing it desperately. The mother finds salvation in the church, as her dazed mind gropes for solace; the father clings to illusions of greatness; James, Jr., comforts himself with visions of vaguely defined accomplishments, and Edmund turns to his poetry. They torture each other with misunderstood tenderness and misplaced self-interest, each hiding from the other as well as from himself. This long play—almost too long, for O'Neill never comes to the point briefly and briskly—is a powerful family drama in which happiness and mutual love, so close to attainment, remain congealed in the human heart.

A Moon for the Misbegotten, the last of O'Neill's work, written in 1942 and published ten years later, centers again on a few characters. The action takes place on the hard New England soil, as it did in *Beyond the Horizon,* his first play on Broadway. James Tyrone, Jr., is now the protagonist, still burying his guilt in alcohol. He cannot accept the fullness of Josie's love, for he bears the burden of betraying the love for his mother which he would never recognize. Years earlier, after Mrs. Tyrone's death, he had accompanied the body east from San Francisco on a train, but had spent his time with a prostitute in a private compartment. Later, he sought forgetfulness in a wild orgy rather than attend the funeral. He lies about his affairs with loose women to cover his loneliness and drunken self-effacement. Josie, vital and warm-hearted, pretends to be a slut, though she is in reality a virgin. Phil Hogan, her father, pretends to be cantankerous and deceitful to hide the grandeur of his spirit.

Masks are no longer needed. Each attempts to conceal his true self from the other, knowing the other's truth, but jesting and laughing to avoid revealing it. Lover and beloved are laden with guilt. James says to Josie,

"We can kid the world, but we can't fool ourselves, like most people, no matter what we do—nor escape ourselves no matter where we run away."

But when they cease fooling one another and the masks are peeled away, the truth is more unendurable. James becomes a child, the misbegotten, who has always been dead. Josie cradles his sleeping form in her lap as they sit outdoors in the night, and says,

"It's a fine end to all my schemes to sit here with the dead up to my breast and the silly mug of the moon grinning down, enjoying the joke."

As in all the posthumous plays, the exposition is strained, the relationships painfully constructed, the pulling back and forth repetitive, but the total effect is like an avalanche that gathers momentum slowly, then crushes everything before it. A curious reminder of O'Neill's too infrequently used comedic sense in tragic situations is the scene in which Josie and her father frighten off the rich T. Stedman Harder, who comes to purchase their land, their carefree Irish humor contrasting with the stiff formality of the man who believes money can buy everything. Josie and Phil are full of the "joy of life" that Ibsen found so comforting as the antidote to middle-class dullness.

A Touch of the Poet is the only play of the cycle to have been shown on Broadway. The 1958 production won all the critics'

awards and saw Kim Stanley and Helen Hayes star as Sara and Nora Melody. The play has the same structure, the same weaknesses, the same power, as *Long Day's Journey*. Con Melody, an Irish immigrant with pretensions to aristocracy, keeps a thoroughbred mare in the stable, while his wife Nora, whom he spurns as beneath him socially, slaves to keep the tavern going. Sara, his daughter, mocks his boasting, defends her mother, and tries to pull him back to reality with: "It must be a wonderful thing to live in a fairy tale where only dreams are real to you." After a humiliating fight with the police, and futile defiance of the rich Harfords, Con Melody retires to the stable and shoots the mare. His dream protection shattered, his memories of earlier gentlemanly gallantry broken, he reverts to his peasant origins and Irish brogue.

Nora says, "He's dead now and the last bit of lyin' pride is murthered and stinken'." The mare was "the livin' reminder . . . av all his lyin' boasts and dreams." He had meant to kill the horse and then himself, but "he saw the shot that killed her had finished him, too" and "it'd be a mad thing to waste a good bullet on a corpse!" Sara, seeing him now as a living death in life, wants him back with his old pride, prancing around on the mare, telling tall tales of duels and the Battle of Talavera. She says sorrowfully, "He's beaten at last and he wants to stay beaten." When she sees him join the common rowdies at the bar, cheering for Andrew Jackson, friend of the common man, she says, "I heard someone but it wasn't anyone I ever knew or want to know." Nora, who has borne the brunt of his former airs, finds her self-sacrificing love justified. Her husband is aware of her love and his need for it. He kisses her for the first time without complaining of the kitchen smells. Sara has given her love and her body to young Simon Harford. No more dreams surround them. The symbol of the dead past, the mare, is gone. The reality is as stark and uncomfortable as the dream. The earth can endure neither.

More Stately Mansions, which Mrs. O'Neill feels should be produced only in the repertory of the Swedish Royal Theatre, is available in published form. O'Neill left fragments of an enormous play, which were edited by Karl Gierow of Sweden and Donald Gallup of Yale University. This fourth play of the unfinished cycle is a Strindbergian nightmare of mother, son, and wife locked in a power struggle for domination. The love-hate-guilt theme is played against the corruption of the human soul engendered by the fight for possessions.

The two available plays of *Possessors Self-Dispossessed* give some indication of O'Neill's political philosophy. He was always aware of social forces, but the artist in him refused to become involved in political partisanship, much to the discomfort of the Leftists in the thirties, who regarded him as a renegade. After all, had he not been a member of that rebellious group in Greenwich Village which included John Reed, Louise Bryant, and Mary Heaton Vorse? In the early plays there are frequent references to socialism. The I.W.W. office throws out Yank, "the Hairy Ape," for having no class-consciousness. Yank is the brute animal force that supplies the motive power while the idle rich sit above in ignorance and contempt. *Marco Millions* is a travesty on capitalist insensitivity, but O'Neill rejected political theories and turned to man himself. He sensed the deepest contribution of contemporary drama, that human nature is variable. Man and society are constantly changing and interacting.

The suspicion persists that the vast project of his last years was to be a fully orchestrated demonstration that those who pursue gold will be destroyed by the pursuit, that the lust for material wealth changes human nature, and that the possessors will dispossess themselves. It may well be that some day, although the Yale University Library (the repository of O'Neill's manuscripts) has published all the complete plays, some fragments will be released that will reveal O'Neill's final political convictions.

In *A Touch of the Poet,* the prelude of the theme is sounded. In *More Stately Mansions,* the vengeance of things is violent. Each of the three central characters connives to win control of the property and destroy the others. Simon Harford sets mother against wife as a means of being free of both. Each has his separate diversion. Deborah, the aristocratic mother, dreams of unfulfilled romances with the crowned heads of Europe. Sara, Con Melody's daughter, full of greed and passion, runs from the specters of the ancestral mansion to be free in the arms of other men. Simon is writing a book on the nature of man, a book he will never finish, but which gives O'Neill an opportunity to expose the vacuity of contemporary ideas. Simon says,

"Human life . . . is a liar's promise, a perpetual in-bankruptcy for debts we never contracted, a daily appointment with peace and happiness in which we wait day after day, hoping against hope, and when finally the bride or the bridegroom cometh we discover we are kissing Death."

He comes close to a modern glorification of evil when he rejects the notion that man is virtuous, which he claims is responsible for "all the confusion in our relationships with one another. . . . All one needs to remember is that good is evil and evil, good."

The characters move in a complex interrelationship of self-preservation and sacrifice for loved ones, of covetousness and generosity beyond even Strindberg's boldest work. Simon turns from love to hate and back to love, shouting to his mother, "You hated your love for me because it possessed you and you wanted to be free!" Each seeks freedom at the expense of the other, but in the final resolution the mother sacrifices herself to preserve her son, as she crosses the threshold to insanity; but it is to no avail, for, like Con Melody or Billy Brown, he has gone beyond reason and reverts to the innocence of childhood in the arms of Sara, now wife-mother-mistress. In a horrified whisper, she says,

"I see now the part my greed and my father's crazy dreams in me had in leading Simon away from himself until he lost his way and began destroying all that was best in him! To make me proud of him! Forgive me, darling! But I'll give my life now to setting you free to be again the man you were when I first met you—the man I loved best! The dreamer with a touch of the poet in his soul, and the heart of a boy!"

O'Neill also planned a succession of one-act plays to be called By Way of Obit, of which only Hughie was completed. Not produced as yet in New York, it was given its premiere in Sweden, and presented at Salzburg in German. It is a lengthy monologue in which the desk clerk of a small commercial hotel listens to Erie Smith, a traveling salesman, tell of his dealings with gang-sters and flashy women. Hughie, the former clerk, is dead, and as his replacement pays little attention to Erie's boasts of being "a Broadway sport and wise guy," the salesman reverts to the truth, revealing his actual self. As he does so, the clerk becomes more and more like Hughie and begins to show interest. Erie responds by going back to the tales of big-time underworld connections with which the play began.

What can one add about Eugene O'Neill? His enormous body
of work encompasses all the diverse elements in the poet's search
for freedom. He found no solutions in a hostile world which he
loved and of which he was a product. He groped intensely,
demonically, in all directions, challenged every idea, and ended
with a renewed understanding of human love, a love that rises out
of suffering and reaches beyond the self. He tested every dramatic
technique. With the early plays, he made the realism indige-
nously American (*Desire Under the Elms* or *Ile*), adding language of the common folk and blasting the trivial sentimentality
of the effete parlor-drama. He turned to Freud and new insights
into the subconscious (*Strange Interlude* and *The Great God
Brown*). He let loose primitive emotions as solutions in themselves,
with Nina, or Lavinia, or Emperor Jones. He turned to expressionism, dream fantasies, and abstract ideas in torment in *The
Great God Brown* and *Dynamo*. With *A Moon for the Misbegotten*
and *A Touch of the Poet*, he rejected the illusory happiness
that accumulation of wealth provides. He saw men not strong
enough to meet their destiny, trapped by a rationalistic psychology that bereft them of a place in the universe. He set out to
redefine the meaning of God. He molded a contemporary divinity
on a power generator and put his faith in Electrical Energy. He
turned back to his native Catholic mysticism in *Days Without
End*; then, nostalgically, came home to the family—for laughter
in *Ah, Wilderness!* or pain in *Long Day's Journey*. He indicated a
preference for illusion and self-deception in *The Iceman Cometh*,
then turned to meet the truth head-on and found it equally
illusory in *A Touch of the Poet*.

He was the first to introduce honest race relations on stage
(*The Dreamy Kid*), and added the problem of miscegenation
in *All God's Chillun*. He walked in the path of Strindberg, Ibsen,
and Aeschylus; and, like his son-in-law, Charlie Chaplin, he
walked estranged on a lonely road. He caught the speech of
farm and sea folk, and moved away to flights of poetic symbolism.
He did enough to bring down attacks from all sides. The academi-
cian was embarrassed by the crudity of the language, the poet
by his clumsy, repetitive, and obvious metaphors, the social
reformer by his desertion of the political scene, the philosopher
by his awkward, peasant-like certainty of truth. All these
criticisms are valid and the embarrassments justified, but even

Homer nods. Paraphrasing what Lincoln said of Grant, one could add that in the army of playwrights we could use more such generals.

O'Neill was essentially a romantic idealist, hypersensitive to the failure of modern civilization to achieve increased happiness, despite its victories over nature. His integrity is unchallenged. He never succumbed to the demands of the commercial tread-mill, nor did he ever permit Broadway to dictate terms. His overwhelming theatricality, his power, rises from a superhuman drive to pull all the world on stage and tear it apart, if neces-sary, to disclose meaning, to face God or the devil and demand unflinchingly some revelation of truth.

2

ARTHUR MILLER — *Return to the Self*

Paradise keeps slipping back and back . . .

It is a view which does not look towards social or political ideas as the creators of violence, but into the nature of the human being himself.
Author's foreword to After the Fall

In January, 1964, the Lincoln Center Repertory Company inaugurated its initial season with Arthur Miller's first play in nine years, *After the Fall*. Newspaper, radio, and network television coverage was extensive. National magazines featured the event and the *Saturday Evening Post* published the text of the play the week of the opening. The eyes of the nation were focused on the events in a sunken amphitheatre off Washington Square. The theatre was part of American life. For better or for worse, Arthur Miller's play set the tone for a historic new enterprise.

Arthur Miller has been the subject of controversy ever since *Death of a Salesman*. The advocates of private and obscure images of man's disintegration had condemned him for continued adherence to an outworn Ibsen tradition. Eric Bentley had seen in the drama "the little man as victim," evoking pity but detracting from the social implications of the play because Willie Loman's plight is covered with a "sentimental haze." On the other hand, the social realists had welcomed Miller too enthusiastically as a writer who avoided violence and sexuality and personal dislocation as a way out of despair.

Miller, in the European tradition, had set himself up as essayist, commentator, and moralist. While observing an early rehearsal of *Death of a Salesman*, he had written,

> We must be a terribly lonely people cut off from each other by such massive pretense of self-sufficiency, machined down so fine we hardly touch anymore. We are trying to save ourselves separately and that is immoral, that is the corrosive among us.

He repeatedly demanded of the writer "a kind of truthfulness that is larger than the mere imitation of life," and a relentless search for "responsibility and guilt for this world we cannot quite believe we made." He questioned what "is the most human way to live" and "where in all the profusion of materiality we have created around us is the cup where the spirit may reside." But with *After the Fall* Miller denies his own precepts and gives ammunition to his detractors. With one blow, he isolated himself from the purists and the Marxists.

After the Fall is a brooding, sensitive, compelling, and incomplete play, a return to lust and loss of faith, as in so much of the contemporary art that Miller had condemned, whether it be that of Ingmar Bergman or Tennessee Williams or even Edward Albee. Miller recently said the drama that eschews purposeful action reflects "a widespread disbelief in the power of men to affect their own situation, the rejection of all meaning but irony . . ." Of the theatre of the absurd, he wrote, "These plays are most convincing if performed the day before the world ends. Better still, the day after." *After the Fall* comes very close to falling in the same category. Whether purposeful action is possible is the theme of the play.

Nine years of absence from the theatre and two tortured marriages that ended in divorce, plus changes in the world situation, have evidently deprived Arthur Miller of the assurance that collective drives can eliminate social ills and the disease of the spirit. He now holds the view that "does not look towards social or political ideas as the creators of violence but into the nature of the human being himself."

After the Fall does not refer to the bomb, but to the Garden of Eden and the fall of man after woman seduced him to taste of the fruit of knowledge. Miller, in the true Puritan spirit, seeks expiation for his guilt by returning to the problem of original sin. Once doubt exists and God's perfection is questioned, man's fall begins. Suffering and inner travail are atonement on the road to regain paradise, or a transformed paradise after knowledge. Miller is caught in the interim period in which "paradise keeps slipping back."

Quentin, the central character of the play, a thinly disguised representation of the playwright, wants to know why. The opening lines are: "Hello! God, it's good to see you again!" They should have been punctuated, "Hello, God. It's good to see you again!"—for the words are addressed to the Listener, invisible in the front rows beyond the edge of the stage. The Listener may be God, you—the audience, or the psychiatrist, a combination also used in *The Cocktail Party*, where Sir Harcourt-Reilly as priest-confessor-psychiatrist is the voice of T. S. Eliot. Miller has long been wrestling with the Almighty. He now wants to be on more intimate terms, discussing failure, not pinpointing ideals. The play is a trial of man by his own conscience: man, re-enacting his past deeds, turns "at the edge of the abyss to look at his experiences." The long road from Adam to Miller is fraught with uncertainty and disaster as a result of basic human nature. Man knows little of himself and less of woman.

A central theme of Miller's earlier work had been that "we ought to be struggling for a world in which it will be possible to lay blame," but now he writes of Quentin: "His desperation is too serious, too deadly to permit him to blame others." No longer is Miller convinced of a right way of life. He joins the chroniclers of disaster, with a long-drawn-out confessional in which the audience acts as participating analysts reviewing the career of a middle-aged failure. Every intimate detail of his life, particularly his relationships with women, is thrust on stage, and the ordeal ends with the need to continue the agonized quest.

In this sense, the play is historically honest because it is Miller's own history. The diminished note of hope implies a radical realignment of the playwright's values.

The form is equally elusive. Quentin's conversational tone merges with the events themselves, often incomplete, often a shifting kaleidoscope of recaptured images of the past and present, crisscrossing, overlapping, springing up unexpectedly as "the action takes place in the mind, thought and memory of Quentin, a contemporary man." As Quentin unburdens himself his thoughts are acted out, a visualized psychoanalysis, or "an open evolution of a concept on a stage, an attempt to give form to life before your eyes." The form is that of the stream of consciousness, not arranged according to what happened next in the usual time sequence, but as

> a mind would go in quest of a meaning . . . sometimes it stumbles and loses its way, only to try and find its way back. But all of it in the open, before your eyes, creating its own form.

Miller's own words indicate an artist's effort to merge form and content. Once life had meaning, but that meaning is no longer adequate. Having lost faith in the old and not as yet having found the new, Quentin, according to Miller, is in pursuit of

> a moment which he thinks he once had and which he knows he *must* find again, the moment when his life, and presumably life itself, cohered in a form.

Childhood, family relations, rejection by his mother, the loss of the father-hero image, political and business associates, weave in the rambling formlessness of subconscious thoughts around such words as idiot, innocence, blessing, truth, justice, guilt, love. There is a certain disquieting intimacy established with the playwright as he unfolds his analysis from infancy to maturity, for he is friend enough to strip himself naked and hurt before our eyes. He does not grovel or engage in self-pity or even ask for understanding. The play becomes a plea for involvement in a common search for meaning.

In so intensely autobiographical a play the characters are recognizable, for Miller's life has long been public property. Miller, the writer, is Quentin, a lawyer; Marilyn Monroe is

Maggie, a cabaret singer; and even Elia Kazan, who directed the play for the Lincoln Center, is the friend who names names before the Un-American Activities Committee. The question of tact and taste immediately arose, and Miller was roundly condemned for exposing the details of his life with Marilyn Monroe, particularly so soon after her death. In the play, her love is all-consuming, her animal use of sex an outgrowth of an insatiable need to be wanted, and her self-destructive suicidal drive a physical embracement of death as a welcome release. The Maggie scenes attract the sensation-seeker, but the only relevant criterion is whether they function in the overall design.

Miller intended to counterpose the death impulses of Maggie with Quentin's thirst for life, and the innocence of Quentin's complicity in murder with personal guilt for all crimes against humanity. Maggie, sick and reaching for the barbiturates, says, " 'Cause all I am . . . is love. And sex. Whyn't you lie on me?" Quentin rejects her request because it "degrades" him, and adds, "I am not guilty for your life! But I am responsible for my own." As she clings to him and pulls him to the floor, he shouts, "You won't kill me! You won't kill me!" The montage shifts to the tower of a German concentration camp, which hangs suspended over the play's entire action, and now that Quentin knows how to kill and to stay alive, he cries aloud in his agony,

> "Who would not rather be the sole survivor of this place than all its finest victims? . . . My brothers died here . . . but my brothers built this place."

The implications are clear and terrifyingly relevant, but Miller became so absorbed by the Maggie scenes that they overbalance the play. The criticism that they violate the demands of decency and personal privacy is less valid than the esthetic consideration. All artists submit their innermost selves to the world. The creation of art is a form of exhibitionism. Its justification is its meaning, its revelation of truth to others. Such scenes are evidently catharsis for the author but embarrassment for the viewer. In divulging his own failure, a needed therapy, Miller courted the danger of presenting a peephole revelation and losing communion with his audience. It is interesting to note that for the road company, Miller considerably shortened these scenes.

The first half of the play, however, is a towering achievement. The form unfolds as the mind touches various events revealing decisive details of Quentin's life and asking the audience to be concerned with the limits of love, the response of the beloved, the meaning of friendship, justice, truth. Miller imposes no specific dogma, but asks for common speculation into mutual concerns. The second half of the play, with its emphasis on the bedroom scenes, reduces these questions to Miller's own personal involvement. He does not stand aloof with the required objectivity of the artist.

Miller's problems with women unhinge the play. A diminished version could well be entitled "Should I, who have failed twice, marry a third time?" What follows is a public thinking-out of the answer to that question. Miller (or Quentin) reviews his own life, his relations to others, the world around him. Hesitation is not generated by such questions as: Do I love Holga? Can I support her? Will she interfere with my career? Will she make a good wife?—the normal questions of hesitant bachelors. Rather, he raises the questions: Am I capable of love? Is love possible? What has been the cause of previous failure? Is there something rotten inside myself and the world around me that denies creative union? This is a paraphrase of the Hamlet legend.

Hamlet raises the question, "Shall I kill the King?"—and does so only when the deed will not be a limited act of personal vengeance but will spread out to the uprooting of the source of all evil. He leaves the world purged, but in ruins. Hamlet discovers that some men are evil and pervert good for their own ends. Quentin discovers that all men are guilty, all that live "after the fall." An evangelical minister can blame original sin, for his role is to perpetuate an accepted myth, but the playwright's function is to question those myths. Hamlet finds the King guilty and kills him, then pays with his own life. Quentin puts the blame on Adam, too inaccessible for personal revenge, and goes off to marry Holga. *Hamlet* is dramatic conflict. *After the Fall* is dramatic analysis. The comparison with Shakespeare is not intended to disparage Miller, but to indicate the differences between two plays with comparable protagonists. Quentin's decision is based on the need to avoid suffocation and death and to move toward whatever light prevails. The marriage question becomes the allegory for involvement beyond the self.

Five different women rise in a shifting montage to haunt him. There are the three wives, his mother, and a young girl to whom he had given direction and hope by advising her to have her nose straightened by plastic surgery. The wounds of the past reopen, torturing him with his own inadequacy. The young girl regards him as a saviour and returns to bless him. He resents her use of him as the father symbol. His own father-hero myth had been shattered. He cannot play a role for others when the father he believed in has proved unworthy. In *All My Sons* and *Death of a Salesman*, the Telemachus theme is repeated as father and son, representing different worlds, strive to find one another and never meet.* In *After the Fall*, the mother is equally tarnished. She abuses her husband for having lost the family fortune during the Depression, and is deceitful with her young son. Quentin is offered a sailboat to compensate for having been left alone when the parents went on vacation without telling him the truth. The mother's life, a series of frustrations, seeks artistic expression through the son. The simple, naïve girl, his legal client, who would make him God, and the overly adoring mother who would make him her atonement are responsible for two traumatic experiences imbedded deeply in Quentin's memory, which alter the concept of love. As the mother shouts, "I didn't trick you. Quentin, I'll die if you do that. I saw a star when you were born, a light in the world," her guilt explodes in his mind, and his fingers seize the throat of Maggie as she lies gasping for breath. Mother and Maggie become one in his subconscious death impulses. Louise, his first wife, wants to be a separate person in her own right, an outgrowth of Ibsen's Nora and an indication of present-day alienations. The second wife wants to cease being a person in her own right and become completely identified with her husband.

Miller is baffled by the mystery of sex and women against which he must fight for salvation and logical clarity. In his earlier plays, women were submissive like Linda Loman or frigid like Elizabeth Proctor. None was too clearly drawn. Men dominated. Now, sensual pleasures alarm Miller with their overtones of innocence and guilt. Harold Clurman has indicated that an "unmis-

---

* For a fuller discussion of the father-son theme in *Death of a Salesman*, see the chapter on Arthur Miller in *The Contemporary Theatre* by Allan Lewis.

takable feature of Miller's work is its Puritanism," the "hankering for total innocence . . . that cannot possibly be achieved." Even the assumption of moral righteousness becomes a sensual pleasure. Harnessing the passions after full release is an effort to avert complete endorsement of sexual excitement.

In *After the Fall* the men are the vaguely defined characters, all save Quentin, who like Biff and "the misfits" is a lonely figure seeking peace between the social image of himself and what his own awareness of the self is. But this retreat into the self is a dangerous process for a writer whose fantasy and imagination rarely rise beyond external events. Miller, in an intensely personal play, is faced with the problem of transfiguring intimate revelations into symbols of general relevance, or in his own rather ponderous words, building "a bridge of human mutuality." In *After the Fall* Miller remains insecurely moored to the left bank—the bridge, a concept rather than a reality.

The critics did not receive the play kindly. Of the daily newspaper reviewers, Howard Taubman almost alone welcomed it as a major achievement marking the return of Arthur Miller to the theatre. Others felt that the memory of the late Marilyn Monroe had been desecrated, and that the playwright was divesting himself of blame in an undignified fashion, blaming the women in his life for his own failures. The weekly critics, particularly in *The New Yorker* and *The New Republic*, berated Arthur Miller mercilessly for retreating into sordid revelation and spreading personal events on the stage in a haphazard manner. *The Village Voice*, more fond of avant-garde writers, wrote:

> Quentin, at all times, remains Arthur Miller, questing among his moral flash-cards, muscling his way toward the perfect analysis . . . For all its earnestness, the play . . . is incredibly square.

Controversy was not quieted by Miller's own statements denying that the characters of the play were actual people and claiming that he had written a parable for modern man, rather than an isolated and particular analysis of Arthur Miller.

Show Magazine, in its May, 1964, issue, was the most vitriolic. It described a supposed new play "hallucinated" by Lillian Hellman about the five men who adored her, entitled *Buy My Guilt*, an obvious parody of *After the Fall*. This mythical play, "now being performed in the converted tiger cages of the Bronx

Zoo on a most advanced thrust-retreat stage," discusses hypothetical men in Hellman's life, parallels of the women in Miller's
life, and in bitter mockery refers to

> my former husband, Rudolph Valentino, poor, dead, bewildered
> symbol of America's sexual dreams. And now my darling Max—he
> is called Helmut in the play—who has brought me happiness or
> something and has defined clearly my sense of evil, the only man
> I ever knew who could hum the whole of *The Magic Flute.*

Most of the judgments were unduly harsh. Many of the
adverse comments were by critics who had grudgingly praised
Miller because of compelling popular demand, or by others who
had been awaiting the opportunity to attack, for Miller, like
Chris in *All My Sons,* had assumed an inner knowledge of correct
procedure that made him the unpopular prophet of a new age.
Now that Miller was no longer certain, but was prostrating himself in frenzied quest for knowledge, those who had stood by
in reluctant awe enjoyed demolishing an unfrocked messiah.

Broadway's insistence on perfection implies that a writer
is as good as his last play. Critics do not judge by historical
perspective or the totality of a man's work. Bertolt Brecht, Sean
O'Casey, and Sartre are permitted lapses. Each, in investigating
new techniques, did not achieve perfection with his first new
play in a different form. Miller was denied the same privilege
and was gleefully relegated to second-rate status by those who
had never liked a socially oriented playwright. If *After the Fall*
had received comparable criticism as a commercial Broadway
production, it would have closed after the first few performances.
A repertory system saved the play, and public response has
rebuked the critics. *After the Fall* was the most successful play
of the Lincoln Repertory season; once the subscriptions had
expired, it ran the entire summer to packed houses as the sole
offering.

Most of the adverse comments centered around the charge
of formlessness. This is indeed strange, for Miller had been
condemned by the same critics for adhering too severely to the
Ibsen technique of the well-made play. Miller had openly announced his effort to abandon realism and to find a form more
consistent with the loose emergence of recalled images. The

radical departure in structure was at least courageous in experiment. Genet and Ionesco used comparable techniques and were admired by the same critics who dismissed Miller. The failure of the new form lies in Miller's unquenchable devotion to realism. Surrealistic fantasy requires poetic expression to carry it beyond the immediate. But *After the Fall* remains a realistic play with scenes rearranged in time and space.

The unpleasant suspicion persists that had the play been submitted by anyone but Arthur Miller, or had his name not been attached to it, or had it been submitted to a generation not familiar with Marilyn Monroe, it might have been regarded as an unusual and provocative experience. The facts of his life are generally known, and the audience did not help the play by indulging in identifying specific characters in real life. The guessing game was an obstacle to involvement, very much like looking at a Rembrandt painting and picking out the names of the assembled burghers rather than concentrating on the totality of the painting, or reading *Ulysses* and being worried about cross-references rather than the idea. The charge of indecently parading what is intensely private has already been answered, but Eugene O'Neill was not loath to do so in *Long Day's Journey into Night*, which, though staged years after his death, is a ruthless exposure of family secrets and was designed to absolve the writer. Strindberg, who had three unsuccessful marriages, repeatedly exposed his intimate experiences to public view. *Dylan*, more acclaimed by the same critics, is an exploitation of the Welsh poet's sexual and suicidal impulses, and *Who's Afraid of Virginia Woolf?* (voted the best play of the year) lays bare every delicate detail of marital infelicity. Many playwrights have done the same. Miller has a right to, if he so chooses.

Accusations of scandal, sensationalism, private catharsis, incoherence, or poor timing are less valid than the criticism that Miller's tortured and anguished soul is made into a fascinating object for observation rather than for empathy. His retreat from social causation into the intensely personal, making human nature responsible for evil and violence, is a failure to live up to his promise of relating man to the forces that surround him. Quentin, the contemporary man, remains Arthur Miller. In another sense, however, the play does rise beyond the personal, for the American man today is disturbed by inability to love or the conflict between love and career. Miller, unlike others who condemn the American woman, does not cast blame, nor does he render himself blameless. He hesitates with his third marriage. He is unsure even at the moment of decision, but he goes on, weakened and no longer in control. Hope is fragmented and confidence wavering.

In Miller's screenplay, *The Misfits*, we see the lonely man, the maverick, who does not accept the morality of middle-class society. Marilyn Monroe was again the figure around which Miller centered his writing. In the motion picture, published later as a screen-play novelette, Miller deals with men who do not want to work for wages and who live removed from the organized economic and social structure. They roam under the open sky, chasing mustangs, taming the last wild replicas of themselves in nature. They are lost, lonely misfits, as is the woman who comes into their lives. The men seek spiritual independence; the woman, sexual.

Loneliness has always plagued the artist. James Baldwin terms it a natural result of the love an artist bears his society— an endless lover's quarrel in which the artist chooses to reveal the truth about his beloved. Eugene O'Neill was such a tormented lover. Arthur Miller, fascinated by the theme "he is strongest who stands alone," rearranged Ibsen's *An Enemy of the People* to emphasize Stockman's ostracism as a result of his dedication to progress. The isolation of the truthful artist is a necessary complement of his task. He invites alienation once he sets himself apart as the professional visionary. Loneliness is tolerable when the artistic achievement that it nourishes brings other people together. Miller regards the theatre as the means of making men less alone. In his earlier plays he succeeded. In *After the Fall* his protagonists stand at the crossroads.

In this sense the play becomes a significant drama of our times. Generalized slogans and idealized panaceas have not achieved universal brotherhood. Exaggerated idealism invokes cynical disrespect. Commitment is difficult when history has undermined the foundation of long-held beliefs. Miller, whose *Death of a Salesman* helped to pillory success-dreams and false illusions, now seeks his own personal truth, as Biff may have been forced to do after Willie Loman's death. Absorption with the self and analysis of motives stem from Miller's consciousness of personal failure as son, husband, and friend:

The truth is that we have not discovered how to be happy and at one with ourselves. We have only gone far in abolishing physical poverty.

Not knowing where to find spiritual exultation, or even what road to pursue, destroys the tight little world of realistic play-writing, for there can be no third-act resolution. Instead of impos-ing solutions, Miller follows the scientific Principle of Indeter-minacy; the playwright, "observing despair, has likewise changed it, if only by raising it to our common consciousness." He does not renege as visionary in asking the audience to co-operate in the pursuit of a recognizable faith. Quentin does marry for a third time. His act, despite his anxiety, is positive. It may be more relevant and meaningful than any superimposed idealism. "Evasion is probably the most developed technique most men have," Miller had said earlier. The commitment Quentin "makes to life or refuses to make" determines the symbolic relevancy of the character for our times. Unlike Albee or Beckett, Miller does not spell out despair behavioristically, seeking metaphors to enshrine the lament. He surrounds his despair with an evocation of a better life, and if he does not know how to attain it spe-cifically, he has the courage to go on seeking. At least, he has changed both himself and the audience by recognizing the problem. The removed playwright has come much closer to his audience.

Miller's earlier work stood

squarely in conventional realism . . . and tried to expand it with an imposition of various forms in order to speak more directly, even more abruptly and nakedly, of what . . . moved [him] behind the visible facades of life.

His plays have consisted of family dramas in which the social issue is revealed through the personal dilemma. The family is a microcosm of a world beyond, and the behavior of an individual in love, sex, or parental relations is evidence of the choices imposed by social necessity. *The Man Who Had All the Luck* deals with a wife and a hired man who have to convince a successful businessman that he is responsible for his own success, that his wealth is fully merited because he actively redirected his environment and made his luck. *All My Sons* focuses on the difference between two moralities and the way in which money has distorted human relationships. Profit-seeking can ignore social responsibility. These first two plays are well-constructed, conventional suspense-dramas.

Death of a Salesman arches beyond Willy Loman into the death of an ideology, the death of a set of values by which salesmen live and which no longer functions in our present society. The structure of the play is Miller's initial departure from severe realism. When time past and present coalesce, the moment of decision is reached. Miller wrote a contemporary morality play of Everyman, the Salesman. Willy Loman, the most convinced devotee of success and the likable personality, to whom all human values are salable, awakens to the emptiness of his dreams. For an artist to rebel is traditional. For the humdrum salesman, the monument to mediocrity, to refuse to accept his epitaph is catastrophic. A tragedy of classic proportion was in the making. Arthur Miller softened the explosive impact by overplaying the father-son conflict. Willy Loman commits suicide. He cannot sell himself in life. He can sell himself only in death, by bequeathing to Biff his paid-up life insurance. But this final sale does not bring a world down with it. It leaves Willy Loman a pitiful lone adventurer of the road, the survivor of free enterprise at its lowest level. The sons are Willy's divided self of the future—one asserting the continuing validity of Willy's dream, the other rejecting it, but left without alternatives. The social forces are overwhelmed by the mystery and passion of personal relationships, a situation repeated more intensely in the Maggie-Quentin sex struggle of *After the Fall.*

Miller is sensitive to the need for redefining tragedy in the contemporary theatre. Aristotelian concepts weigh heavily on an altered world. Willy Loman need not fall from a great height or a small one, his pride crushed by "an unseen pattern behind the clouds." Miller sees Willy as a tragic figure as long as the intensity, "the human passion to surpass given bounds, the fanatic insistence upon a self-conceived role," is present. *Death of a Salesman,* despite its compromises with the inherent logic of the theme, remains a powerful creation, one of the major dramas of the American theatre.

In *A View from the Bridge,* Eddie Carbone turns informer, deserting his own long-held beliefs when passion derails conviction. When does a man name names? When do principles give way to self-interest and emotional excess? Though Miller indicates sympathy for Eddie he condemns his treachery, but the conflict is weakened by pitting ideals against sex suppressions. Principles are not tested, but Eddie's emotional breaking point and the extent of his incestuous love. In this play, Miller continued his break with form. Alfieri, the narrator, moving in and out of the action like Tom in *The Glass Menagerie*, and the unit set are efforts to give wider scope in time and space to a family drama.

The Crucible exposes a shameful period in American history when fanaticism destroyed reason, and witch hunts reduced man to a fearful animal. Miller fights for the right to dissent. *The Crucible*, which pillories the ignorance that mass hysteria can foment, was his bold reply to the McCarthy investigation. It was also his first attempt at an historical document, with many characters and the involvement of an entire community. (A play of his apprenticeship dealing with Montezuma has never been published or produced.) Despite the large cast, *The Crucible* has been produced by community and college theatres throughout the country; the National Repertory Theatre under Eva LeGallienne's leadership found it the most meaningful to audiences in its widely scattered areas. Social comment is portrayed through personal frustrations. Abigail, rejected by John Proctor, turns her lust into hate and revenge, and invents the devil and the evil witches. Mrs. Proctor, on the other hand, who has been a cold and frigid woman, when faced with the supreme sacrifice discards her Puritan inheritance and kisses her husband passionately and freely, finding freedom in unrepressed emotional fullness. Sex and sorcerers become intertwined. A man's name becomes, for Miller, the symbol of ultimate dignity. Proctor faces hanging defiantly when the inquisition insists that he sign a confession. He shouts out, "How may I live without my name?"—the same problem which disturbs Eddie Carbone and Quentin. Man's ultimate self resides in his uniqueness, his name.

In all the plays, the emphasis is on the small man who finds himself alienated from the accepted morality and searches for happiness, alone and fearful of the odds. Miller's protagonist assumes heroic stature by fanatic insistence on a self-conceived role. In *After the Fall*, Quentin is different. He is Miller's first intellectual hero who has no passion other than self-truth and is overwhelmed by the inadequacy of the male. Miller, however, is too powerful an artist, too sensitive a spirit, too logical a mind, too analytical a composer, to remain overwhelmed at the sexual insecurity that Eve thrust upon Adam. He believes the theatre is the most important of the arts, for here man is placed at the center of the world in "the quiet eye of the storm in which he can witness the age-old revelation of man challenging God in the working-out of his fate."

Though death meets the protagonist in the earlier plays, there arises a hope in man's ultimate triumph, and a confidence that human dignity will prevail. *After the Fall* is no longer reassuring, yet the theme is a re-evaluation of hope. The opening lines counterpoint the underlying despair with the promise of joy.

"Every morning when I awake I'm full of hope . . . for an instant there's some . . . unformed promise in the air . . . I can't wait to finish breakfast and . . . it seeps in my room, my life and its pointlessness."

What happens in the play is an attempt to discover the basis of that hope, to understand its source and to repossess it. After seeing how love could kill, and fearing the death of love within him, Quentin looks to Holga and cries up to her, "That woman hopes!" and then adds in resolution, "That's why I wake each morning like a boy—even now, even now!—I swear to you, I could love this world again!"

Ionesco stated, after the reviews of *Rhinoceros*, that the critics this time condemned him for being too clear whereas they had always condemned him in his other plays for being too obscure. He was damned whichever road he took. So too with Arthur Miller. When he dealt with social problems he was condemned for being a playwright still mired in the thirties. When he writes an intensely individual analysis with a breakthrough in form he is condemned for having lost track of the society beyond the self. Miller's radical shift in point of view from the broader aspects to the intensely individual has not been completely assimilated. Psychiatry, as understood by so many writers today, can be harmful to their art. A case study is undramatic, and attempting to find hidden motivations for guilt can remove self-reliance. A rambling couch disclosure becomes too facile.

McCarthyism, World War II, and the gas chambers of Hitler bred fear and disillusionment. The necessity for survival shriveled human motives. *After the Fall* is a compulsive self-revelation. It may violate the ethics of private therapy, but it may well be the self-catharsis Miller needs to return to a broader perspective of the tragedy of contemporary man. With one magnificent achievement in *Death of a Salesman,* and a powerful indictment of ignorance and mass hysteria in *The Crucible,* Arthur Miller stopped to re-examine himself. He once wrote,

> Each member of the audience is carrying with him what he thinks is an anxiety or a hope or a preoccupation which is his alone and isolates him from mankind.

In *After the Fall,* Miller tried to expose his own anxiety as a revelation of mutual suffering with other men. No other American play of the 1964 season was equally ambitious, yet awards were showered upon well-constructed minor efforts such as *Barefoot in the Park* and *Any Wednesday. Luther* captured honors for the best play of the season, yet John Osborne's work is a confused and truncated document about a historical figure, which has less meaningful contemporary relevance. Albert Finney rescued a flawed work that contained more about Osborne than it did about Luther. *After the Fall* was more deserving of the awards. An imperfect play of a gifted mind is generally decried, whereas the slick product of a mediocre talent is hailed, when kudos are bestowed.

Arthur Miller has written only a few plays, but has consistently aimed high. He no longer feels he has "a solution to the enigma of existence beyond questioning." Quentin cannot move beyond his indecision. "A way of life has to be believed in before it can be breached," and Quentin is struggling without belief. He clings to his own dream very much as did Willy Loman. Writing about conviction has brought Arthur Miller close to the loss of conviction, but he does have a humility before the vastness of the problems of life. He has witnessed deception by high-minded idealists; his trust in social amelioration and human betterment impaired by evil on both sides, he yet begins anew to know himself before he can prescribe for society.

Why condemn Miller for seeking moral values and admire Genet and Ionesco for tearing them down? The critics were unable to abstract Miller from Quentin and judge the play objectively, yet with all its doubts and formlessness, *After the Fall* is a drama for our times. For Miller, the session in the confessional booth is over. The hard glare of the public plaza has to be faced. He is capable of a giant step forward.

Incident at Vichy, which opened in December, 1964, as the second play of the second season of the Lincoln Center Repertory Theatre and the second play by Arthur Miller to be presented in one year, was not a giant step forward, but a reassuring sign of his return to issues beyond the self. The replica of Auschwitz which hung over Quentin's self-analysis in *After the Fall* became the living drama of those who were sent to Hitler's gas chambers. Miller had visited Germany and attended the trials of former Nazi officers. He became absorbed by the question of social guilt, and his long one-act drama is, like Rolf Hochhuth's *The Deputy*, a condemnation of failure to assume responsibility.

The play takes place in a detention room in Vichy, France, during the Occupation. A group of suspected Jews has been rounded up and is awaiting interrogation. The situation is typical of dramas in which men face a common danger and respond according to their different codes of self-preservation. As the terror mounts, some of the men—there are no women in the play —crack under pressure; others discover sources of strength. The electrician has faith in the ultimate triumph of the working class; the actor, out of vanity, believes he is the untouchable Jew, for the German people have applauded his art; an old, bearded Jew resorts to prayer. The two central characters are a doctor who was a former French military officer, and a wealthy Austrian prince, who has been detained by mistake. As a lover of beauty and elegance, the prince has a more detached viewpoint, and in the initial discussion he indicates that the unbelievable act of genocide is possible because of its very unbelievability, that the Nazis have achieved the perfection of vulgarity, and that separate individuals preserving a sense of decency are helpless before monolithic evil.

Once the reality of the unbelievable has been established, the second question is how to act. The doctor proposes organized resistance and escape, but each man clings to the hope that he will be the exception and be granted German clemency. The prince, who knows he will be released, offers friendship and sympathy, but to his amazement is rebuffed because of his own latent prejudice and complicity. The doctor uncovers, even in men of good will, the need to blame someone for personal failure. Each man has his "Jew." The prince cannot be exonerated merely by his mere recognition of guilt. He must assume responsibility through deeds. In their final confrontation, the aristocrat hands his release papers to the doctor and remains with the condemned prisoners. He sacrifices himself to save a man whose life is of more value than his. The doctor is capable of actively fighting the Nazis.

The play lacks Miller's usual careful construction and shows evidences of having been too hastily written. The opening terror is not sustained. The action consists of waiting while the victims, one by one, are called into the next room. Drama becomes discussion. The final resolution takes too long to develop, and the debate is weakened by Miller's continuing insistence that evil is part of human nature, that violence is universal. The strength of the play lies in its statement that the few who assume responsibility can alter the course of history. At least, they can assert the dignity of man.

Miller could have written a more effective play had he concentrated less on the dialectics of debate and more on the dialectics of drama, but his willingness to face major issues of the day with honesty and conviction gives stature to an otherwise complacent American theatre.

3

TENNESSEE WILLIAMS —
The Freedom of the Senses

. . . and shall 'till my brush hangs burning
flame at the hunter's door
continue this fatal returning
to places that failed me before!

Cried the Fox

"Now, honey. Now, love. Now, now, love."

A Streetcar Named Desire

ARTHUR MILLER wrote one play in nine years. Tennessee Williams has written four in the past five years. He is a prolific and compulsive writer who turns out at least one new script annually or rewrites an old one. Twenty-five years of constant literary activity since his days of poverty and poetry-writing for the avant-garde magazines in Greenwich Village have led to world reputation and financial security. Yet his recent plays are not equal to the earlier work. Either he has reached the point of exhaustion or has grown submissive to commercial demands. Almost ironically, he stated a few years ago:

I believe that writing or any form of creative work was never meant by nature to be a man's way of making a living, that when it becomes one it almost certainly loses a measure of purity.

The purity is certainly gone. *Sweet Bird of Youth* (1959), and the plays which followed in successive years, *A Period of Adjustment*, *The Night of the Iguana*, and *The Milk Train Doesn't Stop Here Anymore*, are melodramatic versions of former themes.

Despite his recognized position as a playwright, Williams remains the restless, running poet, seeking solace in privacy and far corners of the world and never finding it. He was deeply influenced by D. H. Lawrence, in whose memory he wrote a play, *I Rise in Flames Cried the Phoenix*, and to whom he dedicated a poem, which tells as much about Williams as of Lawrence:

> I run, cried the fox, in circles
> Narrower, narrower still
> Across the desperate hollow
> Skirting the frantic hill . . .
> Calling the pack to follow
> A prey that escaped them still.

The figure of the fox repeats itself in much of his writing.

I still believe that a writer's safety, especially in his middle years, if he began writing in his adolescence . . . lies in a fugitive way of life running like a fox from place to place. . . . I found one other expedient, which is to stop taking a problem as if it affected the whole future course of the world.

Orpheus Descending, the root play of Williams' work, was entitled, in its motion picture version, *The Fugitive Kind*. Running will not write a better play. Williams has long passed the point of decision. His success in the forties has not been sustained. His "natural joyfulness" has abruptly turned him into "something less than a serious writer and more the latest sensation of the entertainment world," where nothing is staler than yesterday's hero. He is troubled, full of self-doubts, and produces increasingly morbid exhibitions of violence and sexual depravity.

Sweet Bird of Youth is a case in point. The first ten minutes are packed with an unbelievable accumulation of degeneracy

and decay. Two people lie on a huge bed, which dominates the
Moorish room of a still-fashionable hotel on the Gulf Coast. One
is a decaying actress wearing a black, eyeless domino to cover
her face from the morning glare; the other is a blond gigolo in
white silk pajamas ("He has the kind of body that white silk
pajamas are or ought to be made for"). The woman is Ariadne
del Lago, a former movie queen, traveling incognito as the Princess Pazmezoglu. She fears heart attacks, admits having a "death
wish," seeks to capture the legend of her youth, is querulous,
alcoholic, hypochondriac, and savagely sexed, and doesn't know
the name of her companion. The young man is Chance Wayne,
who once played in the chorus of *Oklahoma!* and served briefly
and reluctantly in the Korean War. Now he sells his virility to
the highest bidder. She takes pills, drugs, and uses an oxygen
tank to overcome morning suffocation as she squirms restlessly
on the satin covers. He attempts blackmail by using a hidden
tape recorder for their conversation. She is far more experienced
in jungle tactics and "the language of the gutter," and brings
him to submission by using him in the one way she has of for-
getting a shameful past, and "that's through the act of lovemaking." She says, "That's the only dependable distraction, so
when I say *now* because I need that distraction, it has to be now,
not later."

Chance Wayne has returned to his hometown out of a compulsive need to see Heavenly, a young girl whom he once loved,
seduced, and photographed in the nude when she was less than
fifteen. He discovers from an unscrupulous doctor who is to marry
Heavenly, that he (Chance) left the girl so diseased that an
emergency operation was necessary to remove her sexual organs,
and that Heavenly's father, Boss Finley, has determined to avenge
the crime against his daughter by gelding her seducer.

Hollywood craftsmen regard the four essential ingredients
of commercial success as sex, violence, God, and communism.
Usually, one of these ingredients is sufficient around which to
build a script. Williams combines all four. Sex and violence are
abundantly obvious. Politics is added when Boss Finley turns
out to be a bigoted racist; in the second act, for no apparent
reason, his campaign speeches are projected onto a huge television screen. Religious references course through the entire play.
The action takes place on Easter Sunday; the Resurrection of

the Lord and the castration of Chance Wayne are symbolically related, and Heavenly talks about going into a convent. In her sole conversation with Chance, she looks up at the sky and says, "Oh, Lady, wrap me in your starry blue robe. Make my heart your perpetual novena." So anxious was Williams to toss everything into the play that he ignored Ariadne del Lago. She has little to do after the first scene, but in the end is used as a possible escape for Chance. Discovering that her latest motion picture is a box-office success, she offers to take him with her. For ill-defined reasons he rejects the return to her world of phony duplicity, and awaits his fate with calm resignation. As his executioners enter, Chance advances to the forestage and says to the audience,

"I don't ask for your pity, but just for your understanding—not even that! No, just for your recognition of me in you, and the enemy, time, in us all."

Understanding is not difficult to give, but the effort to render the play universal by making Chance a symbol of man's evil is skirting the ridiculous. Williams is obsessed by time. The actress is fighting the depredations of overindulgence. Chance, at twenty-seven, shows the ravages of time, and both fanatically pursue the vanishing "sweet bird of youth." "The age of some people," says Chance, "can only be calculated by the level of rot in them." Kenneth Tynan, reviewing the play, said, "In *Sweet Bird of Youth*, the level is dangerously high. None of Mr. Williams' other plays has contained so much rot." As fascinated by depravity as a Puritan is by sin, Williams mounted an agglomeration of clichés, with little or no relevance to reality. He states that Chance and Ariadne are both castrated—she by time, he by the vigilantes. Tenderness and warmth vanish. The themes of time, youth, and loneliness refuse to be integrated with political reaction and race hatred. The dream world of unfortunate people becomes a romantic melodrama, and tragedy is reduced to psychopathology. Here indeed is decay in all its odors, a playwright profiting from "the abuse of the terrible" and the exploitation of the obscene. The production was not helped by the circus direction of Elia Kazan, although Geraldine Page rescued the play with a brilliant performance as Ariadne del Lago. Paul Newman, struggling to give credibility to the role of Chance, was hemmed in by the script.

Conscious of adverse criticism, Williams, in his next play, *Period of Adjustment,* made an effort at "light comedy." The editors of *Esquire* magazine, which published the text simultaneously with the Broadway opening, called it the "cleanest" of Williams' works, "virtually Sunday-school reading" as compared with *Sweet Bird of Youth.* The play, they stated, deals with the truism that "love conquers all," and could be subtitled "Sex Can Be Fun." They hastened to add that it was only a *relatively* clean play, fearing that the adjective might drive readers away. Two couples are having marital difficulties. One couple, recently married, is unable to consummate; the other has just split up through over-consummation. How they finally resolve their difficulties and bridge the long road from His to Hers is the comic-strip material of this effort at reform. The setting is a Spanish-type suburban bungalow built over a large cavern into which it is slowly sinking. A student nurse, Isabel Haverstick, is the newlywed who, as the play opens, is still a virgin. Her husband George boasts of his prowess with women, but suffers from fears of impotence. His army buddy, Ralph Bates, has married Dorothea, the homely daughter of a millionaire. She has compensated for over-protective parents by developing an insatiable sexual appetite, which the psychiatrist had mistaken for psychological frigidity. Almost everyone in the play has the shakes. George gets the shakes when he has to perform his nightly marital duties. Dorothea's buck teeth shake from overexcitement at the prospect, and the house itself shivers over the cavern below—presumably the symbolism to indicate the shaky foundations on which society and its moral absurdities rest.

Williams was anxious to reject violence and return to compassion and tenderness. He precedes the play with the lines:

> little words of tenderness
> are those I never learned to say.

And Isabel, as she is shown the house, says, "There is such a tender atmosphere in the sweet little bedroom, you can almost— touch it." And Ralph, in explaining to George how to approach a woman, says, "You didn't appreciate the natural need for using

some tenderness with it." As the curtain comes down at the end
of the play, both couples are reassuringly tucked into separate
beds. The Period of Adjustment is over. It is Williams' weakest
play, never rising above the commercial comedy formula. His
arduous effort to retreat from depravity proved that he was more
effective in the world of Stanley Kowalski.

Fortunately, in his next play, *The Night of the Iguana*, Williams returned to his favorite lost and lonely people whose
private images are shattered by the ugliness of reality. The play
was originally a short piece performed at Spoleto, Italy, and was
expanded for Broadway production the following year. Williams
came close to redeeming his previous failures, for the characters
are alive in suffering and drawn with the old mastery. The play
suffers by being forced beyond its original limits. The introduction of the insensitive German tourists singing the Horst Wessel
song is too obvious, since the theme of the play is clearly apparent after the first act. The locale is a run-down inn on the west
coast of Mexico.

The central character is Shannon, a defrocked minister, who
had been ousted from his church for pronouncing atheistic precepts and seducing young girls. He now works as an unsuccessful
tourist guide. Maxine, who runs the inn, is lusty, foul-mouthed,
and possessive, and wants Shannon for herself. She knows that
as she grows older, she can no longer live with the pleasures of
the flesh, and she needs Shannon as a captive lover and companion. Two unusual characters for Williams are Hannah, the
spinster who sells water colors in the public plaza and accom-
panies Nonno, her 97-year-young grandfather, a poet. Hannah
is reserved, well-mannered, virginal, and sensitive to the sufferings of other people. She stifles her physical passions, denying
herself emotional freedom, but spiritually she is at rest with
the world. She is the reverse of Shannon. He has lost God and
found release in vice. She is the saint, timeless and feminine, but
unfulfilled. These two ill-mated persons deeply affect one another,
each needing what the other has to offer. The iguana, a lizard
whose meat is a delicacy, is captured by the local urchins and
tethered under the porch to be fattened for tomorrow's meal.

As all poets must, Williams uses symbols to express what
lies beyond the spoken word. The glass menagerie, the streetcar,
and the iguana follow in the path of the cherry orchard and the

wild duck, but with Williams the symbol is too removed from the full action of the play, though in one scene it serves magnificently. Shannon, prompted by Hannah, cuts the iguana loose in a positive gesture, thus permitting one trapped creature to reach the darkness of the forest, even though he knows that in doing so he ties himself to a future life of agonized torture with Maxine. With Ibsen and Chekhov, the symbol is woven into the lives of all the characters and enriches the implications of the text. With Williams, it is superimposed, an obvious reference to all the little folk trapped and fattened for slaughter by those more brutal and less sensitive—the division of the world into what John Gassner called the "eater" and the "eaten." Lillian Hellman, in *The Little Foxes*, uses the same figure. Alexandra reminds Regina: "Addie said there were people who ate the earth and other people who stood around and watched them do it." Though Shannon and Hannah are those who will be "eaten," he cuts the iguana loose as a sign of defiance and a recognition that some can be saved.

The most moving scene in the play is the one in which Hannah and Shannon reach out and touch one another as they discard layers of lying and deception. Hannah, the pilgrim, brings to Shannon, the minister, an understanding of Christian ethics and self-awareness. She stands alone in Williams' gallery as a positive character for good. When Shannon rather truculently asks her if she can tell him what his problem is, she replies, "The oldest one in the world. The need to believe in something or in someone." She has discovered something to believe in: "Broken gates between people so they can reach each other, even if it's just for one night only." What gives the scene a delicate poetic quality is the way in which the iguana theme is translated into personal relations. Shannon straps himself in the hammock, pretending to be unable to move, so as to attract Hannah's attention. He rails at his fate and pleads for her to release him. Unlike the iguana, he is responsible for his own captivity. He shouts to her, "You think I like being tied in this hammock, trussed up in it like a hog being hauled off to slaughter?" Hannah calmly reminds him that she understands the game he is playing, and points out that he enjoys the suffering:

"There's something almost voluptuous in the way you twist and groan in that hammock—no nails, no blood, no death. Isn't that a comparatively comfortable, almost voluptuous kind of crucifixion to suffer for the guilt of the world, Mr. Shannon?"

His will sapped, he no longer struggles to be free, and resigns himself to a sensuous enjoyment of his torture, but a conscious direction had been indicated. *The Night of the Iguana* is the most affirmative play that Williams has written. Two characters have comforted one another and reached an inner peace. Shannon returns to an awareness of God, and Hannah knows that her prudishness is a pose, that her body can come alive with love, and old Nonno, before he dies, completes his poem.

The Milk Train Doesn't Stop Here Anymore is unusual, not only for its title, but for being the only play that failed on Broadway, was rewritten, and then reproduced a few months later with a different cast and director. Like *The Night of the Iguana*, it was a one-act play presented at Spoleto and later blown up into a full-length play. Not the least discouraged by its failure on opening night, Williams induced David Merrick, the most successful of Broadway producers, to present it once more with Tony Richardson as director and Tallulah Bankhead as the star. All three versions were failures. Not even the name of Tennessee Williams could keep the play running.

The Milk Train is about a dying actress, old and wealthy, who lives in a mansion on the southern coast of Italy. She is an unregenerate disciple of evil, who drinks heavily, takes dope, and is dictating her memoirs. The young man who appears out of the sea and comes uninvited is the Angel of Death. He pleads with her to recognize God and be aware of powers beyond the self. She woos him with the pleasures of the senses and the sadistic thrills of completely denying the rights of others—a medieval morality play on the libertine and his conscience. To fill in the emptiness of the action and the thinness of the debate, stagehands move about replacing scenery and participating in the conversation. Williams had exhausted the vein he tapped too frequently. The poetic imagery is hollow, the thoughts pretentious. The play sounds like a rehearsal of his own private conversations, and may indicate that Williams was struggling to find theatrical expression for new themes. He had long been a brilliant inventor of emotionally intense scenes, and was pitifully anxious to include a play of ideas. He writes of Flora Goforth, the obscene and vulgar sensualist dying in her villa on the Divina Costiera, that he hopes the audience will pity "this dying female clown, even while her absurd pretensions and her panicky last effort to hide from her final destruction make you laugh at her." Chris, the godlike young messenger from the sea, pure and handsome, is obviously intended as a Hippolytus-Christ figure. In writing a parable of the Resurrection, Williams' intellectual strivings are woefully weak. His greatest gift lies in suggesting ideas through emotional relations.

The Christ figure occurs also in Tennessee Williams' first play, *The Battle of Angels,* which was tried out in Boston by the Theatre Guild in 1940, and did not reach New York. The author was deeply attached to this failure, and kept revising it, until seventeen years later it arrived on Broadway as *Orpheus Descending.* Much of the later plays derive from this work. Val Xavier, the young man with the guitar and the snakeskin jacket, who wanders into the small southern town, is St. Francis Xavier (Saviour) combined with Orpheus descending into Hell. Val, the first of a long series of Williams' pilgrims, brings light and life to the emotionally starved women of an isolated, ignorant, backward community. Chris, of *The Milk Train Doesn't Stop Here Anymore,* attempts to bring spiritual liberation to an old woman approaching death. Sex and violence are underplayed. The play becomes dull talk and no action. Williams is more effective on the Dionysian level, where he equates freedom of the senses with freedom of the spirit. Val is a Christ of the Passions, with mild social overtones. The message he brings to Lady is that "there's just two kinds of people, the ones that are bought and the buyers!"—an early version of the "eaten" and the "eaters." Val, however, adds a third kind—the "kind that's never been branded." In a long, lyric passage that sets him apart from the hard-skinned dullards, he talks of the legless birds that "live their whole life on the wing" and "sleep on the wind" and "never light on this earth but one time when they die." The imagery, excellent though it is, belongs in a separate poem, for it is unrelated to a Pilgrim who must effect miracles on earth.

Val touches the crushed spirit of the sheriff's wife: "You started to paint as if God touched your fingers . . . you made some beauty out of this country with these two soft woman hands." He reaches Carol, whose defiant sex exhibitionism is a struggle against her loneliness. She admits "the act of lovemaking is almost unbearably painful," but she endures it because "to be not alone even for a few minutes is worth the pain and the danger." To Lady's barren frame he brings life, and she shouts, "I've won, I've won, Mister Death. I'm going to bear!" at the moment her withered, malignant husband appears on the landing and shoots her. The child announced on Christmas Eve and illegitimately fathered by the Christ figure will never be born. Val is caught by the posse armed with a blowtorch. It bursts into blue flames against the eerie darkness of the Confectionery, like a scene from the inferno, and since Val's miracles are effected by sex, the Crucifixion becomes the Castration. The Orpheus-Redeemer is cast into a southern Hell.

Though he has been attacked for such explosive melodramatic endings, they are no worse than the blood-and-thunder scenes of Jacobean drama. Their power is that they reach beyond the immediate locale to wherever brutality and ugliness suppress the cry for beauty.

The next two plays are distinctly different in theme and structure, the product of Williams' richest creative years. *The Glass Menagerie* is one of the finest moments in the American theatre. Four characters and a one-purpose set are closer to Ibsen's aims, but a double scrim, off-stage music, effective lighting, and the glass figurines superimpose an atmosphere of dreams and unreality. In a mood piece of tender beauty, form and meaning are skillfully merged into a minor masterpiece. Amanda, foisting her illusions on her unwilling children, lives in the past with pretensions to glory. She resents her present poverty and escapes from it by self-deception and invented romance. Tom, the son, is unable to restore the family fortunes. Laura, crippled, retires to her own dream world. The structure of the play is simple—the preparations for the Gentleman Caller, his arrival, and his departure—but in the process the characters are clearly revealed as inevitably doomed to heartbreak and pain, lost in a struggle against a reality they do not comprehend. No one is wittingly cruel, but all are deeply hurt. Even the Gentleman Caller, once a high school hero, has been reduced to mediocrity and a belief in popular success myths. Tom runs away, beyond

the confining room to the open sea, but finds no rainbow's end. Laura, the victim of misplaced love, is broken like her glass unicorn, and resigned to continued rejection. Amanda's silliness is gone. A quiet dignity enshrouds her defeat as she comforts her daughter. Tom, "attempting to find in motion what was lost in space," returns to urge Laura to blow out her candle, "for nowadays the world is lit by lightning!" Images of light and darkness weave in and out in a chiaroscuro of unattainable happiness.

In *A Streetcar Named Desire*, the insensitivity of Stanley Kowalski is pitted against the delicacy of Blanche DuBois. They fight for the love of Stella, "its voice an instant in the wind." Stella is caught between duty to her sister and the physical need for Stanley. The final scene is terrifying when Stella surrenders her last hold on refinement and chooses the brutal sensuality of Stanley. As Blanche is taken away to the asylum, Stella stands weeping on the porch, whispering the name of her sister, conscious of her guilt. Stanley pulls her to him, touches her body, and whispers voluptuously, "Now, now love. Now, love." Inside, the men are drinking beer, as Steve says, "This game is seven-card stud."

Stanley and Blanche are worthy opponents using different techniques and weapons. Blanche cannot triumph, for the world belongs to the Stanleys, and he must eliminate her if his own values are not to be threatened. The rape on the night Stella gives birth in the hospital is unbearably brutal but dramatically essential. Stella is life and Blanche is death, and sex, which can create new life, can also destroy the delicate balance and drive Blanche to insanity. Blanche is another pathetic victim who descends from emotional shock to whoredom to mental decay.

Williams' imagery plays again with variations on light. As Blanche tells Mitch, her gentleman caller, of the suicide of her first husband, who turned out to be a homosexual, she says,

"The searchlight which had been turned on the world was turned off again and never for one moment since has there been any light that's stronger than this—kitchen—candle."

As Mitch offers marriage, which for Blanche means safety, protection, and her only salvation, she cries out fervently, "Sometimes—there's God—so quickly!", a line Williams clung to as his personal credo.

The plays that followed are variations of the themes of his first three works. They range from the nymphomania of the minister's virginal daughter who becomes a prostitute in *Summer and Smoke*, the family violence of *Cat on a Hot Tin Roof* and the cannibalism of *Suddenly Last Summer*, to the disintegration of the old actress writing her memoirs of evil in *The Milk Train*. Present-day critical evaluation has been unfavorable. Men like Alan S. Downer and Gerald Weales point out literary defects, the repetition of theme and character, the use of melodramatic clichés, and inferior craftsmanship. Even the lyrical quality of the prose that established Tennessee Williams as the poet of the theatre has been minimized. An American playwright, it seems, is never forgiven his failures. Williams could well have stopped writing after *A Streetcar Named Desire* and been considered a major playwright. He is guilty of heeding the call of commercial success and relying on sex and violence as solutions to human problems. He dissipated a rare talent, but much of the criticism leveled at him is overanalytical. Only a one-play playwright is exempt from the charge of repeating his themes and characters. Shakespeare was concerned with the problem of good and evil in all of his tragedies, and Iago is repeated in Edmund, Goneril, and Richard III. Many scenes, such as the dropping of the handkerchief in *Othello*, or the accidental failure of the Friar's letter to arrive in *Romeo and Juliet*, are contrived, and Shakespeare never hesitated to use melodrama. A writer's work flows from an overall point of view, and all his plays are variations on a theme. Williams' problem is that he achieved mastery with his first plays and has gone downhill ever since. The natural expectation was for him to surpass *The Glass Menagerie*.

The basic conflict of all major drama is good and evil, as it is in life. Shakespeare gave it the scope of all human existence. Tennessee Williams carves out one corner of a vast problem and explores it in depth, a corner that is dark and shadowy, peopled by the hurt and the haunted, surrounded by evil in ugly forms. The victims do not rise in splendid opposition, but retreat more deeply into their aberrations. Revolt is expressed in sexual freedom. Williams, himself, is like a character in his plays. He is so conscious of his Puritan heritage that he carries his opposition to defiant exhibitionism.

The overall perspective validates the claim that no playwright of our times has created greater magic in the theatre. He writes for the stage and for actors. Laurette Taylor, as Amanda in *The Glass Menagerie*, gave stature to the art of performance. Geraldine Page rose to fame after *Sweet Bird of Youth*, and *A Streetcar Named Desire* propelled Marlon Brando to such success that the next generation of actors imitated his mannerisms and his inaudibility.

Times have changed since 1940, but Williams has continued to pursue the same course. Frail derelicts with false dreams may no longer be pertinent in an age accustomed to extreme negativism or desperately searching for a positive faith, yet Williams cannot be easily dismissed. When his artistry controlled and shaped his material and held it in check, an incandescent beauty glowed in the theatre. His fault lies, not in pursuing the same theme, but in failing to expand and enrich it. At his best, he is the American Baudelaire, crying aloud to shield the sensitive and running for protection to the power of evil.

4

THORNTON WILDER AND WILLIAM SAROYAN
— The Comic Vein and "Courage for Survival"

"Oh earth, you're too wonderful for anybody to realize you."

Our Town

"Well, that's what life is: disappointment, illusion."

The Matchmaker

"Fire your feeble guns. You won't kill anything. There will always be poets in the world."

My Heart's in the Highlands

"Seek Goodness everywhere and when it is found bring it out of its hiding place and let it be free and unashamed."

The Time of Your Life

THORNTON WILDER and William Saroyan are grouped together as prophets of optimism, a rare commodity in the serious theatre of today. Though ordinarily one would hardly pair the quiet dignity of Wilder with the undisciplined rebellion of Saroyan,

66

the two playwrights are alike in an affirmative response to life. Neither has been too active in the theatre of the past decade, but the first signs of an upswing against the theatre of negativism have given new impetus to revivals of their plays and to a reconsideration of their influence. Both write of simple human beings surrounded by the mystery and enjoyment of life. Saroyan is more instinctive, responding on the immediate emotional level. Wilder coats his small-town folk with philosophic overtones. Both come close to the sermon of a Unitarian minister who has had his fling in Greenwich Village. They seek to break with the "box set" of conventional realism, and are unabashed at giving full lyric expression to the homespun message of heart-warming faith in man.

Wilder is the more careful craftsman, planned and deliberate. After painful analysis, he arrives at the awe and wonder of the simple things in life. Saroyan is reckless and impulsive and responds to life's beauty instinctively. Wilder revises painstakingly: "I constantly rewrite, discard, and replace . . . There are no first drafts in my life. An incinerator is a writer's best friend." Saroyan appeared on a motion picture set in London with the first line of a screen play and informed those present that the rest of the story would unfold from combined improvisation, while they were shooting. Wilder is the leisured writer with financial means for intellectual detachment; Saroyan is headline sensationalism, dissipating energies and money—yet both have consistently refused to conform to the demands of the commercial theatre.

In the theatre, Wilder has been the more active in the past decade. *Plays for Bleecker Street* was presented at the Circle in the Square Theatre in 1962. Only the first three of a projected series of fourteen one-act plays were offered by the off-Broadway Bleecker Street Theatre, for which they were expressly written. *Hello, Dolly!* (a musical play based on Wilder's *The Matchmaker*) was the outstanding box-office success of the 1963 season and gives every indication of equaling the sustained record of *My Fair Lady. A Life in the Sun,* based on the Alcestis legend, was performed at the Edinburgh Festival in 1955, was retitled *The Alcestiad,* and then became the libretto for an opera by Louise Talma, produced in Frankfurt in 1962. Paul Hindemith wrote the music for *The Long Christmas Dinner,* which Wilder

revised for the premiere in Mannheim in 1961. Leonard Bernstein, composer and director of the New York Philharmonic
Society, has indicated his interest in writing the score for a
musical play of *The Skin of Our Teeth.*

Wilder's reputation was first earned as a novelist with *The
Cabala* (1925), *The Bridge of San Luis Rey* (1927), and *The
Woman of Andros* (1930). He has written only four full-length
plays: *Our Town, The Skin of Our Teeth,* and *The Matchmaker*
(*The Alcestiad* is still unpublished and unperformed in this
country). Like many European writers, particularly the French
and the Russian, he turns to the theatre for an immediate relationship with audiences and for a definitive summation of his
philosophy in human terms. His admiration for the theatre is
based on his belief that

> in the great ages it carried on its shoulders the livest realization of
> public consciousness. The tragic and comic poets of Greece, Lope
> de Vega, Corneille, Racine, Shakespeare, were recognized by their
> contemporaries as expressing what every citizen felt dimly and
> rejoiced to hear concretely.

The theatre should stir the passions and direct the mind. In a
recent interview Wilder recalled longingly the time when, at
the first performance of Euripides' *Medea,* "strong men fainted
and several children were prematurely born." The theatre can
be restored to its commanding position if it pursues its role as
a critic of society and becomes "the art form by which a nation
recognizes its greatness."

Our Town, first produced in 1938, achieved this mission. It
has come to be considered the most typically American play—
a classic of our time. The plot need not be repeated, for the
play is known to every high school student, performed by every
community theatre, and regarded as an essential element in the
repertory of most professional groups. It is a miracle of theatrical
magic. By eliminating the usual techniques of realistic representation, and avoiding all pretense, greater illusion was achieved.
Wilder is interested in people and ideas, in "reality not verisimilitude." He merged form and meaning in a rare example of artistic
unity.

The absence of scenery and elaborate costumes or props,
other than a few chairs, a stepladder, and similar simple physical

devices, may invite production by budget-conscious producers, but Wilder regards the physical accessories as the least necessary of the theatre's demands. The inner reality of each individual is unique, and imagination is preferable to mechanical devices to achieve it. "Our claim, our hope, our despair are in the mind, not in things, not in scenery," he wrote in the preface to his published plays, and insisted that since the play is a parable of modern times, the language which conveys the meaning should be "heard, not diverted." Such statements by any playwright are usually more theory than fact. *Our Town* appeals to the eye as well as to the ear, and audiences are amused by the bare upstage brick wall.

Wilder substitutes a different "scenery"; in *The Skin of Our Teeth* it becomes elaborate at times. Brecht was equally anxious to put an end to the Belasco era, but he used the complementary theatre arts for his purpose, to overwhelm through multiple sense appeals—music as well as words, props as well as costumes, reading as well as hearing. Wilder is likewise not recounting an anecdote or telling a story, which proscenium stage encourages. The unencumbered set reaches into "the truth operative in everyone. The less seen the more heard."

Wilder's departure from the staging of the well-made play was not original. He knew the work of Pirandello and the German expressionists. He had translated André Obey's *Le Viol de Lucrèce*, and *The Merchant of Yonkers* (later *The Matchmaker*) was an adaptation of a work by the nineteenth-century Viennese playwright, Johann Nestroy. More influential, perhaps, was his admiration for the Oriental theatre, which he knew well from his many years in the Far East when his father served in the diplomatic corps. A platform and a passion were the only indispensable ingredients; reducing the theatre to its skeletal requirements made it free to reach beyond the immediate. But no recital of influences can diminish Wilder's originality. All writers take from others. Wilder was skillful enough to add new touches, which, in turn, were seized upon by his European contemporaries—Brecht, Duerrenmatt, and Max Frisch in particular. His techniques made a deeper impression abroad; his story received wider acceptance in his own country.

The Stage Manager, who acts as narrator, commentator, and judge and participates in the action in several roles, is a genial creation. It is he who unites the play, disarms the audience, speaks for the author, and breaks the limitations of time and space. He is Greek chorus, Laudisi of Pirandello's *Six Characters in Search of an Author,* the poet in many guises of Strindberg's *Dream Play,* and Thornton Wilder. Narrators have been used with increasing frequency ever since, as in *The Glass Menagerie, After the Fall,* and *The Ballad of the Sad Cafe.*

Our Town summarizes the totality of life in a small New England village. The first act is labeled "Daily Life"; the second, "Love and Marriage"; the third, obviously, "Death." Grover's Corners is a community set against all of time. The characters are not specific individuals, psychologically revealed, but types. The Webbs and the Gibbses are representative of American middle-class life. Emily and George are young boy and young girl. They have already become legendary, ingrained in the myths of a nation. The method Wilder employs is quickly apparent. The smallest daily chores, the most repeated of living action, the local events—doing homework, listening to the Albany train, watching the boy down at the stable, ironing a dress—are magnified to equality with the movement of the stars. Whatever *is,* belongs to an intricately connected and meaningful system. Just as the earth is a speck in an endless succession of planetary units, so each moment of breathing is part of the history of man. Timelessness and pancakes are discussed in the same everyday language.

Most of the scenes could be inserted into a realistic play. Even the dead talk as though they were gathered around a New Hampshire cracker barrel. Pain and suffering are tolerable, for what we endure is both unique and common to all. Emily's early death in childbirth touches our hearts, but she is still with us in death. Her final statement is the lesson we never learn:

> "We don't have time to look at one another . . . Oh earth, you're too wonderful for anyone to realize you . . . Do any human beings ever realize life while they live it—every, every minute?"

Simon Stimson, the local drunk, now with the deceased, answers:

> "That's what it was to be alive . . . to spend and to waste time, as though you had a million years."

Middle-class life is given dignity by relating it to the cosmos. Wilder objected to the theatre which arose in the nineteenth century with the domination of the merchant. "They wanted their theater soothing . . . they distrusted the passions and tried to deny them." The rules that developed for the situation play which did not disturb deprived the theatre of vitality. Wilder, resenting middle-class domination, broke all the rules and wrote the most complete middle-class play.

The Skin of Our Teeth uses the same technique, but carries it to the logical conclusion of relating the seemingly unimportant to the grandiose. Mr. and Mrs. Antrobus, of Excelsior, New Jersey, are Adam and Eve, Renaissance figures, and also the suburban neighbors next door. All history is merged with the present, picturing the rise from primordial ignorance to the continuing problem of survival. In the first act, man is pitted against the destructive forces of nature. The audience is called upon to help, Prometheus-like, by passing up chairs to keep the home fires burning during the glacial age. In the second act, man is ranged against the moral order, and in the third, against himself. A typical American family is the Human Family. The allegory borders upon the fantastic and the incredible—Mr. Antrobus' arrival on time at his office is as important as the invention of the wheel and the alphabet.

Wilder's use of composite historical characters was similar to that in *Finnegans Wake*. He had lectured on the work of James Joyce at the University of Chicago, and was taken to task for not indicating his sources. Wilder dismissed the charges by adding to the preface of the published version of the play:

> I should be very happy if, in the future, some author should feel similarly indebted to any work of mine. Literature has always more resembled a torch race, than a furious dispute among heirs.

The play is a brilliant example of expressionistic theatre. Unities of place and action are abolished. Man's fate is compressed into a circus satire in which burlesque and vaudeville antics combine with tightrope-walking on the razor edge of despair. Like Max Frisch in *The Chinese Wall* and Bertolt Brecht in *Mother Courage*, Wilder indicates that man has learned little from experience, but must go on laughing and striving. He cannot renege now and permit chaos to triumph. Somehow or other, he will survive. At the end of the play, when Antrobus has lost "the most important thing of all: the desire to begin again, to start building," Sabina, who is Vice and Virtue, Sex and Self-interest, Love and Deception, admonishes him, as she prepares to go to the movies, that she will work with him if he has any ideas about "improving the crazy old world." Antrobus adds:

> "I've never forgotten for long at a time that living is struggle . . . all I ask is the chance to build new worlds and God has always given us that . . . we've come a long way."

As Sabina comes downstage to tell the audience good-night, she reassures all that as far as Mr. and Mrs. Antrobus are concerned, "their heads are full of plans and they are as confident as the first day they began."

Though hailed in Europe, the play had a mixed reception in New York. Many regarded it as a silly extravaganza, a sophomoric lampoon of history. Brooks Atkinson was enthusiastic, terming it "one of the wisest and friskiest comedies." The play won for Wilder his third Pulitzer Prize, his second for a dramatic work. It ranks with the best of Brecht—an example of historical realism in which the accumulation of evidence permits audiences to pass judgment.

The Merchant of Yonkers was Wilder's only failure, despite the fanfare that attended a production by Max Reinhardt, with an all-star cast headed by Jane Cowl and June Walker. Wilder refused to let the material die. He was determined to pull it through to survival, in the manner of Antrobus with mankind. Rewritten as *The Matchmaker* and directed by Tyrone Guthrie, the play did prove a success sixteen years later. The retired and professorial Wilder had become the maverick with three consecutive triumphs.

A libretto by Michael Stewart and music and lyrics by Jerry Hyman transformed *The Matchmaker* into *Hello, Dolly!*—the outstanding musical play of the 1964 season. The production was a triumph of the theatre arts, a vindication of the major trend in musical theatre. Choreography, costumes, design, and songs were interrelated with plot. Gower Champion, the director, exercised an overall control that fashioned a unified experience in the tradition of *Oklahoma!* Wilder's play gained in the process. As an acted piece, it was handicapped by reliance on verbal appeal. The musical version gave fuller scope than Wilder's original prose to the joyous sensation of being alive. The appeal to the eye, which Wilder had discounted, the multiple appeal to the ear, the evocation of unheard songs, enhanced a mediocre work and achieved a refreshing reiteration of "Isn't the world full of such wonderful things?" Sentimental and nostalgic, *Hello, Dolly!* restates the trite maxims that love conquers all, that woman is the greatest work of God, and that money is good only when it becomes "manure to be spread around to help young things grow." Despite Wilder's efforts to convert the middle-class theatre from its devotion to the soporific and its ignoring of the

> questions about the nature of life which seem to be sufficiently answered by the demonstration of financial status and by conformity to some clearly established rules of decorum,

the hit musical inspired by Wilder's work is a *soothing* play.

This raises the question of Thornton Wilder's amazing gift. He deals with the most commonplace, the most trivial, relationships and gives the impression of being exceedingly profound. Remove the deceptive overtones, and his work all winds up with a simplistic philosophy—live every moment of your life, for life is beautiful; the tragedy is human wastefulness. Such nostrums, as in the case of Saroyan, fall short of revelation. The arts of the theatre, skillfully employed, can cover dross with an alluring sheen.

A defense of Wilder can be based on his similarity with Camus. Both explore consciously the absurdity of man's plight, reject irrational remedies, and end by asserting that at least one can live by not adding to the suffering of mankind. Both recognize the anxieties that plague the world, but rather than welcome defeat, they rely on man to effect solutions as he always has. Optimism is better conveyed in song and dance. *Hello, Dolly!* may be Wilder's most explicit statement.

Plays for Bleecker Street is an attempt to express in dramatic terms a definitive summary of Wilder's beliefs. The cycle of one-act plays will constitute a morality of the twentieth century. The theatre, Wilder feels, can be strengthened to achieve its role as the "signature of an age."

The overall title, *Plays for Bleecker Street,* is added proof of Wilder's opposition to the picture-frame stage, which "militates against belief" and squeezes the drama into a "removed showcase." A precondition for a revitalized theatre is to "kick the proscenium down." Wilder enjoys reminding us that in the great theatre of the past the audience encircled the acting area on three sides. The plays were entrusted to the Circle in the Square Theatre, a pioneer in the growing arena theatre movement. Though Wilder can afford artistic independence, his action was a courageous defiance of Broadway commercialism and its reluctance to experiment. He gave a boost to the struggling little theatres of New York by proving his willingness to have his work seen first at a small, off-Broadway organization.

The cycle consists of two series of seven plays each, entitled respectively *The Seven Ages of Man* and *The Seven Deadly Sins.* The first will be for five actors, the second for four. Eventually, when completed, all fourteen will be presented in sequence on several successive evenings in the theatre. The only ones available so far are *Infancy* and *Childhood,* the first two of *The Seven Ages of Man,* and *Someone from Assisi* or *Lust,* number four of *The Seven Deadly Sins.*

Infancy deals with two children in perambulators being taken for a walk by their parents. The parts of the children are played by grown actors dressed in baby clothes, who comment on the world situation, the adult world, and their own growing pains. Their highly imaginative response to their environment is reminiscent of Wordsworth's "The child is father to the man." *Childhood* reveals the gulf that separates the inner worlds of children and adults, no matter how wholesome and loving their relationship may be. In both plays, the child's struggle for improvement is thwarted by those who are older. "The reason why the world is in such a sloppy state," Wilder has remarked, "is that our parents were so stupid." The third of the plays deals with a fictionalized incident in the life of St. Francis of Assisi, when he was seized with desire for the beautiful Mona Lucrezia.

On the basis of but three examples of a large undertaking, judgment can be only tentative. *Infancy* is in the gay mood of *The Skin of Our Teeth,* and is by far the most effective on stage. *Someone from Assisi* is a disappointment. It lacks purpose and gives the impression of being removed from context. It is a serious sermon about the nature of lust, and Wilder is much more comfortable in the comic vein. The total concept of the cycle, however, is on a grand scale—the use of the theatre to crystallize views about "our lives and errors" from birth to death.

> I am interested in the drives that operate in society and in every man. Pride, avarice, and envy are in every home. I am not interested in the ephemeral—such subjects as the adulteries of dentists. I am interested in those things that repeat and repeat in the lives of millions.

With this statement, Thornton Wilder, at seventy, becomes the youngest of our playwrights.

With the Group Theater production in 1939 of the long one-act play *My Heart's in the Highlands,* William Saroyan became the most controversial figure on the American scene; Saroyan provoked further discord himself with his sensation-seeking antics and public defiance of the critics. To those who were insensitive to his play, he recommended "rest, recreation and reading." His meteoric rise was short-lived; he became, just as quickly, the forgotten man of the theatre. A dark world, doubtful of survival, ceased to look kindly on his glib reiteration of the joy in the human heart, yet he has never retreated from his original position.

Untouched by a changing world situation and undaunted by adverse criticism, Saroyan continues to be a prolific writer. One new play, *The Cave Dwellers,* appeared on Broadway in 1957, but two have been presented in Europe and others are scheduled. *Sam, the Highest Jumper of Them All* was directed by Saroyan himself in London, and *Lily Dafon* was well received in Vienna. Television and motion pictures have also kept him busy, and short stories continue to pour forth, although Saroyan now admits the necessity for "sitting working." He still belongs to the "action school" of writing, with a careless disregard for form and a reckless prodigality of language. Thirty years ago he published a series of short stories that won immediate recognition. Recently, he again sat down to work at the rate of one a day, thirty-seven stories in thirty-seven days, published as *After Thirty Years: the Daring Young Man on the Flying Trapeze*—an omnibus collection of his works. The small prose form is readily adaptable to his unique style of rambling dialogue and impromptu situation, and is logically related to what Saroyan has to say, as well: Beauty and love are spontaneous and unpredictable. His gentle folk find happiness in the intuitive perception of emotional truth. Organized plot and calculated action only impose rigidity on feelings. His loose construction is an effort to capture the meandering spontaneity of life, but the theatre is a more demanding taskmaster.

Born among the Armenian farmers of the Fresno valley, Saroyan saw people caught in the grip of major forces they little understood. The human spirit was chained by mass production and corporate power. After World War I, he saw Europe in the throes of a spiritual depression and the United States exhausting lives in an economic depression. He returned to the simple things of life to find understanding. With the farmhands of the vineyards and the patrons of the waterfront bars of San Francisco, he reached for the fundamentally good behind the impersonal mask of social aggregates. The form that evolved was similar to improvisational music, a developing of themes as they occurred, a creation of words and atmosphere that overshadowed plot.

Today, though the message is foreign to current cynicism, the form has found new adherents. Frequently off-Broadway revivals of his plays indicate renewed interest. *Hello, Out There*, written in 1941, was revived in 1961. This moving one-act play could well be the model for scores of more recent works in which two people, particularly boy and girl, find each other. Jack Richardson's *Gallows Humor*, Lewis John Carlino's *Snowangel*, and Murray Schisgal's *The Typists* are examples. But form alone will not sustain a welcome reception. In *Hello, Out There*, the young man is killed, the young girl hurt, and goodness destroyed by deceit. What a devastating comment on changes in accepted thinking that what is most un-Saroyanesque should be the basis for contemporary acceptance.

To Saroyan, however, *Hello, Out There* is a play of exaltation. The two young people, surrounded by dirt and death, find love and life, if only for one glowing moment. She cleans the jail. He has been framed on a rape charge. Little hope awaits them, yet they talk of sharing their future together. When she says: "Nobody anywhere loves anybody as much as I love you," he shouts, *as if to the world,* "Hearing you say that a man could die and still be ahead of the game." Saroyan does not close his eyes to ugliness and brutality, but he refuses to hate mankind. John Gassner quotes a line of Saroyan's in answer to the charge that his love of the human race is excessive: "As long as I am willing to go on being a member of that race, it goes against both nature and truth for me to hate it."

The casual, explorative improvisation in dramatic writing is increasingly evident, but it has produced few plays as lyrical as *Hello, Out There*. The content, though aborted, may well percolate through to another generation, riding out the tide of contempt.

Saroyan is gifted enough in impulsive bursts to rise above the saccharine fairy-tale level and cloak his work with fantasy and fable. *The Cave Dwellers* is an excellent example. In an abandoned theatre in the midst of a slum-clearing project, with the sounds of demolition in the background, live three ragged outcasts from the real world—the Queen, now old and sick, a former actress; the King, a circus clown; and the Duke, a prizefighter. A young Girl joins the group to share their poverty. Though not a performer, she is welcomed into their special world, for she too has fled from conformity. With what they beg on the streets, they survive, sharing food and warmth. Though they know their temporary home will soon be destroyed, they are happy. A man accompanied by his wife and a black bear begs admittance on a cold winter night. The frightened occupants of the stage hesitate to let them in. They have "three beds for four people. Rags for clothes. No food. No fire." How can they be of help to others? The King answers: "There's a whole world out there, full of fortunate people in their own homes. Not in a hulk of a haunted theatre. Let them help." The Queen answers that they can help "by not being afraid," by bringing the visitors "into the human circle of love." The strangers are accepted, and a short while later the wife of the man gives birth to a child in the backstage alley. The King worries whether the newcomers will remain when there is so little to share. The Queen gives the theme of the play:

"These people—and I include the bear—are *here*. Beyond that door, beyond this theatre, is a whole world of wealth, in which no door opened for them. Why, I don't know, and I don't care. They're here . . . and friends, and members of the family."

The workers of the wrecking crew bring food. A young man falls in love with the girl, and takes her away.

Saroyan forces his symbols, not letting them speak for themselves as he did in *My Heart's in the Highlands*. He translates the obvious. The dark cavern of the stage in which these people live is "the womb, cave, hiding place, home, church, world, theatre." The birth of the child is the Nativity, with the slum clearance as background to the modern manger. "God's in his heaven, all's right with the world" becomes "God's heaven is man's heart." Art, in the guise of these forlorn vaudevillians, *is* life. The ivory tower —or the empty stage—becomes the highest art, the art of living, possible away from the organized arrangement of material comforts which corrupts and hardens and breeds loneliness. When art someday invades politics, humanity may be served. Saroyan wrote: "The trouble with politics is that it inspires poets only to mockery and scorn."

The purest statement of Saroyan's optimism occurs in *My Heart's in the Highlands,* which the author unabashedly admitted to be a classic. The play was warmly greeted by Brooks Atkinson and George Jean Nathan, but condemned as obscure by the more conservative critics. Saroyan, young and bellicose, and never averse to publicity, fired back with,

> It is surely impertinent for me to believe that the greater and truer American theatre shall begin its life after the appearance and influence of this play, but, God forgive me, that is what I believe.

The running battle with critics demonstrated Saroyan's ability for self-promotion but detracted from the play. Like all good art, it needed no defense. Saroyan, rebuking "those intellectual giants who can explain everything and understand nothing," said,

> . . . the meaning of the play is the meaning of reality itself . . . the moral of the play is the oldest in the world . . . it is better to be a good human being than to be a bad one. It is just naturally better.

Little Johnny, who lives in a run-down shack with his poet father, and the old actor with his bugle, a refugee from a mental institution, insist on the reality of their dream world. They bring music and beauty to the neighbors and are rewarded with food and love—the same situation as twenty years later in *The Cave*

Dwellers. The bugler dies. The father's poems are rejected. There are sadness and tears, but there is rage as well. Though the United States was not yet at war when the play was written, the danger was imminent. The poet rises to denounce a mad world:

> "Befoul the legend of the living, you maniacs, whose greatness is measured by the number you destroy. You frauds of the world! You wretched and ungodly! Go ahead, fire your feeble guns! You won't kill anything!"

And then, his fury spent, he adds quietly, "There will always be poets in the world."

The Time of Your Life, which won a Pulitzer Prize in 1940, is Saroyan's finest achievement. Gathered in Nick's waterfront saloon in San Francisco is a colorful assortment of hangers-on who thirst for life and help one another. All are removed from the self-seeking success-demands of the mainstream of American life. Saroyan's prefatory explanation of the title of the play sounds like an evangelistic plea for goodness.

> Place in matter and in flesh the least of the values, for these are the things that hold death and must pass away. Discover in all things that which shines and is beyond corruption. Encourage virtue in whatever heart it may have been driven into secrecy and sorrow, by the shame and terror of the world.

The play is a warm, naïve *Lower Depths* of friendly folk who laugh and sing and defeat the law. Tennessee Williams' *Camino Real* and William Inge's *Bus Stop* are comparable dramas of wayward souls miscast in modern society who are thrown together by the unconquerable need for love.

Saroyan violates all the rules. In a brief essay, "How to Write," he states that the one rule is to ignore all the rules, for each set of admonitions has been "set up by some writer to protect himself." Such bravado would be more impressive if Saroyan himself had been able to go on endlessly creating new variations, but he became a victim of his own planlessness. His plays became repetitive and too easily fashioned. By the time of World War II, he had talked himself out; his defiance was too personal to find willing ears. His earlier work had caught a nation in need of enthusiasm and willing to enjoy his almost childlike ebullience.

Thornton Wilder was more detached. Saroyan never stopped insisting. In *Get Away, Old Man* (his wonderful titles have become the fashion), Jonah is pure Pollyanna when he explains that every life is a miracle, a miracle every minute, and every minute is filled with beauty. The awakening of the spirit can eliminate "stress and fretfulness and fear." What matter if there is no food, shelter, or clothing, so long as the heart is free. Saroyan would brush away the present-day complicated superstructure and reinstate Rousseau's natural man. Such disregard for the realities of modern urban living provokes a condescending smile, but even sophisticated audiences will respond to this plea, so long as it is dramatically effective and communicated in poetic imagery.

Saroyan's unpredictability and spontaneity were quickly dissipated. He did not fly off in a new direction. The rebel found that art, too, can rebel and refuse to accept the uncontrolled. Joy in life is a theme capable of endless exploitation, if endlessly evoked with fantasy, which demands, despite its apparent looseness, stern discipline. But Saroyan works in the only way suitable for him—running from acceptance, he hits occasional bull's-eyes. He did bring to the theatre rare moments of unusual beauty and tenderness in *My Heart's in the Highlands, The Time of Your Life,* and, occasionally, in *The Cave Dwellers.* He may still return to the theatre with a play of stature. As one of his characters says, "Farewell, and welcome!"

5

THE FUN AND GAMES OF EDWARD ALBEE

"When you get down to the bone, you haven't got all the way yet. There's something inside the bone . . . the marrow . . . and that's what you gotta get at."

Who's Afraid of Virginia Woolf?

"I cannot touch another person and feel love . . . I no longer have the capacity to feel anything . . . I have been drained, torn asunder, disemboweled . . . I use what I have . . . I let people love me."

The American Dream

EDWARD ALBEE has been the most widely acclaimed of the new playwrights. His work is performed everywhere in the Western world. He has been the subject of acrimonious critical debate, condemned by the established hierarchy and loudly applauded by the iconoclasts—the sure signs of the arrival of a major voice in the American theatre. His rapid rise to fame and international acceptance could be considered precipitous and premature, for to date he has written but four one-act plays, the stage version of Carson McCullers' *The Ballad of the Sad Cafe,* and one full-length original play. Yet, with *Who's Afraid of Virginia Woolf?* Albee indicated a command of form, a mastery of dialogue, and a poet's insight that may make him the outstanding playwright of the sixties.

If the Russians claim they discovered Van Cliburn, the Germans may well lay claim to the discovery of Albee. *The Zoo Story* opened in Berlin in 1959, the first production of his first play. The script had been rejected by New York producers and the chance intervention of friends in Europe made the production possible. Albee's second play was likewise given its first performance in Berlin, a further evidence of the reluctance of American producers to risk their investment on the experimental and the untried.

The Zoo Story, also the first of Albee's plays to be produced in New York, opened prophetically in January, 1960, the start of the new decade. It was paired at the Provincetown Playhouse in a double bill with Samuel Beckett's *Krapp's Last Tape.* The combination was intentional and emphasized the kinship of the two playwrights. Both adhere to a philosophy of despair and emptiness and sterility. In Beckett's brilliant tour de force, Krapp reviews a life without meaning, fond only of his tape recorder, struggling to find contact with his youthful self. In Albee's play, Jerry tries to establish contact with a person other than himself, and succeeds in the moment of death. The two characters in each play (considering the tape recorder as a character) engage in a complex skirmish which results in the self-annihilation of one. Both plays couple a sardonic view of life with pantomine, mounting tension, varying rhythms, and both are tightly drawn with an abundance of words that belies the economy of structure. Both keep jabbing away at a single point as Krapp circles around his tape machine and Jerry around his victim. Both are realistic but leap beyond the surface revelations to a semiabstract metaphorical quality.

In *The Zoo Story,* written in a more traditional manner, two men from different social levels meet, warm to each other, then clash, and both participate in the suicide-murder. Jerry is the lost animal, seeking, sensitive, belligerent; Peter is the contented vegetable, successful, well-mannered, respectful of others' rights. Jerry lives alone in a drab rooming-house on the West Side. Peter lives in the elegant East Seventies with a wife, two daughters ("You couldn't even get your wife with a male child"), parakeets, cats, and $18,000 a year as a publishing executive. Jerry, who has walked in a "northerly" direction from the Zoo, forces his attentions on Peter, who is quietly reading a book on a bench in Central Park on Sunday afternoon. The time is midday, the place a public park, yet it is more lonely and isolated than a dark alley along the waterfront. The bench is public property, but becomes the place each seeks to carve out as his own, the object to be possessed, the arena for assertion. The book is Peter's intellectual escape, the mark of the vegetable. The knife is Jerry's savagery, the mark of the animal. The mounting clash between the two, always menacing, moves from the discussion of literature and from psychological confession to the physical struggle for the bench—from the surface amenities to violent brutality—when Jerry says, as he slaps Peter every time the word "fight" is mentioned:

"You fight, you miserable bastard; fight for that bench; fight for your parakeets; fight for your cats, fight for your two daughters, fight for your wife, fight for your manhood, you pathetic little vegetable." (*Spits in Peter's face.*)

Peter defends himself. Jerry tosses him a switchblade to make the fight "more evenly matched," and as Peter holds it in his outstretched hand to defend himself, Jerry impales himself on the knife. The two men are joined by the death weapon. Ionesco in *The Lesson* used the same symbol for sexual relations between the Professor and his young student. With Albee, the knife may represent a macabre love affair of latent homosexual relations, but it also is the meeting of two separate worlds in the heart of a modern city, held together at the point of a switchblade. Jerry's more sentient world demanded recognition. It will find it in tomorrow morning's headlines.

The Zoo Story is splendidly conceived, with its careful build-up of the love-hate theme between Peter, whose only offense is that he is inoffensive, and Jerry, who is full of hatred, self-pity, and imposed isolation. The opening encounter, hesitant, slow-paced, monosyllabic, mounts skillfully with the energetic flow of words, the rhythms changing from the curt staccato interplay to long confessional passages, until the final physical shoving for possession of the bench. Jerry does most of the talking. He is the more articulate of the two. In Harold Pinter's *The Dumbwaiter,* another two-character play, horror is achieved through what is left unsaid, the pauses of the unknown. Albee's play achieves horror through what lies behind what is said, particularly in Jerry's long account of his adventure with the dog, which led him to visit the Zoo to study the life force of animals. He discovers they can be mastered and trained, but they pursue and bite even though they know the hand that feeds them seeks friendship.

The play has been regarded as a search for communication. It is hardly that, for these two men always communicate, always touch one another, first through words and ideas, then with bodily contact, and finally with the knife, the instrument that symbolizes life but brings death, as used so frequently in the plays of García Lorca. Jerry dies, but he is joyous and reaches beyond his own self to commiserate Peter, urging him to flee, returning the book and wiping the fingerprints from the bloodstained knife. Jerry comes close to religious peace: "I came unto you . . . and you have comforted me, dear Peter." Peter, who lives, is forced to face a continuing anguish, roused from his cultured complacency to awareness of the destructiveness below the surface of comfortable living. He is now an accomplice in murder.

The play gives no answers. It ends with Peter's repeated cry of "Oh, God," and Jerry's mimicking supplication, echoing the refrain. Peter rushes off to a troubled conscience; Jerry sits in full possession of the knife and bench, but he is dying. Despite the ugliness and sadism and despair, the audience is deeply moved by the plight of both men.

Krapp's Last Tape is more abstract, more geometrical. Krapp never becomes a real man. Albee's characters are terrifyingly real. The end is perhaps too sudden, too explosive, but the play grips with its beautifully concealed artistry and was able to hold its own alongside Beckett's work.

Albee's second one-act play, *The Death of Bessie Smith,* is cinematic in its technique. The hospital admissions room, where the main action takes place, is downstage center. An upstage ramp is used for scenes that occur elsewhere—short episodes that go back in time and merge in the sickening crisis when Bessie Smith, the famous blues singer, hurt in an automobile accident, bleeds to death before she can be admitted to the hospital for whites only. Bessie Smith never appears. The characters are those who surround her at the moment of death—the Nurse who listens to records of Negro blues, and her die-hard segregationist father; the Orderly, a handsome, resilient, quietly rebellious Negro; the Intern, a young doctor with liberal ideas who would rather help in the Spanish Civil War, not knowing until the end that the same battle is being fought more subtly, and equally dangerously, right here.

The action moves in fast shots from the home of the Nurse and her father, to the admissions room of the hospital and the love duet between the Nurse and the Intern; dissolves to Jack, the companion of Bessie Smith, rushing into another hospital and being rejected; then back for the final scene with the Nurse and the Intern, when Bessie Smith is lying dead in a car outside. Again, characters come alive with short, deft strokes. The dialogue stings. Bessie Smith hovers over all like a pursuing fury. In death, she is more disturbing than in life. The play does not hammer away at race relations, but implies that when prejudice is the order of the day, all who live by it are trapped. The Nurse, the most bigoted, cries out:

"I am *sick*. I am sick of everything in this hot, stupid, fly-ridden world . . . I am sick of going to bed, and I am sick of waking up . . . I am tired . . . I am tired of the truth and I am tired of lying about the truth . . . I am tired of my skin . . . I WANT OUT!"

The play deals with a group of people who live in this segregated environment, and whose passions and emotions have also become segregated. It is a drama of helpless and hopeless lives.

The American Dream and *The Sandbox,* a brief sketch with the same characters, were produced the following year and had their premiere in New York. *The Sandbox* had been commissioned for the Festival of Two Worlds in Spoleto but was never performed. Henry Lutz, a producer interested in new playwrights and a writer himself, presented it at the Jazz Gallery with a collection of other short pieces. *The American Dream* opened off-

Broadway together with a one-act opera, *Bartleby*, by William Flanagan, an intimate friend of Albee. He is now at work on a longer opera, *The Ice Age*, for which Albee will do the libretto. *Bartleby* failed to win support, and *The Death of Bessie Smith* replaced it for the first full evening of Albee's work.

The American Dream, Albee wrote, is an attack

> on the substitution of artificial for real values in our society, a condemnation of complacency, cruelty, emasculation, and vacuity; it is a stand against the fiction that everything in this slipping land of ours is peachy-keen.

Reaction to the play was mixed. Although the majority of critics again hailed the continuing talent of a young writer, Walter Kerr of the *New York Herald Tribune* admonished him to "add flesh without losing his mind," and Howard Taubman of *The New York Times* admired the "sardonic freshness," but though it was a "short play," wished he had left "before the end." In London, the audience response was not favorable. Albee, in an ill-considered move, replied to the attacks:

> May I submit that when a critic sets himself up as an arbiter of morality, a judge of the matter and not the manner of a work, he is no longer a critic; he is a censor.

Certainly, if the playwright sets himself up as an arbiter of morality—and he does—so may the audience (which includes the critic), and it is asking the impossible as well as the undesirable to demand that manner be judged without including the matter. A play about race relations, as is *The Death of Bessie Smith,* must stand as a dramatic experience, but it would be a betrayal of the critic's function if he did not point out the validity of attitudes on a social issue. This play depicting empty lives ignores the affirmative aspects of the one recent movement that has aroused dedication and courage.

The American Dream is a wildly imaginative caricature of the American family. The technique and even the matter are imitative of Ionesco, particularly of *The Bald Soprano*. The characters are dehumanized types, played in a mannered, marionette style—except Grandma, who is honest and therefore a real person. The American woman and mother is subjected to a scathing denunciation. Mommy emasculates her husband and reduces him to a trained seal, dismembers her adopted child, falls in love with his long-missing twin, and sends her mother to an asylum. No *joie de vivre* courses through her, yet she is always seeking satisfaction—the undercurrent of the play—in buying a hat, fixing the plumbing, or mending a man. The play ends with Mommy, happy that the muscular young man is present, ordering a bottle of sauterne and inviting all to drink to "Satisfaction! Who says that you can't get satisfaction these days!" Albee is the angry young man, tearing apart the antiseptic mirage of American middle-class happiness.

This vaudeville is an improvisation on absurdity, a comic travesty on "peachy-keen" vacuity. The technique is to act out the cliché as though it were a recently discovered truth. The obviously dull is performed enthusiastically. The illogical is accepted as commonplace.

When the long-expected Mrs. Barker arrives and no one knows exactly why she has come, Mommy says to her guest: "Would you like a cigarette, and a drink, and would you like to cross your legs?" All of the social amenities crowded into one question. Mrs. Barker, not at all nonplussed, replies: "You forget yourself, Mommy; I'm a professional woman. But I will cross my legs." A bit later, Mommy asks: "Are you sure you're comfortable? Won't you take off your dress?" Mrs. Barker does so, and for most of the remainder of the play moves about in her slip.

In a mechanical, standardized existence, individuality ceases to exist; therefore, characters either do not have names, or do not remember their names, or interchange names. (In the New York production, an empty picture frame draped in American flags hung on the wall to indicate the emptiness of their lives.) The search for satisfaction is counterpoised by emotional sterility. Years ago, Mommy ordered a child for adoption, paid handsomely for it, and wanted a customer's satisfaction, but, annoyed by the child's independence, cut off all its vital organs, one by one, until it died. Albee himself is an adopted child, and the theme of nonfertility and maternal destructiveness is repeated in his next play in the mythical child of Martha and the childbearing fears of Honey.

The American dream is the young man who is all appearance and no feelings, represented in the play by the twin of the adopted child. He has escaped Mommy, but the removal of his brother's vital organs produced a sympathetic transferred reaction in him. He says:

> "I cannot touch another person and feel love . . . I have no emotions . . . I have now only my person . . . my body, my face . . . I let people love me . . . I can feel nothing."

Grandma, the only likable character, lives in both worlds—that of the ridiculous and the illogical, and that of cynical common sense. She is always waiting to be carted off by the van man, but she is sane enough to be the only opposition to Mommy, and as though she were wearing different masks, she steps out of the play to comment on events to the audience.

The Sandbox takes the same characters out of doors at the beach, where the young man, always doing calisthenics, becomes the angel of death, and Grandma buries herself in the sand with a toy shovel. It is very much in the style of Beckett's *Happy Days* or *Endgame*. Albee evidences a continued mastery of structure, a disciplined dialogue, and a command of rhythmic variations, but these two plays are his weakest. They are forays into comic-strip exaggerations, a juxtaposition of incongruous symbols, which are riotously funny in brief, slapstick bursts. Lacking people, they become wearisome. Dullness parodied can become dull.

The four one-act plays created a mild sensation. Albee's reputation, however, would not have carried beyond the limited avant-garde audiences were it not for his major breakthrough with his first full-length play, *Who's Afraid of Virginia Woolf?* The plot, on the initial realistic level, is simple. George, associate professor of history, and Martha, his wife, daughter of the president of a small New England college, return home early in the morning from a party for new faculty members, given by her father. George and Martha are drunk when they enter and continue drinking throughout the rest of the play, which takes place in their living room, from two to five in the morning. They are joined by a young couple, the newly appointed teacher of biology and his wife. In the drunken orgy that follows, Martha and George engage in a harrowing battle to destroy each other, taking deliberate delight in pain and venom and cannibalism as they feed on each other's weaknesses.

Strindberg, whose *The Bond* is the forerunner of Albee's play, portrayed a primitive sex struggle for domination, between equals, in which one triumphs. With Albee neither triumphs. Both are contemptible, the woman more so, for Martha is coarse and obscene, as depraved as any woman in Genet, but terribly more human, and disgustingly more vulgar because she is representative of an established institution of traditional culture.

The sex duel is divided into three parts. In Act One, called "Fun and Games," the guests are greeted and all engage in the games of childhood and the games of fantasy, a fantasy which excites sexually as the drinking invites confession. The games are cruel and have man-made rules, as does life. Martha violates them as a means of torturing George. The guests are bewildered and helpless. At the end of the first part, Martha is triumphant.

The breaking of the rules, which have held together a tenuous structure, particularly the mentioning of their son to others, leads directly to Act Two, the *"Walpurgisnacht,"* in which the campus game of musical beds results in Martha's committing adultery while her husband is in the house and fully aware of her actions, and while Honey, the silly younger wife, is lying on the tile in the bathroom peeling labels.

The third act is called "Exorcism," the title Albee originally intended for the play. George exacts his revenge by playing the final game of killing their son on the day of his maturity, a hypothetical son who exists only in their games. The exorcism serves to remove all that is unreal from both George and Martha, an exorcism of final despair, which eliminates all fantasy and returns them to reality, or to the point where new rules and new games can be devised. The old fun and games are gone forever. Only the new are possible.

This seesaw battle of brilliant equals, with the younger couple watching and becoming involved, is played with the weapons that each sex has perfected. Martha has instinct for the right wound, her tongue for the cutting word, and her body for the most humiliating insult. She is most alive when most savage. George has reason and knowledge, a greater vision of cruelty.

The single theme is worked out in complex variations. The characters are arranged in all possible combinations. The deadliness of the blows intensifies from moment to moment, each precise in its triphammer effectiveness. The unities of time, place, and action are all carefully observed—a few hours, one setting, four characters—to permit action in depth. The language is pruned. Though the play lasts for more than three hours, hardly a phrase can be eliminated. The language varies with the emotional quality of the scene—sharp, staccato, lean for the lightning jabs; slow, delayed, wordy for the heavier blows.

On the level of the sordid revelation of lives on stage, the play is an absorbing drama of sex and violence. Audiences are repelled or shocked or full of admiration as they see themselves, or those they know, uncompromisingly portrayed. Empathy and insight, as spectator requirements, are fully satisfied, but the play goes beyond this and reaches out to different symbolic levels. Herein lies the crux of the vitriolic debates the play has inspired, for the symbolism requires judgment and analysis and is therefore subject to personal preference. Most interpretations are plausible and even demonstrable, but also can be easily rejected on the ground that too much is being read into the play. Many prefer to see the play as an insight into domestic butchery. Were this its sole achievement, it would have exhausted its potential quickly. The symbolic references are what make any play continuously intriguing. Through the poet's metaphor, they reach beyond the immediate to the general condition of man. Ibsen's white horses and Chekhov's sea gull are richly suggestive of human relations beyond specified boundaries. Albee has his mythical child and his fun and games.

Such overtones may not be apparent at a first viewing of the play, but they are sensed. Consciously or not on the part of the playwright, they exist as his poet's vision transforms appearances. The conventional formula play that dominates Broadway invites no such experience. It remains on the surface level. Its appeal is to those who insist they "do not have to go to the theatre to think." The joy of experiencing greatness in art consists in both thinking and feeling, on ever expanding, freshly suggestive, constantly interweaving possibilities. The audience of *Who's Afraid of Virginia Woolf?* wanted to talk about the play, to hear what others had to say. They sensed the forbidden and could not be restrained from exploring further.

George is a historian sensitive to world forces and the decline of civilization. Nick is the scientist in the present-day position of preference, already part of the Establishment, the new conformity in charge of reordering the world toward a mechanized dehumanization of the future. The antagonism between the two is intellectual as well as physical. George, mocking the wave of the future, taunts Nick on experiments that will "assure the sterility of the imperfect," and make history "lose its glorious variety and unpredictability." He voices the cry of the artist against mechanical control: "I, and with me the . . . the surprise, the multiplexity, the sea-changing rhythm of history, will be eliminated . . ."

George is more the philosopher, Nick the technician. Both are impotent, without direction. George finds no meaning in his life, his career, his thinking. There is no purpose in being chairman of the department or college president or himself. His brilliance is verbal and directionless, without belief to focus its intensity.

Nick is no match for George, for he is a scientist without vision. He compensates by being handsome, young, muscular, the American success boy who boasts of his sexual prowess and his boxing skill. He asserts himself in the bedroom, but even there cannot give "satisfaction." He is lifeless technology, the personification of Eric Kahler's insight into our present-day world "where technics have become ethics."

The women move in smaller concentric circles. Martha, sophisticated, outwardly assured, cannot create either through her husband or herself as a woman. Honey, naïve, simple, cannot have children because of psychological fears. Her pregnancy is illusory but physical, Martha's completely imaginary.

The relationship between George and Martha has many ramifications. One overbold commentator has even discovered references to George and Martha Washington. In spite of such exaggerations of zealous scholarship, this relationship, the core of the play, is Albee's most inspired achievement. Martha is the professional bedmate, the courtesan of the campus, but she is also a woman of tremendous energy who is unfulfilled. Promiscuous sex is an outlet for Martha as Mother Earth, comfort to all men, but a deformed Cybel whose body seeks pleasure but will never bear a child. Unable to create, she destroys. She is a direct descendant of Hedda Gabler, who, caught in middle-class dullness, burns Lovborg's manuscript, his brainchild; then, discovering she is pregnant, commits suicide, so as not to give birth to her own child. Albee's obsession with sterility has Martha destroy George's novel by ridicule, so that it is unborn; then provoke him to kill their imaginary child.

George and Martha are worthy opponents, incapable of love, skillful in the destruction of another's self, enjoying the negation of love, in a "total war" that brings a sexual elation without completion. Locked in mortal combat, they need each other to destroy each other. Barred from giving life, they exult in the preparations for humiliation and death.

They are college beasts, the perversion of the passions and the intellect. Martha "fake-spits" at George, and he warms to the fight, saying, "Be careful, Martha. I'll rip you to pieces." As he prepares for the final slaughter, he slaps her face to get her truly mad. They claw and tear not only "through the skin, all three layers," but through the muscles, the organs, the bones, and then: "You haven't got all the way," says George. "There's something inside the bone . . . the marrow . . . and that's what you gotta get at."

The play is a series of games and rules. The games are seriously playful imitations of the social games we play to stay alive. The beginning games are comparatively harmless, like "Getting the Guests"; then they turn to open adultery, and finally to killing the child. The rules designed to preserve outward harmony conceal the truth, and once violated, lead to pain. Fantasy, which generates new games, contains the seed of its own destruction, even to the destruction of self, for it is sprung loose out of falsity and hypocrisy.

The final revelation that George and Martha have a mythical son has been called "a most unlikely trick" or "hardly worth waiting all evening for." It is central to the play. This final, elaborate fantasy deals with the creation of life, of which they are not capable. It involves the heavy responsibility of man's assuming the role once held by God. Martha broke the rules of the sacred game, played privately for twenty-one years, and George punishes her by committing premeditated homicide. The child born of the mind for secret pleasure is killed by an act of the mind for public pain, and on the day he is to assume manhood.

Medea destroyed her children, those she had given birth to, to avenge a husband who had betrayed their love and abandoned her for career and self-advancement. George, the man, not the one who gives birth, destroys his child by an act of the will. His act is bloodless and intellectual, symbolizing the last stage in a world where love and life and passions and the creative act are machine-made.

Mention of God invites speculation about the religious overtones of the play, evidences of which are numerous. Such implications are passed over in witnessing the play, but are more apparent in listening to the recorded version, and quite definite in the reading of the script. *Waiting for Godot* may deal with two men waiting for someone who never comes, a parable of life's fruitless waiting for what will never arrive, but it gathers dimension when the reference is to God who will not come. *Who's Afraid of Virginia Woolf?* deals with more recognizable symbolism, but Martha's opening lines are a coarse reference to Christ and lead to the climactic scene in which she loses her child. As she writhes in agony, George intones a Requiem Mass, the benediction for an intellectual abortion.

Christ, the Son of God, was crucified to redeem all men. The son of George and Martha is sacrificed, not for redemption, but for the catharsis of marital infidelity. Martha is purged, punished, and barren. Regeneration, in an ugly age, can occur—if at all—out of a sickeningly low level of rot. Lorca's barren Yerma kills a husband who will not plant a fertile seed. Albee's impotent George revels with barroom glee in their continuing sterility.

The bloodless purging at the end is the attainment of the existentialist freedom, the point of the final "no" from which there is no return. They are both free from the old fun and games, free from falsity. The ruthless battle has ended with the contestants torn and wounded, lying on the floor, ready to pick one another up. The rules have dehumanized them. Now stripped of false myths, they may be able to reach beyond the self. This final scene slips into a new rhythm. The sharp] .ing of the in-fighting gives way to a slow, ritualistic beat. 1 .rtha admits she is afraid of Virginia Woolf. What this implies is vague, perhaps intentionally so. It may be part pun, a play on "Who's afraid of the big bad wolf?"—with the emphasis on the fear—or it may refer to the distinguished English writer herself and the search for freedom, the consciousness of woman's role, and the need for "the separate room."

Be that as it may, the more important element is the exorcism, the incantation, which removes the body of her son from her fantasy. Martha is subdued and crushed, and reaches out to George in a restrained counterpoint of yes and no and maybe, the uncertainty coupled with the negation that is the possible beginning of an affirmation.

Where they will go is left unanswered—Albee leaves his victims cleansed but without purpose. Ugly as the battle has been, we feel deeply for George and Martha, two uncompromisingly brutal but human people. Albee's negativism is rounded with a latent compassion; cruelty for its own sake "is of little value," he has said. In reviewing Lillian Ross's novel *The Vertical and the Horizontal*, he wrote:

> . . . the most miserable of men, the man who knows he suffers but cannot grasp his suffering, cannot feel it, is not any less a human being, only a much sadder one . . . It is Miss Ross's compassion that surfaces. Without it, the book would be cold, cruel and distasteful. With it, the book is a triumph.

The four characters in Albee's play repeat the life of Dionysus, god of theatre and debauchery, who, cut to bits and boiled in the cauldron, returned to life. Albee has captured in modern terms the dramatic power of man, destroyed by his own acts, still clinging to life, still groping for meaning.

The campus setting is appropriate for the theme, intensifying the bitter irony. The college is the cultural and intellectual center where tradition and values are preserved. More revealing of the nature of our society is its preoccupation with drinking and sex orgies. The campus, too, is directionless and impotent, reduced to imitating the vacuous business world of success.

With all its grim unpeeling of sadism and defeat, *Who's Afraid of Virginia Woolf?* is a funny play. Situations and lines crackle with savage humor, then shift to terrifying sadness. The games they play have vaudeville theatricality. The comedic spirit is a dramatic device to intensify the pain beneath the surface gaiety—a laughter of horror, the gallows humor of those sentenced to die. Beckett and Ionesco and even Giraudoux have explored the comic vein to expose the underlying anguish. Albee follows suit.

The New York production captured the changing rhythms of the play, the broad laughter, and the characterizations of human beings caught in traps of their own devising and the world around them. Rare are the occasions when the script and performance combine to give the charged excitement that makes the theatre an enduring experience.

Such was not the case with the New York premiere of *The Ballad of the Sad Cafe*. Albee's adaptation of the McCullers novella did not generate dramatic power. It remained a static representation in visual form of a literary work. Scenes from the original story were pieced together, and to achieve cohesion and replace the role of the novelist, a narrator was added who popped up on all corners of the stage with comments on the action and quotations from McCullers' prose. Though the action takes place in a nondescript southern town, Negroes are not involved; but a Negro actor played the narrator. The race problem was thereby needlessly introduced, diverting attention from the grotesque and distorted lives of the protagonists. Though this casting was a director's choice, and would occur only in production, it was done with Albee's approval.

Adaptations are perhaps permissible if the dramatist refashions the material to his own medium. Albee, however, seemed unwilling to effect major surgery on the novella; he superimposed theatrical devices, such as the one-act, no-intermission form, which was not essential for mood or continuity, nor demanded by the content. The result was an awkward form, as though Albee had been playing with a "mythical child" he never permitted to be born.

The Ballad of the Sad Cafe had been planned long before *Who's Afraid of Virginia Woolf?* It will not add to Albee's stature as a playwright, but it is important because it re-echoes his continuing obsession with sterility. Although the play is pure Carson McCullers, Albee gave it his paternal blessing and assumed responsibility by adoption. The play centers on the fight in which Amelia, muscular and inarticulate, engages Marvin Macy, her husband, who has been denied his conjugal rights, in as brutal and vulgar a battle of the sexes as has ever been witnessed on stage. The physical contact of the greased bodies, in a strug-

gle to the death, is the substitute for the marriage act. Contact
does not arouse sexual passion but ceremonial hate. Violence and
destruction replace any joy of human association. Marvin Macy
says to Amelia, "The night you said you marry me, no man
ever been happier . . . ever. I gonna come back some day and
kill you!" Amelia, herself deceived by the homosexual dwarf on
whom she has bestowed her affection, crawls off to isolation
and decay, a woman destroyed by two men—one who boasts of
his evil, and the other a misshapen, twisted soul drawn to evil.

Albee quotes McCullers' lines on the imbalance between
the lover and the beloved, which are spoken by the narrator:
"The lover craves any possible relation with the beloved, even
if this experience can cause them both only pain." This is philosophy removed from what happens on stage, for in the play there
are no loved nor beloved. The word *love* and its meaning are
foreign to these lives, save in a perverted sense. Cousin Lyman,
the dwarf, says at one point, "Oh, Amelia, I do love you so,"
and Amelia stops him with, "Those are words I don't wanna
hear"; then she adds, hesitantly, "I am . . . fond of you, Cousin
Lyman."

Destruction is total. Even the cafe, the one place that could
brighten for a brief moment the empty lives of the townsfolk,
is wrecked. Amelia dies. The gray shutters are closed. The two
men go off together. The dwarf, who had appeared mysteriously
from nowhere, fastens his love on a man who abuses and reviles
him, a man who has thieved and been in the penitentiary. His
romance is a step in the hierarchy of crime to which he wants
to belong and from which he derives satisfaction. Both will
become part of the chain gang, whose song is heard in the distance as if it were the choir of the twelve disciples.

These two are devoted to evil, but all the others are twisted
and stunted shadows of giants and pygmies, a Gulliver's adventure in a nightmare of non-love. Amelia never endures the act
of sex. Woman does not fulfill her natural function. A scoundrel
like Peer Gynt or a hapless victim like J.B. can fall into a woman's
arms and insure the continuity of life, even a life of continued
suffering. With Albee, the world need not go on. No child will
be born in or out of wedlock. *The Ballad of the Sad Cafe* is
a ritualistic celebration of the end of man. Non-regeneration turns
on itself and finds comfort in annihilation.

Such action is parasitic and self-defeating, for a fertile seed has to be planted for a man to continue even to be absurd, for problems to be faced which the cynic can mock, and for Albee to continue writing plays about sterility. With no offspring, sex turns on itself and delights in perversions. With Albee, symbols of impotence replace life-giving images. If there will be no future existence, there is no recourse but to build additional violence and evil to destroy more hastily this final generation.

In this sense, Albee bears a derivative kinship with Genet. Genet, however, being French and a criminal, takes men apart from the established social structure—the thief, the prostitute, the homosexual—all removed from acceptance; all of them are non-reproductive but feed off existing society. In his separate world, Genet can pursue evil to its sanctification, equating crime with Christ. The thieves of the Cross become the Apostles. Genet glorifies with its own morality a newly established hierarchy of evil, substituting it for traditional morality. Albee, a moderate Genet, American-style, mocks middle-class "peachy-keen" vacuity and takes it to its self-elimination. Sartre could well have written of Albee as he did of Genet, "the pure form of the opposition carried to impotence." Genet's characters, like Albee's, can never give life. They can only feed off life. Genet carries a rejection to his own self-contained brutality. Albee, lacking a belief or a philosophy, even a negative one, walks dangerously in a field strewn with booby traps. The adoration of destruction is comparable to Jean Tinguely's sculptures, which consume themselves, often in a blaze of fireworks and cannon shots.

The theatre at its best is a source of illumination. Albee seeks out the dark alleys, the hidden recesses of the malformed and the diseased. He imparts no knowledge of paths toward enlargement of life. Gassner's reference to Albee as a writer in a direct line from O'Neill may apply to the similarity of their careers rather than their qualities as playwrights. Both were apart from the commercial groups who dominate the professional theatre. Both started with one-act plays which broke with convention. Both saw their first full-length plays create new directions for Broadway playwrights. Successors to O'Neill carved out a new commercialism; those who follow Albee may do likewise, but Albee has none of O'Neill's relentless pursuit of massive themes to uncover the dignity of man. Albee is more adroit, more subtle, more like Tennessee Williams of the earlier plays.

O'Neill looked for the heroic in the tradition of the Greek masters of tragedy, forging towering figures doomed to disaster but courageous enough to wrestle with gods to assert the innate divinity of man. Albee's characters are non-heroic or anti-heroic. Perhaps he does not believe the heroic is possible in our age, as Artaud has repeatedly declared, but Albee at least does not leave his people bereft of will, acted upon but not acting. Jerry Talmer, a critic and a friend of Albee, cautioned him not to remain too close to the garbage heap. It is like telling Williams to write about healthy people. His one effort to do so resulted in Williams' worst play. Albee can write only about what moves him, and his own growth will determine the direction he pursues.

Unlike O'Neill, Albee has not explored new forms nor ventured into new techniques. He contains a bit of Ionesco, some Beckett, more Strindberg, and a dangerous dose of Genet, but he writes plays that grip an audience, that hold with their elusiveness, their obscurity, their meaning; and he has functioned in the true role of the playwright—to express the human condition dramatically and metaphorically, over and above the story line unfolded on stage. He has the courage to pursue the truth relentlessly, without compromise, no matter what the truth may be or where it may lead, even if it hurts, and *Who's Afraid of Virginia Woolf?* hurts.

The play deserved all the awards showered upon it, and the failure of the Pulitzer committee to make the record unanimous reflects the power of the play. Most of the judges with final authority for the Pulitzer Prize are men who endorse campus life and are dedicated to preserving the myths of our time, who enjoy the fun and games as now played. With all its weaknesses, the play is a pace-setter in establishing the new myths, and it revealed the power of the drama to have a direct and meaningful impact on audiences.

6

THE SURVIVORS OF THE DEPRESSION —
Hellman, Odets, Shaw

"The world is out of shape when there are hungry men."
Watch on the Rhine

"It's getting late to play at life. I want to live it."
Rocket to the Moon

"We must not be martyrs—we must be seeds."
The Assassin

THE THREE MOST PROMINENT playwrights to come out of the economic depression of the thirties were Lillian Hellman, Clifford Odets, and Irwin Shaw. All were committed writers, deeply concerned with the fight for social justice, and critical of long-held myths that induced complacency in times of success and panic in the face of disaster.

The decade was not a pleasant one. It began with industrial chaos, the collapse of the financial structure, and mass unemployment. It ended with a second world war. A re-examination of the basic structure of the American way of life was in order. The belief that rugged individualism and free enterprise, left unfettered, would result in the greatest good for the greatest number gave way to demands for state planning and government controls. The New Deal instituted Social Security and Federal Works Projects to replace the dole and the breadline. Militant trade unions insisted on a voice in management policies. The issues were critical and the fate of the nation at stake. The theatre became an active participant in the struggle to arouse a disheartened people to renewed conviction. It was sobered, socially conscious, seeking constructive belief to oppose national disintegration. The plays of Hellman, Odets, and Irwin Shaw were a response to a special period of American history.

The advent of another war restored the economy to full production and united a divided nation in the common struggle against totalitarianism. Almost every serious writer was responsible for at least one anti-Hitler play, passionate and partisan—and rarely produced today. The war itself was fought out of a sense of duty, out of a dogged determination to get a job done, rather than from devotion to a crusade. Few war plays of merit resulted. *Mr. Roberts,* the popular comedy by Thomas Heggen and Joshua Logan, deals with the boyish pranks and sexual adventures of sailors caught in the boredom of an isolated supply ship. It has little reference to the cause for which men are fighting. *A Bell for Adano,* the dramatization of the novel, by Paul Osborn and *The Home of the Brave* by Arthur Laurents are accounts of human relations intensified by war. No World War II plays, however, equaled the lusty laughter of *What Price Glory?* by Laurence Stallings and Maxwell Anderson, or the grim plea for peace of Irwin Shaw's *Bury the Dead* or Paul Green's *Johnny Johnson,* all written long before Pearl Harbor.

With the unprecedented prosperity after the second world war, the theatre of social protest fell into disrepute. A public enjoying a booming economy preferred not to be reminded of the terrifying days of the Depression and Hitler's rise to power. The United States in a position of world leadership needed leadership in the arts as well, to rally reluctant and divided allies.

Instead, during the days of Senator McCarthy, it fostered the suppression of critical dissent and created a climate hostile to the free expression of the artist. The writer, in particular, fearful of ubiquitous investigating committees, remained silent or was silenced. The theatre concentrated on light comedy, lush musicals, and case studies of psychological frustrations. Advocacy of social issues was suspect. Plays dealing with the results of economic dislocation gave way, in a society of affluence, to dramas of personal dislocation. The future of the nation became less important than the preservation of the self.

The writers of the thirties found it difficult to make the transition. Hellman was the most resilient. She has also been the most active, even though she once said of the theatre,

> It is a tight, unbending, unfluid meager form in which to write, and for these reasons, compared to the novel, it is a second-rate form.

After an adult libretto for the musical play *Candide*, she reappeared in 1960 with an original play, *Toys in the Attic*, followed in 1963 by a satirical comedy, *My Mother, My Father, and Me*.

For years Odets and Shaw were rarely heard from. They worked in motion pictures or retired for personal reassessment, though the theatre drew them back periodically. Odets, restless in his lucrative employment in Hollywood, returned to Broadway in 1949 with *The Big Knife*, an attack on the destruction of talent by those who control the motion picture industry. This was followed by *The Country Girl* (1950) and his last work for the theatre, *The Flowering Peach* (1954). His personal vendetta exhausted, he went back to Hollywood, which he now admitted was favorable to creativity. But, like most people who have been part of the theatre, he still could not resist its appeal. Not having a new work, he started the revision of *Golden Boy* for production as a musical play. At the time of his death, he was writing a dramatic series for television.

Irwin Shaw lived in Europe and wrote novels. For the theatre he contributed *The Assassin* (1945), a war play that deals with the problem of guilt and self-sacrifice, a retelling of the assassination of Admiral Darlan; and later, in 1959, an adaptation of *Patate* from the work of the *boulevard* writer Marcel Achard. His most recent effort and his third successive failure is *Children from Their Games* (1962), an ill-formed unleashing of invective against all the ills of society.

Though many survivors of the thirties still work in the theatre, even though sporadically, those who are closest to ardent partisanship have found it most difficult to adjust to a politically changed climate. Their failure raises a disturbing and rarely examined question of the relationship of the artist to his times. The living theatre of the thirties was in the hands of the "socially conscious playwright." His work, if not the most successful financially, was the most meaningful, yet those playwrights who maintained a distant perspective, who were removed from the fight—Saroyan, Wilder, O'Neill—have shown greater endurance. Three decades later, the situation is reversed. Most writers are completely absorbed by personal problems isolated from the current of history; they have produced a vast accumulation for the theatre of the trivial. A few are angry enough to face the social implications of our time—Miller, Baldwin, Albee—and are responsible for our important plays.

The problem of the playwright today can be better understood after a brief glance at the problems besetting the playwright in the thirties. The national conditions that gave rise to the variety of unprecedented government agencies and new institutions also created three developments in the theatre which were unique: the Federal Theatre Project, the trade union theatre, and the Group Theatre. All three were major forces in the enrichment of the theatre—and all three failed to live out the decade.

When Harry Hopkins, in charge of the government Works Projects, asked Hallie Flanagan of Vassar College to head a theatre program, he was interested in giving relief to unemployed actors. What resulted was a subsidized national theatre, the first in American history. The Federal Theatre Project is significant if only for the immensity of the operation. Theatres of all types and forms, from circus and marionette players to grand opera, were set up in every state of the Union. Children's theatres were established in local communities, as well as Negro theatres and theatres for minority groups. Mobile units played to mountaineers in Appalachia, farmers in Kansas, and schoolchildren everywhere. Memorable productions were a musical version of *Macbeth* in Harlem, and the simultaneous premiere of Sinclair Lewis'

It Can't Happen Here in twenty-one theatres. The Harlem *Macbeth* was also notable for being the first directorial assignment of a young actor named Orson Welles.

The numerous companies, mostly repertory in character, included both classical and contemporary plays. Longer rehearsal periods were encouraged and nominal admission prices were charged. The success of a show did not depend on its ability to recoup an investment. The tyranny of the box office was overthrown for the first time in our history, and the theatre, reaching new audiences, bridged the gap between spectator and performer. Most of the plays presented in the drama division were established successes of the past, but new plays were also attempted and many of our present-day writers received their first opportunities in a theatre sponsored by the government to relieve unemployment.

The fruits of this varied activity and a favorable climate were incalculable. A huge reservoir of actors and technicians served their apprenticeship and were available later to the professional theatre. A vast popular audience was recruited which did not consist only of those able to pay high prices. This audience, in turn, influenced the nature of production. The project, though always concerned with entertainment, faced the need to educate as well and developed an original form, the "Living Newspaper," written by members of a trade union, the Newspaper Guild, under Morris Watson and Arthur Arent. Important issues of the day were presented in dramatic form, using short scenes, blackouts, large casts, and technical devices very much in the style of Piscator and Brecht. Among these documentary dramas, which made powerful propaganda pieces and effective theatre, were *One-third-of-a-nation* (housing), *Power* (TVA), and *Spirochete* (venereal disease). Though the writers acknowledged indebtedness to German expressionism, they had learned from our own propagandistic techniques and from such radio programs as "The March of Time." This socially oriented theatre developed its own audience and its own means of artistic expression, proving that Times Square need not be the only center, and that once there is no pressure to preserve conventional form, originality will flower in bewildering variety.

The growing trade union movement used the theatre as an organizing weapon. Independent groups, mostly with Marxist leanings, sprang up everywhere, and in 1935 the New Theatre League was founded as a clearinghouse of labor-oriented theatres, and a magazine was issued, which was well edited and highly literate. These aggressive, uninhibited groups were responsible for experiments in technique and content, following the example of foreign-language groups, which had always existed in the United States, such as the Artef and the Ukranian Dramatic Club. The Prolet Bühne presented improvised sketches called "agit-prop" (short for agitation-propaganda), which were performed at union meetings, on street corners, and wherever crowds were gathered. This ad-lib theatre, a working-class *commedia dell'arte*, spread to other groups and was the forerunner of our present improvisational theatre. Union theatres were responsible for the first performance of Irwin Shaw's *Bury the Dead* and Clifford Odets' *Waiting for Lefty*.

The high point of this activity was the action of the International Ladies Garment Workers Union, a powerful organization which had pioneered in cultural programs for its members. The union rented a Broadway theatre and produced a proletarian revue, *Pins and Needles*, which was highly successful with the carriage trade as well. It was the first time a labor organization had turned producer, and indicated the possibilities of trade union sponsorship of theatres similar to what had been happening for years in Germany. Later, Marc Blitzstein wrote *The Cradle Will Rock* for the Federal Theatre Project. When political pressure forced the cancellation of the show, the entire company, led by Orson Welles and John Houseman, loaded the piano on a truck and moved twenty blocks farther south to the empty Venice Theatre, where they performed the operetta to a capacity house that had marched through the streets with them. This musical play with little scenery and only a few props was a sort of American *Threepenny Opera*. The work was even dedicated to Bertolt Brecht! And this was twenty years before the work of Brecht became well known in this country. A 1964 revival of *The Cradle Will Rock*, directed by Howard Da Silva, who played the role of Larry Foreman in the original cast, proved the enduring quality of Marc Blitzstein's proletarian operetta.

Much of the labor theatre was crude and more enthusiastic than polished, but it was vital and dynamic. As happens in so many popular movements, the material degenerated rapidly into a set formula—the worker always triumphed and the capitalist was always the villain. In the Soviet Union, such dramas have stifled the playwright's initiative. In the United States, under our multiple pressures and freedom of expression, the movement could have developed into a mature and significant theatre, but it collapsed with the end of the Depression and the acceptance of trade unions as equal partners in the power structure.

The third significant development was the birth of the Group Theatre, an offshoot of the Theatre Guild. Essentially an actor-dominated theatre modeled on the Moscow Art Theatre and its several studios, it attempted to eliminate chaos in the preparation of an actor for his profession. Emphasis was on group relationships, the elimination of the star system, and the development of an ensemble with a single unifying style. Moreover, in addition to revolutionizing acting techniques, the Group Theatre discovered such playwrights as Clifford Odets, William Saroyan, and Irwin Shaw. However, its failure to maintain a continuing central theatre as a growing organism and the over-insistent dogmatism of its self-styled "method experts" vitiated the health of the movement and led to the encouragement of new mannerisms. Today, "the method" or one of its many variations is the accepted procedure in teaching acting in almost every school in the country, but each proponent stoutly maintains his particular interpretation as the sole road to discovery. With the scattering of the members of the founding company, the original purpose has been variously defended by warring factions, and "inner truth," the oft-quoted slogan, has become the private possession of the actor rather than a quest shared with the playwright.

The Actors Studio with Lee Strasberg, one of the founders of the Group Theatre, as its mentor continues the work, but has become too divorced from the social reality that gave birth to the Group, and evidences of cultism and preciosity have become apparent. Now that the Studio has gone into long-awaited production, these failings may be eliminated, and with a permanent theatre an ensemble method of acting may yet evolve.

The strength and the weakness of the writers of the thirties derive from the forces that molded them. Critical judgments, as Mr. Dooley said of the Supreme Court, follow the elections.

Lillian Hellman, not associated with the Group Theatre or any other collective organization—her plays were produced and often directed by Herman Shumlin, a representative of Broadway's commercial theatre—has best withstood the test of time. In recent years she demonstrated her versatility by writing a delightfully sophisticated and witty book for Leonard Bernstein's musical play *Candide* (1956). Voltaire's theme that "all is for the best in this best of all possible worlds" was rich material for Hellman's acid humor. As a musical play *Candide* is superior to most, and its revival by the City Center Theatre will serve to rescue it from the obscurity to which the critics relegated it. The gullible Candide is beset by villainy at every turn, yet keeps on singing his optimistic refrain. He sees evil in the world but refuses to recognize it.

The problem of good and evil is basic to all of Hellman's work, but in her own plays the well-intentioned are destroyed by "the little foxes," who are always around to "eat the earth." The evidence of a satiric touch, so rare in contemporary theatre, was reinforced by her dramatization later of *My Mother, My Father, and Me.* Her adaptation of Emmanuel Robles' *Montserrat* (1949) and Jean Anouilh's *The Lark* led to the charge that her talent was exhausted and she had been reduced to rewriting the works of others. *Toys in the Attic* (1960) put such fears to rest.

In *The Children's Hour* and *The Little Foxes* the forces of evil are clearly marked. Mary Tilford, the malicious brat, destroys good people in a world where evil is too prone to be accepted. In Regina, all human values have been destroyed by the lust for power and money. Mary confesses, but the harm has already been done. Regina triumphs, and her only defeat is her rejection by her daughter. In *Toys in the Attic*, Cyrus Warkins, the millionaire, is the one consciously malicious character, and he never appears. People who are outwardly good, who presumably sacrifice their lives for others, are now the instruments of human suffering. Misplaced or possessive love can destroy. Julian is beaten up physically and his pride broken through the actions of a spinster sister who secretly prefers to keep him close to her, and by a silly, sex-hungry wife who mistakenly fears Julian will leave her. Both loves are selfish and devastating. The innocent are the tragic victims—Karen and Horace and Anna.

Hellman's dark world of those who triumph through a calculated disregard of moral values is as grim and full of pain as in the most extreme theatre of the absurd. Her dramas differ in that they are portraits of people and not of abstract symbols. Events are causative, and the individual the product of his environment. Her one effort to dramatize immediate social forces resulted in her weakest play, *Days to Come*, an obeisance to the times, in which workers and capitalists line up in opposing ranks.

In her best plays, the cycle of New Orleans family dramas, specific historic events are left in the background, implying the conditions of modern civilization which alter human motives, and the major interest is focused on richly developed, multi-faceted characters involved with forces they dimly understand. Rarely are these protagonists heroic. Kurt in *Watch on the Rhine* is an exception. In the fervent years, his heroism stirred a willing audience. Today he is far too noble to be convincing. His cause is just, but his absolute certainty of righteousness removes him from tragic stature. Regina, her most memorable creation, is a savage, determined woman. Carrie, of *Toys in the Attic*, is quietly obsessive. Julian is a well-intentioned, none too capable young man who finds an easy way to get rich and runs foul of a husband's jealousy and his own wife's innocence. Good characters are more difficult to portray dramatically. Albertine, the wealthy southern aristocrat, and Henry, her Negro consort, are admirable in their philosophic calm and mature understanding, but are nebulous figures.

Lillian Hellman's strength lies in the dramatic power she can extract from the realistic form. *The Little Foxes*, like *Ghosts*, is almost flawless in economy and structure, realization of character, and pertinence of dialogue. Characters generate events and in turn are influenced by them. *Toys in the Attic* has a weak first act with too much preparation for what follows, but its final resolution is explosive. Hellman's mastery of technique has led to the accusation that her plays are too contrived, too adroitly arranged by the author. Such charges are valid, but it is a pleasure to watch the work of a skilled craftsman. All writers rearrange life and impose their own will on the chaos of reality. The test in the realistic theatre is whether the characters appear to be self-propelled, as they do in *The Little Foxes*, a masterpiece of the Ibsen-influenced theatre. *Toys in the Attic* shows bits of the machinery, perhaps because family plays of psychological insight have become too familiar, but is so artfully contrived that it becomes compelling drama. Hellman does not use her skill to exhibit technical prowess, but to expose the extent to which greed and avarice have corrupted the human soul. She strives for a Chekhovian complex of frustrated and unhappy people, but her use of violence and sexuality brings her closer to Tennessee Williams. At the end of the second act, Anna, the older sister, tells Carrie that her need for Julian is incestuous. Carrie has asked for the truth, which is what she least wants to hear: "When you love, truly love, you take your chances on being hated by speaking out the truth." Anna replies, "All right. I'll take my chance and tell you that you want to sleep with him and always have."

Hellman's bitter complaint is that greed and avarice have eroded love, and that the cause is a social system in which human relations are a product for sale. She is a moralist, and her major weakness, by her own confession, is the obvious addition of the moral, either by an all too obvious explanatory speech or through an arranged resolution that borders on the melodramatic. *The Children's Hour* could have ended with Martha's suicide. The visit of the grandmother, which follows, and the hammering away by Karen that she has come to relieve her conscience are superfluous and aesthetically disturbing. Kurt's final speech in *Watch on the Rhine* about the need to kill if necessary, to destroy Hitlerism, has already been implicitly stated in what went before. *Toys in the Attic* avoids this weakness, and as Julian moans that he "will have to start all over again," we know that he will forever be cared for by his sisters.

Most writers who master the well-made play can ill afford to experiment in other directions. Failure on Broadway is too catastrophic. Odets never varied. Hellman took a chance in *My Mother, My Father, and Me*, and though the piece was not a financial success, it indicated a surprising gift for humor. The play is a travesty of American middle-class life, with abundant laughter, absurd situations, and high comedy, and is expressionist in form. It was probably poorly received because of its failure to concentrate on a few targets, for it lashes out bitterly on all fronts, bordering at times on the petulant and vindictive without reason. Hellman deserted her psychological introspection to concentrate on comic-strip stereotypes in a wild extravaganza of the Jewish family plagued by wealth and removed from dedication to any vital issue. The dominant mother, the complaining and submissive father, the crazy grandmother who is more sane than the rest, the bohemian son, are all here. The scenes shift from the family home to an old folks' asylum, to an Indian reservation to which the young Berney escapes to find American roots. He will spend the rest of his life making silver bracelets and selling blankets to middle-class tourists. He informs the audience that his father

> "is back in the shoe business, and seems to be doing all right with what he calls an 'Honor' shoe, a shoe to be buried in, a shoe in honor of the dead,"

and that his mother was wild when he left and sent him a postcard saying:

> "The eye that mocks the father and does not obey the mother, the ravens shall pick it out, and the young eagles shall eat it."

He giggles and adds, "There are plenty of eagles and ravens here, but nothing's happened." "Nothing's happened" distinguishes the comfortable sixties from the Depression era. Most writers of the thirties had something to say, but didn't say it too well. Most writers of today have little to say and say it extremely well.

Hellman's alert sensitivity is able to find varying means to express her major theme. Her problem is her loss of certainty. Her attacks have become negative and as impotent as Rona in *My Mother, My Father, and Me.* When she was stimulated by the social upheaval of the thirties she wrote a powerful drama in human terms, *The Little Foxes,* in which an entire society in decay is revealed. It ranks with Gorky's *Yegor Bulitchev* and Henry Becque's *Les Corbeaux.*

The most acclaimed writer of the thirties was Clifford Odets. He rose out of the Depression to give voice to a world in crisis. He put the Bronx Jewish middle class on stage and gave them courage, dignity, and stature. His association with the Group Theatre supplied that organization with its own writer and material suited to its "method" acting, very much as Chekhov had done with the Moscow Art Theatre.

Paradoxically, Odets was the playwright least able to maintain persuasive drama in the sixties. His exodus to Hollywood, together with many members of the Group Theatre, removed him from his natural nourishment. When he returned to Broadway ten years later with *The Big Knife*, he no longer was a man of social anger. Success had deprived him of identification with the downtrodden. Of the next plays, *The Country Girl* (1950) was an outright attempt at a superficial success, and *The Flowering Peach* (1954), a drama that never focused precisely on what it had to say.

The human dislocation caused by the Depression supplied Odets with his strength as an artist. He rallied a nation to action and hope. When a workers' theatre competition for one-act plays was announced, he locked himself in a room and in three days wrote *Waiting for Lefty*, a long one-act play about the taxi strike in New York. Strikes had long been a favorite subject of dramatists, for they represent a moment of decision when the working class is in battle array, when opposing forces are engaged in a test of strength. Odets, wisely, did not include the actual strike. The formula of proletarian plays prescribed a third-act resolution. Waves of marching workers faced the drawn police lines, flags waved, guns were fired, a hero died, but the momentary setback was an augury of eventual triumph. Odets pictured the events leading up to the strike, using episodic flashbacks and the waiting for Lefty, who never appears, as the unifying factor. The result is theatre in its oldest form, an Epic theatre technique involving the audience and propelling them into open participation. *Waiting for Lefty* has a hard-hitting, bare, cumulative power, very much like a tribal war dance.

The members of a thug-dominated, taxi-drivers' union belong, for the most part, to the middle class that has fallen socially —the American dream in reverse. No longer do they have hopes of rising beyond their station. To Odets, as to Bernard Shaw, the greatest crime is poverty. Not psychopathic disturbances, but failure to support the family, turns men to desperate actions or makes them submit to failure. In *Awake and Sing* and *Paradise Lost*, a disintegrating family is held together momentarily by a courageous mother. Bessie Berger and Clara Gordon are Bronx descendants of O'Casey's Juno.

The language Odets used was fresh and invigorating—twisted,

torn images of rare strength, a poetry of the people often excessive and at times brilliant. In *Awake and Sing*, Moe says to
Hennie, "So take a chance! Be with me, Paradise. What's to
lose?" And she answers, "My pride!" He grabs her and says,
"What do you want? Say the word—I'll tango on a dime. Don't
gimme ice when your heart's on fire!" Or in *Paradise Lost*,
Kewpie, the gangster, who has replaced Ben Gordon in Libby's
bed, says to him,

> "Libby don't care for you three cents. You're sand in her shoes. I
> buy her clothes, keep your house running. The new fancy carriage
> for the kid? My dough! The money in your pocket? Mine! *I'm in
> you like a tapeworm.*"

Though *Waiting for Lefty* is expressionist in form, its content is realistic, as is all of Odets' work. The small people crushed
by economic forces are pictured magnificently as they give way
or rise in dignity. Too often, the final affirmation is tagged on
mechanically. In *Waiting for Lefty*, the rank-and-file voice of
Agate shouts out like a Communist leader on the barricades,

> "WORKERS OF THE WORLD . . . OUR BONES AND BLOOD!
> And when we die they'll know what we did to make a new world!
> Christ, cut us up to little pieces. We'll die for what is right! Put
> fruit trees where our ashes are!"

The final metaphor of the fruit trees may be misplaced, but it
is followed with the actors in the audience shouting over and
over again, "Strike!"—until everyone takes up the chant. Leo,
in *Paradise Lost*, ends that play with,

> "No man fights alone . . . I want to see that new world . . . What
> is this talk of bankrupts, failures, hatred? . . . They won't know
> what that means. Oh, yes, I tell you the whole world is for men
> to possess."

These final exhilarating but inconsistent affirmations were
requirements of the play of the Depression, for actuality was full
of heartbreak and terror. Pain and suffering make up the substance of the Depression play. Lives are destroyed, but there
is hope for a better world, if people fight for it, a world in which
people will be able to "awake and sing." In a recent interview

published in *Theatre Arts Magazine*, Odets said of Leo's speech that he did believe in the possibilities expressed in this theme, and that it was a logical outgrowth of the text. "I believe that older and more crushed human beings can pass on some lifting values to the younger generation."

In Odets' plays, the Depression, as a special moment in American life, is evident in every scene. Today, the working class has risen to middle-class comfort, and Odets' former Bronx characters now live more comfortably in the suburbs. Audiences no longer have the same identification, save for the underprivileged and the oppressed minorities. Lorraine Hansberry's *A Raisin in the Sun* is an Odets drama with Negro replacements. In his own day, Odets was a man with a mission and his plays burned with furious intensity. He gave vitality to the theatre of an era and established a memorable place in our history, but today his early plays are rarely revived. A production of *Waiting for Lefty* at Williams College was greeted with loud applause by the sons of the wealthy, all of whom shouted at the end, with playful enthusiasm, "Strike!" The work has become a museum piece, a sociological document.

When Odets returned to Broadway with *The Big Knife*, his first play after many years of financial success in Hollywood, he retreated to the personal drama. Charley Castle seeks to escape from Hollywood's erosion of his artistic integrity, but he really wants the physical comfort that Hollywood offers. The drama never reached beyond Odets' own dilemma. Everyone attacks Hollywood, particularly those who have been its best-paid hirelings. No one yet has made the attack significant. Satire would be a more effective weapon.

Odets seemed troubled by success and his desertion of a cause. *Golden Boy* is his own story, raising the question of whether art and commerce mix. Odets wanted big money, but his voluntary submission to its code became the big knife. No one else was particularly concerned.

Odets has stated that *The Country Girl* is a superficial play, and that he himself directed it to have "a swift, tense, strongly paced production," which would be a box-office success. The trite story of an actor who has become an alcoholic, and blames his wife for his failure, can be sustained by clever direction, skillful dialogue, and the excellence of separate scenes. *The Country Girl* is headed for summer stock productions.

The Flowering Peach was an effort to return to broader social issues, but the story of Noah and the ark became the intimate bickering of a Jewish family rather than the broad problems of man. Odets hesitates when he is on the verge of saying something meaningful about man's relation to God, and slips too easily into glib evasions and modern slang. The biblical characters belong more appropriately to the Borscht Belt than on Mt. Ararat, although Odets could still be counted on to create poignant moments, as in the scene in which the commanding Noah learns humility. Most of the play deviates from the implied pursuit of faith. Shem loves money, Ham wenches, Japheth is the progressive-minded intellectual. The mother, with her wisdom, is able to handle the irate Noah and keep the family together—but Odets' fire had been extinguished by the flood. No new insight into man's relation to God resulted, merely a merry family fight, with God in the background. As one wag aptly said, "Odets, where is thy sting?"

Odets' technique kept him afloat in the less demanding medium of the motion picture, but he longed to return to the theatre with another try at socially significant drama. Before his death in 1963, however, he was back in Hollywood preparing a television series for Richard Boone's acting company, which encouraged serious work. Only two scripts were completed.

Odets betrayed his own talent. He was a sensitive man who believed in a better world to come, but he was unable to sustain that belief under difficult and changing social conditions. He was a lonely writer, but too weak to become a great one. In the thirties, however, he rose splendidly as the playwright most able to dramatize an injured nation in need of hope and unity.

Irwin Shaw's case is similar to that of Odets. Both men, passionately devoted to social justice, were unable to eschew the compromises that curtail insight. O'Neill shifted constantly in his groping for truth, but each different moment was true. Brecht had an overall point of view that shaped his material but left him in control. T.S. Eliot or Sartre can select and fashion material within a disciplining philosophy. Odets and Shaw attack evil in the world, but are more like second-line troops who rescue a beleaguered outpost. They avoid the main battle.

Bury the Dead (1936), Irwin Shaw's first play, written in the heat of conviction, is one of the finest antiwar plays. Soldiers who refuse to be buried and who rise from the grave, realizing the futility of war, and walk out to rejoin the family of man are a magnificent invention. Their refusal upsets the established code, and all the forces of society are called upon to convince them to lie down peacefully. If men won't die, war is useless. O'Neill tried it on a cosmic scale in *Lazarus Laughed*. Shaw is immediate and personal. The play is written in a series of flashbacks that give the past lives of the soldiers, much the same technique used in *Waiting for Lefty*. In Odets' play, the unifying force is the union meeting; in Shaw's play, it is the grave. Both are long one-act plays, the best of the theatre of social awareness. For whatever may be the reasons, Irwin Shaw has withdrawn all permission to produce the play.

The Gentle People (1939), staged by the Group Theatre, is a warm and tender parable of little people with their backs to the wall, who stand up, finally, against brutality. Try as he would, and he attempted it frequently, Irwin Shaw could not write another play to equal these two. He turned to motion pictures, novels, became a success, but never wrote another successful play.

In *The Assassin* (1945), a fictionalized retelling of the assassination of Admiral Darlan, Shaw's favorite subject is repeated—the conditions under which men rise to heroism and reach beyond themselves. The characters are poorly drawn and the basic idea diluted. In his preface to the play, Shaw wrote,

> I happen to be a writer who, to my sorrow, cannot help writing on political subjects. This is a savage jungle for the playwright and I regret ever having got into it.

Later, he said,

> A playwright owes nothing to the theatre. He owes a great deal to himself, and he must continue to write plays if all the world howl against him.

It did indeed, as it did also at his adaptation of *Patate* by Marcel Achard, the story of a heel grown rich and his companion fall-guy (*patate*). With *Children from Their Games* in 1962, Shaw lashed out at all the ills of our present society. Like Odets, he retreated to personal apologetics.

Shaw never mastered dramatic form. He craves a success on Broadway, but his skill lies more with the short story and the novel. He believes, as Odets did, in fighting for a better world, but always seems to be doing penance for his success. He lacks the brash, uninhibited anger of the younger generation who can snipe at present-day conformity far more capably.

Paul Green deserves mention, for in contrast with the avowed rebels, he may have chosen wisely. After winning the Pulitzer Prize in 1927, he wrote *The House of Connelly*, an early production of the Group Theatre, and a forerunner of the Lillian Hellman–Tennessee Williams depiction of the decay of the southern aristocracy and the hopeful rise of a more vigorous new order. *Hymn to the Rising Sun*, a superbly written one-act play, tells of the sadistic brutality of a chain-gang boss. *Johnny Johnson*, one of the best productions of the Group Theatre, is the tale of a simple man trapped in a world of greed and corruption. It is a delightful pacifist fantasy, with music by Kurt Weill, and is close to the theatre of Brecht with its skits, songs, dramatic scenes, and horror at the insanity of war. Green was among the first to depict the Negroes' need for education and dignity. With *In Abraham's Bosom*, he dramatized the forces of decay in the South, and responded to the pressures of the thirties by exposing the stupidities and callousness that lead to war.

Paul Green belongs to the social theatre, an able spokesman who could write with lyric brilliance and employ the combined arts of the theatre. But he refuses to be involved in the success pattern of Broadway or Hollywood. He now devotes his time to outdoor spectacles, extravaganzas of music, song, and dance. His re-creation of American history, *The Lost Colony*, is an annual presentation which has given rise to a national movement for comparable theatres in different sections of the country. Paul Green faced the sixties by turning in a direction of his own choice—the rediscovery of human values in our own past.

With the present revival of interest in the one-act play, an enterprising producer could serve the public well by presenting *Bury the Dead*, *Waiting for Lefty*, and *Hymn to the Rising Sun*.

7

MAN'S RELATION TO GOD —
MacLeish, Chayefsky

Job accepts *to live his life again . . . because he is a man.*
ARCHIBALD MACLEISH

"To love you, God, one must be a God himself."
Gideon

THE RELIGIOUS THEATRE has had an extraordinary rise in the past
decade. A precise definition of what is meant by religious theatre
is difficult and perhaps not possible. In one sense, all drama in
search of spiritual values lies within the scope of religious drama,
and even Jean Genet, who sets up an ecclesiastical hierarchy in
his private world of evil, is in search of religion. In the narrowest
sense, however, religious theatre is that sponsored by established
churches for the propagation of the faith, drama in which contemporary writing is used in the manner of the miracle and
morality plays of the Middle Ages, to win back those who have
strayed from the fold.

All religious groups have been increasingly active in the field of the theatre. The National Catholic Theatre Conference is the official organ of the Roman Catholic Church. The National Council of Churches of the Protestant groups has held regular conferences to promote its theatre work, using Union Theological Seminary and Boston University as focal points. The Jewish religion has no national theatre organization, but interest in the drama has been widespread on the local level. The American Educational Theatre Association has set up a thriving religious drama project. Most attention has been devoted to the selection of plays and the encouragement of writers, and to producing T. S. Eliot and Graham Greene as counterweights to Tennessee Williams. In this narrow sense, the religious theatre is an educational instrument with specific propagandistic purposes.

Totemic rites in tribal cultures, the origin of theatre, were used to transmit the tradition of the clan. They were usually efforts to propitiate forces beyond man's comprehension and arose out of ignorance of natural causes. Today's religious theatre stems from increased knowledge, from the failure of modern science and rational proof to answer questions about man's existence. It is a search for God in an age of doubt. For many it represents a retreat from reality, a rejection of materialism, and a return to the solace of the church. For others, the lost and the lonely, the disenchanted and the uprooted, it holds out the comfort of what was or is presumed to have been, in preference to the uncertainty of what may possibly be. On the most courageous level, the adventure in religion today is an effort to discover meaning beyond the furthest advances of modern thought. Einstein spoke of an intelligence guiding his mathematical research. The God of an age of science may be, not the creator of a planned and ordered universe, but the guardian of the awesome force hidden in the smallest particle of matter, or he may be the more impersonal and recalcitrant Withholder of explanations from the conscience of a world disturbed by questions of guilt and justice.

The theatre as temple has existed from the days of Aeschylus. Prometheus, in the first religious drama, defied almighty Zeus on the ground that divine law is not absolute. The debate is between two gods, powerful opponents, and when Prometheus will not yield to Zeus's command to preserve universal harmony, the earth opens to swallow him up. We sympathize with Prometheus' defense of man, but Zeus may have won the long-range argument. By giving fire to mortals Prometheus encouraged the growth of knowledge, the sin that has resulted in our present woes. Change, no matter where it leads, is opposed by established order, and increasing power in the hands of man diminishes his reliance on the supernatural. The Renaissance turned man free to find his own god, even it be within himself, and intensified the continuing dialogue between reason and faith. Defiance or acceptance of God's will has inspired great religious art, whether by Dante, Bach, Rembrandt, or Goethe.

Today, the situation has been qualitatively altered. Man has forged his own thunderbolts capable of destroying all life. The colloquy is between man and his terrible responsibility. The playwright, in responding to the challenge, has given new vitality to the religious drama.

Most notable has been the work of the French writers. The gifted Paul Claudel has contributed a modern masterpiece in *Le Soulier de Satin* (The Satin Slipper), in which the entire universe becomes a stage for man's ascent to divine love. He is closely followed by Mauriac, Bernanos, and Montherlant. Sartre, professional atheist, indicates how deeply the problem disturbs him by devoting an entire play, *The Devil and the Good Lord*, to proving existentially that God does not exist. Samuel Beckett, in *Waiting for Godot*, has written a modern morality play. On a barren hill man waits for Godot or God hopelessly, but goes on waiting. With a broken strap he attempts futilely to hang himself on the tree of life or knowledge, which forms an ironic background for the entire play. Though depicting the neglect of man by God, Beckett pursues the question of faith and meaning.

In England, Graham Greene as well as T. S. Eliot, both converts to Catholicism, are ardent proselytizers for an established church. In recent seasons on Broadway, *Luther*, *Becket*, even *A Man for All Seasons*, and more recently *The Deputy*, all of which were commercial successes, were evidence of the quest for spiritual values.

Though the oldest of theatrical forms, the religious drama, like the younger and more arrogant theatre of the absurd, easily gives way to a set formula. Typical is the work of Graham Greene, which has the third-act miracle of the restoration of faith. Usually a modern saint, like the young priest in *The Deputy*, re-enacts the Passion of Christ. Even Tennessee Williams in *Orpheus Descending* has Val Xavier, the southern saint, rekindle life in others through the redeeming value of sex. In *The Milk Train Doesn't Stop Here Anymore*, the parable is entrusted to Chris, the young messenger of death. With Williams, the Saviour becomes the body beautiful. Popular writers, anxious to please an affluent society, substitute the mystery of Love for the holy miracle. Romance is equated with God, as in *The Tenth Man* of Paddy Chayefsky and the musical plays of Meredith Willson. Most resolutions are mechanically imposed. Spanish and Latin-American plays are endless repetitions of the cliff-hanging end in which rescue is effected through the vision of the Cross. Few American plays have approached the stature of *The Satin Slipper*, Montherlant's *Port-Royal*, or Eliot's *Murder in the Cathedral*.

As in the case of most developments in the American theatre, Eugene O'Neill led the way. He sought to defy death in *Lazarus Laughed*, set up his own modern God of Electrical Energy in *Dynamo*, then retreated to the Catholic church for spiritual peace in *Days Without End*. For a consideration of religious drama in the current decade, however, the unlikely combination of Archibald MacLeish and Paddy Chayefsky has been selected.

Archibald MacLeish is, like Thornton Wilder, a leisured playwright who can avoid the hectic demands of the professional theatre. *J.B.* is his only full-length play, although he has considerable experience in radio and shorter forms. The theatre has always attracted him, but his interests have turned in diverse directions. His education at Hotchkiss preparatory school and later at Yale, where he excelled both as student and athlete, was followed by graduate work at Harvard Law School. He turned to letters, and after serving in World War I, remained in Paris with other expatriates as part of the Eliot-Pound coterie. His first volume of poetry was *Tower of Ivory* in 1917; *The Happy Marriage* was published in 1924, and *Conquistador*, for which he received the Pulitzer Prize, came out in 1933.

The great depression of the thirties turned him, like Hellman and Odets, toward questions of political and social reorganization. He joined with President Roosevelt in the New Deal program, was active in government service, and wrote his first one-act play,

Panic, in 1935, an experimental verse-drama about the stock market crash and its effects on the American way of life. His gift for language led to radio dramas. *The Fall of the City,* a powerful anti-facist work, and *Air Raid,* an attack on Franco and the Italian air force raiding Spanish cities, indicated his alignment with liberal causes. He was honored by being appointed Librarian of Congress, the equivalent of being designated American poet laureate, and did not return to the theatre until 1952, with a one-act verse-drama *The Trojan Horse* (intended for reading). *This Music Crept by Me upon the Waters,* a year later, was performed by the Poet's Theatre in Cambridge. By this time, MacLeish was professor of rhetoric at Harvard and only occasionally ventured into the theatre.

The Trojan Horse is an attack on the hysteria of the Mc-Carthy period. Laocoön becomes the victim of the city's war fever when reason gives way to superstition. He defies the religious demagogue and is thrown to the serpent, while the shouting warriors admit the wooden horse inside the walls of Troy. *This Music Crept by Me,* performed first by the British Broadcasting Company, is an attempt to discover the nature of happiness and learn whether its pursuit is not more valued than its achievement. A group of people influenced by the quiet of the moon on the waters in the Antilles live without the confusing devotion to convention and duty. They almost succeed in finding love and happiness, but the rules return to keep the dream from ever becoming reality. All MacLeish's work stems from the impact of the thirties.

Despite his reputation at home, MacLeish was relatively unknown abroad, and none of his work would have earned him a theatre reputation were it not for *J.B.* First produced at Yale University, it has since been played in most European countries, translated into many languages, and serves as an excellent example of the present-day religious drama. When brought to Broadway in 1959, the original script was drastically revised. Elia Kazan, who directed the play, persuaded MacLeish to make revisions necessary for increased theatricality. In the original version, for example, Sarah returns with her gift of love and urges J.B. to "blow on the coal of the heart." These lines were given to J.B. to make him the active protagonist. The reasoning is in accord with standard practice but not consistent with the logic of the play.

The Yale production emphasized the final minimum note of survival—unknowing blind acceptance, not of God but of life. The Kazan production was replete with directorial devices—lighting, music, and active use of the circus. To French audiences, discussion can be drama. Broadway, on the other hand, perpetuates its condescension to American audiences by insisting on action-packed melodrama. The Yale version was more austere, more poetic; the New York version more grandiose, more spectacular. The use of the circus tent as the symbol of the universe, with the high platform as heaven, the central playing area as the earth—the "ring of home," as Kazan called it—and a stage-left, slightly lower area for Satan, is not a strikingly original conceit. It was also used later by Lionel Bart in his English musical play *Stop the World, I Want to Get Off!*, in which all of man's life is re-enacted under the big top.

J.B. defeats itself right from the start. Mr. Zuss (Zeus) and Nickles (St. Nicholas? Nicodemus?) are circus vendors who become actors and put on the masks of God and the devil and then become the parts they play. The play within a play to indicate differing levels of reality and myth in the manner of Pirandello pulls the spectator back into the theatre, rather than transporting him to the awesome spectacle of man and God. The scope of the theme is diminished by making a mighty confrontation a triple play of confused identity. Putting the supernatural on stage is a tricky problem, like figuring out how best to dramatize the ghost of Hamlet's father. The Almighty can be a distant voice, as MacLeish makes Him in the final scene and as Goethe did in the prelude to *Faust*. Lights and shadows have been attempted. Making a peddler of balloons and another of popcorn the voices of destiny is a bold but dangerous device. Having less than ordinary men assume cosmic roles emphasizes the divine response in all of us. In the Italian production, the parts were played by two comics. Too much, however, depends on the imagination of the audience, and the effect is too frequently that of Charlie Chaplin playing the Almighty, adding a touch of the absurd to a serious concept.

The American businessman, addressed by his initials, is the modern parallel of Job. J.B., "possessed of a lovely wife, fine children, everything that the heart of a man could desire," accepts his success as deserved. He believes in God as he does in his dividends. When all the afflictions are visited upon him—including a car accident, a sex crime, the atomic bomb—and he stands alone, deprived of everything, he shouts out, "Show me my guilt, O God!" In the Bible, God's purpose is to test Job's blind faith that rises above worldly suffering. Job is a religious figure, part of God's order. J.B. is concerned with rational answers to senseless, irrational cruelty. The play becomes a debate between God and Satan, between J.B. and his wife, between J.B. and the Comforters, not a direct confrontation in which the essence of faith is revealed.

Bildad, Zophar, and Eliphaz, who represent the psychiatrist, the Marxist, and the theologian, attempt to relieve J.B.'s anxieties by assuring him that guilt is impossible. J.B.'s inner conscience resists. He wants the dignity of being a man, and says:

> "You tell me
> One man's guilt is meaningless:
> History has not time for guilt—
> Science has no sign for guilt—
> God created all men guilty."

To J.B., the elimination of guilt makes God unthinkable and demeans man. He repents, cries out his remorse, which is the beginning of the acceptance of God. The Distant Voice answers with a recital of the wonders of the Lord, as Nickles looks on unbelievingly. How can a tortured soul, finding no explanation, go on living, enduring the repeated stupidity? In the Bible, Job is silenced, awed, and rewarded. J.B. will not bow his head again. God does not win, nor does Nickles. God leaves before the final curtain to resume his role as a vendor of balloons. Sarah returns, a sprig of forsythia in her hand, to indicate rebirth and renewal, even after the fall of nuclear radiation. Both will go on, "the dark behind . . . and still live . . . still love." J.B. pushes God to one side as something that *is*, accepting His existence as a fact, but placing his faith in love, which permits man to create, to live, to suffer, to be himself.

Job needed no explanation, and is rewarded with more possessions than he had before the test. Job accepts, to go on with everything gone that he had at the beginning. This puzzles MacLeish, for a man who has "cried out to God for death . . . regretted the womb that bore him," goes on bearing children again, repeating the same cycle, awaiting the same onslaught. The only explanation MacLeish can arrive at is that J.B. "is a man." What that means is left obscure. But since man must go on, MacLeish finds his answer in love. Such a conclusion is the application of modern liberalism to theology.

Job is a devastating monolithic parable of man, not knowing why, or never being able to know why, whose belief in God rises beyond suffering, pain, illogicality, in unswerving obedience to the unknowable. The purpose is clear—a lashing warning to all who doubt, a threat of God's fury to all who waver. With J.B., there is no return to faith, but a resignation to go on, with Love as the Redeemer. The mystery of life lies in man's own re-creation of life. Not knowing how to resolve the question, MacLeish harks back to T.S. Eliot's morbid comment,

> "Birth and copulation and death.
>   That's all, that's all, that's all, that's all."

Peer Gynt falls into the lap of Solveig to find comfort in her love and their misshapen child, and clings to life. Nickles urges J.B. not to repeat his miserable life, to "spit his broken teeth out," and "reject the whole creation with a stale pink pill." He is sure

> "Job will make his own cold peace
>   When God pursues him in the web too far."

Sarah cries out to "curse God and die," but J.B. will "sweat it out alone," still trying to know, not bending to God's will:

> "Neither the
>   Yes in ignorance . . .
>   The No in spite . . .
>   Neither of them!"

In utter darkness, he will "blow on the coal of the heart," his doubts unanswered, his ignorance preserved.

J.B. is religious drama in that it raises the question of God in today's world where the vast forces of nature have been harnessed. Science moves to outer space for answers, to the origin of matter; the playwright turns to man himself, having advanced no farther than the man to whom Prometheus gave fire. MacLeish reached for the stars, made the theatre the arena for a mighty debate; unfortunately the results were less commendable, for he had neither the depth of insight nor the gift of poetry nor the theatrical magic worthy of his intent.

The verse-drama has come in for considerable discussion. Unquestionably, nobility of language is absent in the realistic theatre, though O'Casey and Odets have added a richness of common speech that outshines the mechanical imposition of verse. Preoccupation with psychological case studies and middle-class problems, since Ibsen, has reduced language to dull reportage. Yeats and Lorca, our best writers of poetic drama, return to legend and folklore. Maxwell Anderson, Arch Oboler, Robinson Jeffers, and William Carlos Williams have written in verse despite Broadway's indifference. Among the younger playwrights, Jack Richardson and Lewis John Carlino employ a boldness of imagery and rhythmic structure. Few have been successful. For example, *The Cocktail Party,* though arranged on the printed page as verse, reads like accentuated prose.

There is no absolute virtue in either prose or poetry. Theme and content demand their own form of expression. In the contemporary theatre, poetry unrelated to character and theme becomes embarrassing. (Maxwell Anderson made the judge in *Winterset* sound like Elizabeth and Essex.) MacLeish is a poet more than a dramatist. His material calls for grandeur of language. He is successful at times, but the occasionally magnificent images are weakened by obvious straining and become too scholarly to achieve mystery. He repeats a phrase, twists it out of shape, plays it as a pun to obtain elusive meanings, but the effort is too apparent, as for instance:

> "If God is Will
> And Will is well
> Then what is ill?
> God still?
> Dew tell!"

To overcome the overliterary quality of which he is too conscious, MacLeish will suddenly inject a four-letter word or shift from the most elevated thought to immediate reality. Zuss says,

> ". . . searchless power
> Burning upon the hearth of stars—"

and Nickles interrupts with, "Where did I put the *popcorn?*"

Milton's verse account of the fall of man leaves little to Adam. He wisely chose to let Satan and the archangels do most of the talking. Goethe has a superman defy God's restrictions, a man worthy of debate with Mephistopheles, and God takes Faust back because he realizes that so long as man strives he will err. Mac-Leish's play leaves man a passive figure, acted upon but not acting. J.B. is the man in the center of the arena, watched by others, but he never acquires dignity. Kazan, perhaps wisely, resorted to pageantry and theatricality, yet the excitement of a good circus never swept beyond the rafters. Brooks Atkinson and Walter Kerr admired the work as a relief from the usual tedium. Kenneth Tynan and John Ciardi, among the weekly reviewers, found it pretentious. But MacLeish deserves credit for rejecting the limitations of the writers of the thirties and attempting a play of ideas with a universal theme.

Paddy Chayefsky, not as well equipped as MacLeish but a more skillful technician, likewise does not hesitate to tackle the question of faith. His first effort was *The Tenth Man*, a contemporary version of *The Dybbuk*, the Salomon Ansky play, which has become a classic of the Habimah Theatre. *The Dybbuk* is based on the superstition that the soul of a dead man who has suffered an injustice in life, and cannot find solace in heaven, becomes a dybbuk and enters the body of a living person until the wrong is righted. The entire action of Chayefsky's play takes place in a shabby Orthodox synagogue, to the accompaniment of Jewish prayers and ceremonial ritual, which proved extremely popular with the New York audience. Ansky's original play evokes the mystery of folk legend and carries with it an underlying condemnation of orthodoxy. With Paddy Chayefsky, the play becomes an attack on present-day intellectual cynicism and advocates redemption through love. The language is a combination of demonology and Freud, fantasy and realism, but is cheapened by the patter of Jewish whimsy, the stereotype of inverted sentence structure, and the juxtaposition of chant and wisecrack. The rabbi, talking to a friend over the telephone, bemoans his plight in being assigned to this impoverished synagogue, saying,

> "My congregations dwindle and disappear into a morass of mortgages. I'm afraid there are times when I don't care if they believe in God as long as they come to the synagogue."

A girl is to undergo the exorcism of the dybbuk which possesses her. The young lawyer, Arthur, with whom she falls in love, cannot accept faith in anything and certainly not the religious faith of his fathers. She says to him, "Why can't you believe that I love you?" And his answer—"I simply do not believe anybody loves anyone"—is Chayefsky's comment on contemporary emptiness of feeling. The most powerful scene of the play is the one in which the exorcism is performed. The Cabalist chants the prayer and blows the ram's horn and shouts for the excommunication from the world of the living and the dead of the being that inhabits the girl's soul. The girl remains unmoved. Instead, the lawyer falls to the floor as the dybbuk of cynicism is removed from him. When he returns to consciousness, he has a reason for living, a "desire to wake in the morning, a passion for the things of life." As he and the girl leave, one of the old men says, "What a miracle! This young man who didn't believe in God, now does." His wiser companion adds, "He doesn't believe in God. He simply wants to love."

The play is sensational in its setting, its use of folklore material, and the contrast of the acceptance of religion by the older people and its rejection by the young. Those with faith would defy the dybbuk; the lawyer would send the girl to a psychiatrist. However, the play never gets beyond the resolution of a young man in love finding a meaning for life. Boy meets girl in a synagogue and wins her by losing his dybbuk. The basic question of how, in today's world of fragmented values, man is to redeem himself with a new faith is never touched.

Chayefsky further pursued the religious theme in his next play, *Gideon*, produced in 1961, in what might well be termed a television writer's approach to God. As in MacLeish's play, God appears on stage. The Greeks could do this perfunctorily, for their gods talked to humans, but the Hebraic God is the terrifying Unseen, save to a chosen few. Chayefsky uses The Angel, who forgets his role and calls himself God. He needs a messenger on earth and raises the peasant Gideon to leadership of the Israelites. The dull clod whom God has arbitrarily chosen to be a great leader attempts to discover himself. Gideon refuses blind obedience, and as modern man has done, assumes the role of God himself. He puts on the golden ephod, and pleads with the Lord to release him from his contract, saying,

"I am a plain man . . . I shall betray you many times, and you shall rise in wrath against me and shall punish me . . . I cannot continue in this way, my Lord. . . . I do not love you, Lord . . ."

The Angel is startled at Gideon's effrontery and furious at his own failure to inspire love, which God wants more than anything else. Gideon tells Him, "To love you, God, one must be a God himself. . . . You are too vast a concept for me . . . It makes me a meaningless thing." God wants to be loved, but for man to comply would make him a mindless pawn of destiny. In his final defiance, Gideon says, "I must believe in my own self and if you do love me, God, let me do that." The play ends with Gideon offering to the people a "historical, economic, sociopsychological, and cultural" explanation of his victories (the same ideas represented by the Three Comforters in *J.B.*). God bursts into laughter, turns to the audience, and says,

"God no more believes it odd
That man cannot believe in God.
Man believes the best he can,
Which means, it seems, belief in man."

Both Chayefsky and MacLeish build on biblical references, then try to liberate the audience from them. Man must outgrow God, take on His glory, and provide his own morality.

The dialogue is often warm and touching, and occasionally poetic, but Chayefsky drips seriousness with sentiment and exploits all the commercially accepted topics: God, psychiatry, love, and the petty problems of the middle class. When Tolstoy faces God, two bears engage in a wrestling match. O'Neill has some of the same quality. Chayefsky's play sounds like a debate, not between God and his deputy on earth, but between two enterprising businessmen. Both MacLeish and Chayefsky want their secular humanism to have the authority of Scripture. Chayefsky's God becomes a querulous tribal deity, almost comedic in his insistence on love, and only slightly larger than man. Worse still, in his desire to achieve satire, Chayefsky often stoops to maudlin jokes. He plays too often to what he considers audience preference, in the manner of a successful television writer who cannot rid himself of the demands of the medium.

Though both these examples of religious drama fall short of expectation, they are evidences of a willingness to restore the theatre to its historic grandeur. Chayefsky was aware of the comparisons that would be made with MacLeish's play. He said, "I don't want to compare it with *J.B.* My play is not about God testing Gideon. It's about Gideon testing God." His courage is more admirable than the results, yet he need not be judged by the same criteria used to judge petty plays of contrived situations. These religious dramas are both worthy failures, and they indicate a direction in contemporary writing. Ibsen and Strindberg perfected the theatre of middle-class realism. But they also wrote *Brand* and *To Damascus,* powerful dramas of man's search for God. After automation and the employment of nuclear energy to eliminate want, man will still face the need to bridge the void that separates him from his fellowman.

8

THE TIRED DEANS —
Elmer Rice and S. N. Behrman

*You're an artist, Hugo. What have you to do with feuds and hatreds
and rebellions?*

Rain from Heaven

*Many of our current playwrights have been analyzed or are under
analysis.*

ELMER RICE, *The New York Times*, Nov. 23, 1958

*Nothing is made by men,
but makes, in the end, good ruins.*

High Tor

OF THE WRITERS who gave prestige to the American theatre in
the twenties, few are left. Time has taken its toll but so has history. Those who have survived have little left to say. The same is
true of European writers, for not many can keep abreast of the
changing events of four decades.

In France, of the post-World War I generation only Montherlant and Mauriac remain, continuing their intransigent defense of
the need for Christian martyrs. In England, Sean O'Casey, though
constantly alert to the issues of the day until his death in 1964,
produced feeble repetitions of his earlier work. Eliot writes spar-
ingly. The vitality of the theatre lies in the hands of younger
writers.

O'Neill is the exception. Revivals and posthumous plays
maintain his position as the most significant American writer, both
at home and abroad. Alone, he spans four decades with undimin-
ished vigor. Maxwell Anderson, who had flooded the stage with
romantic verse dramas, returned to the scene in 1958 with *The
Golden Six,* a tale of the emperor Claudius, which opened off-
Broadway and quickly disappeared. Thornton Wilder launched
three of his one-act *Plays for Bleecker Street* at the Circle in the
Square Theatre and later garnered tangential fame with *Hello,
Dolly!* (the musical version of *The Matchmaker*). George S. Kaufman and that intrepid pair, Howard Lindsay and Russel Crouse,
continue to manufacture commercial fare and will be treated with
"Broadway's Boys." John Howard Lawson, after boldly experi-
menting with expressionistic fantasy, devoted himself to Marxist
scholarship and criticism. Only Elmer Rice and S. N. Behrman
remain as the respected but tired elder statesmen of the Broadway stage.

This in itself is a remarkable achievement, for the American
theatre does not enlist many as long-standing and revered practitioners. Writers, as a rule, have one intense fling on Broadway,
acquire credits, and retire to the well-paid and less exhausting
production of screenplays for Hollywood or television. Occasionally, when artistic integrity rebels, they write a play like *The Big
Knife, Nobody Loves an Albatross,* or *Telemachus Clay,* bemoan-
ing their fate, and then, with conscience assuaged, they return to
the mass media and the creative death they have deplored. Behrman and Rice, though they also turned to other avenues of expression, have been dedicated playwrights.

S. N. (for Samuel Nathaniel) Behrman's first play, *The Second Man,* was produced by the Theatre Guild in 1927. Thirty-
seven years later, *But for Whom Charlie* was presented by the
Lincoln Center Repertory Company in their initial season devoted

to American playwrights. Elia Kazan directed, and Jason Robards, Jr., and David Wayne starred. The play was not a success, and the Lincoln Center Theatre was roundly rebuked for selecting a play that could have been done more appropriately by a commercial producer. Brooks Atkinson decried the "obtuse casting and direction." S. N. Behrman, disenchanted by the "mutilation" of his play, declared that he would never write again for the theatre. From a man who has written twenty-six or thirty plays (he himself is not sure of the exact number), the words were not taken too seriously, for he has already indicated plans for two new plays: one about life in the theatre, tentatively called *At Rise*, and the other about Montaigne, who, like Behrman, represents a man of cultivated taste with no program for action, a man who dips his pens "in ink without dipping them in blood."

Behrman described *But for Whom Charlie* as "the most serious comedy I have ever written," and went on to say that he was attempting to show

the conflict between opportunism and the sense of responsibility. Ultimately you have to face whether you are going to behave with integrity or whether you are going to drift with opportunism.

This moral dilemma has little reference to the play; it has been a repeated theme since the melodramas of Clyde Fitch. A comedy of manners is difficult enough to write in these days of little concern with manners, without having it burdened with high-sounding platitudes.

The central character is Seymour Rosenthal, Jr., who runs a foundation established by his father, a wealthy motion-picture tycoon. He would like to help promising authors. An old friend, Charlie, is the executive officer; authors dedicate their books to him, sometimes "sincerely, sometimes satirically." But Charlie has no awareness of talent. He hands out awards as favors in the cocktail set. Seymour is the man of integrity, burdened with the guilt of a ruthless father and anxious to use his vast fortune to make amends. He is surrounded by opportunism, intrigue, worthlessness, and a sophisticated *femme fatale,* a continuing figure in most of Behrman's plays. A young writer of promise is shunted aside for Charlie's own personal interests. Talent is not rewarded, but chicanery is. An old writer, who keeps renewing his grant though he never intends to write another book, acts as a commentator, casting caustic barbs at everyone and everything. An unregenerate drunk and a cynic with enough love of the world left to want to tear down all hypocrisy, he is the only character who comes alive; his lines are an echo of the old Behrman. The rest are cardboard figures that never rise to the symbolic importance the playwright intended.

In the end, the head of the foundation fires Charlie but sends him off to Europe with the *femme fatale* and plenty of money. The serious young writer gets his grant, and conscience presumably triumphs over evil. The play is a long-winded discussion about contemporary morals, but none of it seems important. The foundation will live up to its original intentions but will hardly reshape American letters. The play added little to Behrman's reputation. Sophisticated wit and upper-class drawing-room conversation no longer seem sparkling or significant. Perhaps there are too many of the affluent society today in the audience to find these ideas revelatory.

The same was true of *Lord Pengo* (1962), to which Charles Boyer added his considerable talents in the title role. Based on Behrman's own biography of the fabulous art merchant Duveen, the play deals with the commercial and private life of the compulsive art dealer who finds creative joy in selling art treasures to millionaires. At the end of the first act, which takes place in his opulent private salesroom, Pengo employs his best techniques to sell the cold and unimpressed Mr. Drury a questionable Giorgione. He shuts off the lights, leaving only the electrolier on the painting, and speaks oracularly from the darkness:

> "It is not merely a painting you will observe, Mr. Drury . . . it is music, colored music . . . this picture I fondly believe will confer immortality upon you. People who have never heard of Giorgione will know Enoch Drury. Your names will be linked in this life and through eternity. *The Drury Giorgione*, a distinguished partnership, don't you think?"

The life of Lord Pengo revolves around the standard father-son and husband-wife conflicts. Everything is subordinated to sales and influence. Pengo is a man who runs a world he himself has invented. The play is the contrived, realistic comedy, with

stock characters such as the understanding secretary and the unscrupulous gigolo, with telephone calls at critical moments, but it
did afford an opportunity for caustic comments about art and
human values in general, about old masters and young mistresses.
Pengo's unscrupulous salesmanship conceals his need for human
love. He goes to his death with defiant nobility. His self-justifica-
tion is that, basically, he is a magnificent huckster who brings
beauty to others. It is a delightful play that never quite congeals
—in which conversation is elegant but in which there is no personal involvement. Pengo could very well be Behrman himself, a
self-constituted world which is an oasis in the hard realities of a
destructive society. Behrman is fully aware of major problems but
refuses to commit himself.

The Cold Wind and the Warm (1958) is Behrman's effort to
dramatize himself, the story of the successful writer who returns
to his origins to reawaken nostalgic memories, to rediscover the
small-town boy still present in the famous author. Behrman yearns
for the quiet peace of cultural aloofness. He recently said,

> It seems to me that people write most modern plays out of a sense
> of revenge. There is no more marketable commodity than sadism.
> People love it so playwrights give it to them. The theatre once was
> an adventurous medium, but it isn't any longer.

His return to his own youth, based on episodes from his book
The Worcester Account, first published in The New Yorker magazine, is Behrman's own struggle to find adventure in the theatre
and avoid involvement beyond himself. The basic story is of
Willie Lavin, who is forced to choose between the young girl with
whom he is in love and a rich, adventurous woman with whom
he can reach success. One represents compassion, involvement,
sacrifice; the other, experience, growth, and achievement. Willie,
trapped by his own sensitivity, commits suicide rather than accept
a forced marriage and an illegitimate child.

This play, one of the few of Behrman's works that do not take
place in a lavish drawing room, is again an opportunity for wide-
flung comments about life, literature, and art. Behrman, however,
is too close to the material. He assumes the character of Toby, a
would-be composer, who takes no part in the action but talks in-
cessantly about everyone else. It is a diffuse and discursive play

in which the Jewish lower-middle-class characters take on again
the semblance of caricature—the warm-hearted clown, parents
who speak in upside-down sentences and make fun of their
own people with embarrassingly bad taste. As a series of nostalgic
reminiscences in *The New Yorker*, the stories had a convivial
charm, but the dramatic adaptation demanded a point of view
and greater concentration. Eugene O'Neill, in *Long Day's Journey
into Night*, achieved power through standing aside and observing
his own family at a moment of crisis, as did Tennessee Williams in
his best play, *The Glass Menagerie*. But just as Arthur Miller got
too close to his material in *After the Fall*, so did Behrman in *The
Cold Wind and the Warm*.

Behrman's best work was written thirty years ago. Although
his own favorite is *The End of Summer*, there is little doubt that
his first play, *The Second Man* (1927), and *Rain from Heaven* in
1934 are the highlights of his career. In the turbulent twenties,
when American playwrights were deeply concerned with transforming the world, *The Second Man* was distinctive in that it re-
asserted the values of the good life of upper-class society and the
virtues of being rich and avoiding involvement. Behrman has
never wavered from this position. To him, charm, wit, dialogue,
cleverness, and observation are sufficient for the theatre. The
quotation he took from Lord Leighton—"There is always that
other strange second man in me, calm, critical, observant, unmoved, blasé, odious"—might be Behrman's own comment about
himself. With few exceptions, his central characters stem from
good society. Hiram Sherman, an actor who played in a Behrman
motion picture, once said, "Even his bums are fairly affluent."
And in *Rain from Heaven*, the line "What's wrong about liking
Duchesses? They're as good as other people," made Behrman the
idol of the first-nighters, whose man—or rather, second man—he
always was.

From *The Way of the World* to Noel Coward, the comedy
of manners pursues its elegance to S. N. Behrman, the American
Congreve. His plays essentially deal with the way in which the
elite, not the common man, face basic problems. His characters
are aware of social issues as they dally in adultery and intrigue.
The Depression, fascism, anti-Semitism, are treated in many of his
works, but Behrman holds his characters within limits. They
never go too far in their preservation of sophisticated detachment.

In the frenzy of the twenties and the outspoken conviction of the thirties, Behrman remained an unusual writer, avoiding being engulfed in popular enthusiasms. He is a skilled craftsman with a brittle mind, who prefers to give no answers or resolutions but relies on good sense—the reason and harmony of the French. His people ultimately collapse, but they go down with grace and dignity.

Typical is the charming and lovely upper-class Lael in *Rain from Heaven*. Hugo, the dedicated revolutionary, is leaving to sacrifice his life, if necessary, for a better world. They both see man standing at the edge of an abyss. He is willing to fight; she stands aside and says,

"In the sixteenth century, when people went to the Tower to be executed, it always struck me how casually they died. Something beyond gallantry . . . we've lost that."

And later adds,

"I believe in gradualness. I believe in muddling through. I believe that, in the main, people are reasonable and courageable and sweet—fragments of God."

Behrman recognizes the need for involvement—for other people. The artist or the downtrodden may rise in uncontrolled fury, seeking self-expression, but neither Behrman nor his central characters can ever join anything because it disturbs their serenity. He knows his cultured, superior individuals are doomed to disaster because they lack vitality and creativity. He does not permit his passions to run wild with a cause. He holds his mind in suspension and his heart aloof. Joseph Wood Krutch, commenting on Behrman's plays, pointed out that they deal with "an artificial and privileged section of society, and . . . the characters . . . are less real persons than idealized embodiments of intelligence and wit." In an age of decision, Behrman's choice is intelligence. His plays, therefore, are brilliant displays of consciousness and inaction.

Dramatic intensity occurs when man chooses to fight, not comment. Behrman limits his dramatic power by remaining calm. He would like to be an American Anouilh, but Anouilh's brilliant discourses on love, sex, and world problems are based on a rejection of reason and a cynical pessimism, which provides the

Frenchman's classical detachment. Behrman puts all his faith in reason and wealth, and both are deceptive allies in a no-holds-barred battle. It is a pleasure in the theatre to listen to Behrman's dialogue. It is a shame the lines do not belong to living characters.

Elmer Rice clings to the contemporary theatre by providing a new play with increasing irregularity. His most recent work, *Cue for Passion* in 1958, was written forty-four years after *On Trial.* Unlike Behrman, Rice did have a cue for passion. He was always a man committed to causes, a fighter for drastic social reform. He wrote anti-Nazi plays (*Judgment Day*), plays about labor and censorship (*We, the People*), and calls for responsible liberalism in government leadership (*American Landscape*). *Cue for Passion* is a far cry from his earlier work. It is a modern re-telling of the Hamlet story. Not only the title but the characters and plot are based on the Shakespearean play, and audience interest lies in making the correlations. Everyone from Polonius to Horatio is present in a tricky parallel, reaching to a hallucinatory reappearance of a dead father.

Tony Burgess comes home from two years in Asia, sulky, per-verse, intractable, a melancholy suburbanite. He believes his step-father, Carl Nicholson, had been his mother's lover and was the murderer of his father. On a palatial California estate he sets out to avenge his father's death, but Tony has a mother fixation and a reverse Oedipus complex. He identifies himself with the lover's role and is unable to kill his stepfather, for that would be to de-stroy himself. His anger is not directed at the evil represented by Carl, but at his own guilt. Carl did what Tony had only dreamed of doing. Tony does not kill his "uncle" because he himself had wanted to kill his father. *Hamlet's* richness, its multiple overtones, its relationship to basic problems of good and evil, give way to Tony's multiple neuroses. This Hamlet story with a Freudian twist still retains Rice's strong dialogue and shows a keen mind commenting on modern living, but it bogs down in the present-day obsession with psychiatry. With too many playwrights—and Elmer Rice falls victim to his own warning—drama becomes a case study. Rice, like Behrman, is aware of the contraction in the contemporary theatre; he said recently, "Too many playwrights today seem to be beating their breasts and feeling sorry for them-selves."

Rice's recent miscue should not obscure the contribution he has made to the American theatre. Any playwright who has written as much as he has is entitled to an occasional lapse. In the early twenties he was courageous enough to experiment in his finest and most enduring work, *The Adding Machine*. Four decades later, the tale of Mr. Zero has continuing relevance. A machine-dominated world that reduces individuality to numbers and makes soulless manipulators of its servants has never been more dramatically represented. Zero is capable of one moment of passion—he murders his boss and goes to the Elysian Fields. Here, where he is relieved of all mundane problems, he can be happy, but Zero has become unalterable. He remains an adding machine. He is compelled to go back to earth for his reincarnation, but the heavenly agents know that Zero is beyond redemption. Even in Heaven, he remains a Puritan. Not only is he tied to the machine; he has become a machine himself in his response to love, life, and beauty. The Theatre Guild production, with Zero running back and forth in a forest of man-sized adding-machine keys, was a triumph of the theatre of fantasy and a powerful social commentary.

Street Scene (1929), Rice's Pulitzer Prize-winning play, was a radical departure from drawing-room intrigue and middle-class drama, with its depiction of the swirling life in the slums of New York. The story has the melodramatic ingredients of a drunken father, an unfaithful mother, young lovers, revolver shots, and police arrests, but employs the arts of the theatre in kaleidoscopic scenes, to make the protagonist an entire community rather than specific individuals—an American *Lower Depths*. The people cluttered in the vast loneliness of New York tenements are depicted as the helpless victims of social forces. Poverty destroys beauty, compassion gives way to cruelty, and neighbors derive pleasure from the downfall of others. Public charity and social work are shown in their scheming inadequacy. On a large canvas, a cross-section of urban depression was given dramatic form. *Street Scene* was a forerunner of the Living Newspaper and one of the early demonstrations of the power of theatre as historical documentation. With a score by Kurt Weill and lyrics by Langston Hughes, the musical version has become a popular favorite.

After World War II, Rice wrote less frequently. His association with the Playwrights Company gave him a continuing outlet for his plays, even though they were of dubious merit. *The Grand Tour* (1951) was a sentimental romance about a schoolteacher on a European trip; *The Winner* (1954) was a last stab at legal evidence as drama. *Dream Girl* (1945) and *Cue for Passion* (1958) are further evidence of the change in Rice's outlook. He no longer is fighting for social causes, but has, like so many others, retreated to personal psychological studies. At heart, despite his plays of social protest, Rice is an incurable romanticist.

A skillful performer in varying styles, Rice was able to learn from European developments. *The Adding Machine* is reminiscent of expressionistic plays by Ernst Toller and Georg Kaiser. *Street Scene*, in sharp contrast, moves from abstract concepts and anonymity of the individual to the detailed realism of Emile Zola combined with the reportage devices of Epic theatre. *On Trial* initiated the flashback technique, now so widely used in motion pictures and on the stage. His many plays of courtroom evidence, derived from his training as a lawyer, are close to Bertolt Brecht's plea for the theatre as tribunal, even though Rice imposes a suspense-crisis thriller structure.

He retained enough vitality to depart from all his previous styles in the ebullient and witty fantasy *Dream Girl*, an engaging comedy of a daydreaming young girl who fancies herself in love with three different men. As her agile imagination pictures events, they unfold on stage. The technique is again cinematic, although, on stage, revolving platforms and blackouts replace the dissolve to effect rapid changes from reality to fantasy. Georgina Allerton, the young lady, is a delightfully incurable romantic; her scenes have become audition exercises for aspiring actresses, and the play is assured of endless revivals as summer stock fare. The plot is weak, but clever dialogue and ingenious staging have made the play a perennial favorite. Under its innocuous boy-gets-girl triviality lies the maxim that dreams should be balanced by at least a minimum of practicality and that too acute a preoccupation with dull reality should burst into flights of fancy, lest it degenerate into cynicism and apathy.

For Elmer Rice, champion of the underprivileged, to have written a Freudian *Hamlet* and a teen-age love story is no cause for condemnation. The finest writers will turn out a potboiler now and then. George Bernard Shaw offered his "pleasant" comedies to a reluctant Victorian audience, but an acute wit and an undeviating social commitment give meaning to his most contrived action-melodramas. Rice was not a profound or an original thinker, but a talented adaptor of current ideas, even those that were unpopular. His courage was admirable, but the McCarthy era, which quieted rebellious minorities, gave him no inspiring causes to defend. A skilled veteran of his craft, he could always turn out a well-constructed play sprinkled with brilliant comments on contemporary life, but the fire was gone. A generation without a cause left him without the "cue for passion" that had raised a rich talent above mediocrity. The one movement that has now inspired the young and aroused their willingness to sacrifice for others came too late in his life. He would have written, otherwise, a stirring tribute to the fighters for civil rights.

Elmer Rice is in the unique position of being both a playwright and an active worker in behalf of other playwrights. Like Edward Sheldon, that great human being who, though practically blind and suffering from his own anxieties, never failed to help other writers, and whom Rice knew in his youth, he has never failed to come to the assistance of others. His own life may be his most enduring monument. Always a man of principle, he did not hesitate to act when moral issues were at stake. When he was New York area director of the Federal Theatre Project, he resigned in protest when the State Department refused to permit the opening of *Ethiopia*, the first of the Living Newspaper presentations. In 1951, he left the Playwrights Television Theatre when the networks and agencies intensified the use of a blacklist of actors. In an open letter he declared,

> I have repeatedly denounced the men who sit in the Kremlin judging artists by political standards. I do not intend to acquiesce to the same procedures as followed by police commissars who sit in the offices of advertising agencies or business corporations.

As the dean of American playwrights, Rice has been a member of the board of directors of the Dramatists Guild and of the American National Theatre and Academy, and retains his chairmanship of the National Council on Freedom from Censorship. More directly connected with the theatre was his active participation in the formation of the Playwrights Company, an effort to eliminate the commercial producer. His force as a personality has been felt, and his love of the theatre is indestructible. He commented a few years ago on the dearth of good plays, "Fantasy is too deeply rooted to be eradicated. So long as people continue to dream and to dramatize themselves there will be theatre." Here, perhaps, lies the motivation for *Dream Girl* and *Cue for Passion.*

From the twenties had come a solid corps of professional playwrights. A number of them have been dealt with already. Among those not previously mentioned, Philip Barry has had one play, *Second Threshold* (1951), produced since his death. Robert Sherwood remained close to Broadway until he too died, just before the opening of his play *Small War on Murray Hill* (1957), and George Kelly, master showman of earlier days, was still heard from with a futile comedy, *The Fatal Weakness* (1946). Their era was long past. These later plays were by men who knew no other way of life than writing for the theatre.

Maxwell Anderson belongs with Rice and Behrman, if for no other reason than his continued activity and his inability to transfer what he had to say to relevant terms. There is nothing reprehensible about repeating a valid theme, but repetition without variety is to rewrite the same play. Certainly Shakespeare does not vary from his persistent concern with man's triumph over evil, but each play is a variation on the theme, with new characters to champion the cause. Anderson keeps on telling us that the noble cannot survive in a world of gangsters and that a courageous death is the final deed of revolt.

His latest play, *The Golden Six,* was offered at an off-Broadway theatre and barely survived the reviews. Turning to off-Broadway may not necessarily indicate decline in popular favor. An increasing number of established writers prefer to launch a new work away from the hazards of Broadway, particularly if the play is an experimental personal statement or a probing in new directions that invites less fanfare and a special audience. But the tale of Claudius in *The Golden Six* was Anderson in decline. Yet, though his reputation has suffered more than that of others, his contribution to the American theatre cannot be so lightly dismissed.

His work since World War II has not equaled his stirring

though somewhat sentimental dramas of the earlier period. *Truckline Cafe* (1946) was a failure, but *Joan of Lorraine* (1946) and *Anne of a Thousand Days* (1948) were well received. *Lost in the Stars*, the musical version of Alan Paton's warmly human South African novel, *Cry, the Beloved Country*, had a book by Maxwell Anderson and music by Kurt Weill. His first play of the fifties was *Barefoot in Athens* (1951), a story of Socrates' final days, which was followed by the long-run success of *The Bad Seed*, a gruesome melodrama of a disturbed child who enjoys murder, based on the novel by William March. Like so many others, Anderson has resorted to adaptations, as he did with *The Day the Money Stopped*, from the novel by Brendan Gill.

Anderson's early work prompted many to hail him as the worthy successor of O'Neill. The strange collaboration of Anderson, Stanford University graduate and schoolteacher, with the hard-hitting journalist Laurence Stallings had turned out the lusty, raucous deflation of wartime heroics in *What Price Glory?* —the first of many plays with question marks in the title. His co-operation with Harold Hickerson produced the burning anger of *Gods of the Lightning*, a defense of Sacco and Vanzetti. On his own, Anderson attempted to rewrite the same tale in *Winterset*, in which gangsters, lovers, and Judge Gaunt speak in an awkward blank verse within the shadows of a metropolitan bridge. Elizabeth of England and Mary, Queen of Scots, may deserve the dignity of poetic speech, but its use is justifiable only if demanded by the nobility of concept. Anderson's verse is consciously literary and superimposed, but one cannot gainsay the moments of hope it engendered of a theatre striving to soar beyond realism into grandeur of language. The weakness is twofold. Language should rise out of situation and character. Anderson's people recite rhetorical speeches and move in prearranged directions.

The *Winterset* theme repeats itself in all of Anderson's work. He had professed a faith in gradualism in his earlier plays, but he was quickly disillusioned by a world in which corruption flourishes and goodness of spirit goes unrewarded. Young Mio and Miriamne die. Esdras, the philosopher, stands over their bodies, which are riddled with machine-gun bullets, and says, "I find no clue, only a masterless night, and in my blood no certain answer . . ." Man's glory is "not to cringe . . . but standing, take defeat implacable and defiant . . ." Stirring words for the lost and spiritually isolated, but hardly a courageous cry to those under the heel of Hitler or Mussolini. Anderson may have a secret admiration for the gangster, for though Trock knows he is to die in six months, he goes on killing, acting, living. For the sensitive, there is no way out but the dignity of death. Victor in *Key Largo*, choosing to remain with the remnants of the International Brigade in Spain, repeats,

"I have to believe there's something in the world that isn't evil. I have to believe there's something in the world that would rather die than attempt injustice . . . something positive for good . . . that can't be killed, or I'll die inside."

In the harsh world of America's rise to material power, such words cast a glow of spiritual longing. Although he ranks among the most incorruptible of playwrights, Anderson dwindled into the most sentimental, and the most defeatist. The Indian in *High Tor* says, "Nothing is made by men but makes, in the end, good ruins." A Mio or a Victor needs roots in American soil. Anderson remains his own High Tor, a memorable historic event, but of another day.

9

THE EMERGENT DEANS —
Kingsley, Inge, and Company

. . . The theatre, in this country, in this decade, was primarily a place not in which to be serious, but in which to be likeable.

WILLIAM GIBSON, The Seesaw Log

The theatre, if it is to survive at all, must remember its entertainment function.

WILLIAM INGE, Saturday Review of Literature

The work is then no longer proof of the validity of the artist's intentions: his intentions have to prove the validity of his work.

JOHN BERGER, Toward Reality

IN THE THEATRE, as in all the arts, a few lead the way. The rest follow. Regardless of what one may think of their work, Tennessee Williams, Arthur Miller, and now Edward Albee are our leading playwrights and so recognized nationally and interna-

143

tionally. Behind them follow a score of lesser lights, mostly imitators or pretenders, some with limited talent striving vainly to reach the heights, others with still unfulfilled potential. From their ranks may come the next distinguished play, or a breakthrough in traditional form or content, but most of them prefer the safety of the accepted formula-play, the slick success they think the public wants. And so it must be, as long as Broadway's demand for new plays continues unabated.

In recent years some fifty new plays have been produced on Broadway each season, and a similar number off-Broadway; not so far back, there were close to two hundred productions in the New York area in one single season. Most playwrights are part of the assembly-line production that feeds this demand. The same is true in other arts. One may not admire the work of Jackson Pollock, but his leadership in having created a new art form cannot be denied. After him, the hoard of imitating abstract expressionists follow. They vary from those with integrity and talent to those who crassly crowd the clichés of the hour into skillfully arranged and outwardly glittering synthetic works. John Berger, writing of contemporary art in his book *Toward Reality*, says, "If you take a long-term historical view, ours is obviously a period of mannerism and decadence . . ." and adds, indicating how easy it is to sympathize with most artists:

> If you accept what they themselves are trying to do, you can admire their effort. The work is then no longer proof of the validity of the artist's intentions; his intentions have to prove the validity of his work.

From the long-range historical point of view, few second-line artists are significant, but in the theatre they do turn out plays that win awards, have long runs at the box office, and indicate the quality of our contemporary culture.

The contented craftsmen, the success boys, the unabashed non-pretenders like Leonard Spigelgass, Norman Krasna, and Harry Kurnitz, will be discussed separately as "Broadway's Boys." We are here concerned with such serious writers as Sidney Kingsley, William Inge, and William Gibson, who are persistent performers, whose body of work is considerable, yet who have fallen short of meaningful drama.

What determines a better play? What separates the significant from the mediocre? What are the elements that deprive a Kingsley or an Inge of superior achievement despite his good intentions? Such questions can be easily dismissed by attributing the failure to lack of talent, but talent too can be abused. Analysis of the problem proves elusive when terms like "genius" and the "mystery of creation" are brought into the discussion. In the plastic arts there are many imponderables and uncertainties. These exist in playwrighting too, but its basic components are expressed in a language more comprehensible than that of color, line, space, or sound. It is possible to know what makes a good play. Above all, a writer must follow the logic of his material relentlessly, no matter where it leads. Once situations are established and characters alive, they must develop in a world of their own making. Art demands truth. As Henry James said, "Our doubt is our passion, and our passion is our task. The rest is the madness of art." The lesser artist cannot resist rearranging his material or cannot summon the courage to follow wherever it leads. In *Two for the Seesaw*, an otherwise touching human document, Jerry returns to his midwestern life and an unhappy marriage, although his entire experience with the understanding Gittel denies this superimposed resolution. In *Dark at the Top of the Stairs*, the adolescent problems of the children and the material dislocations are not resolved honestly, when Ruben at the top of the stairs urges Cora to come to bed with him.

Paradoxically, such writers take their role as creator too seriously. They impose a prearranged plan on lives they have called into existence. They hold off from conclusions that have begun to assert themselves, and manipulate events to re-establish a minimum of dislocation. The pulling of the strings and the mechanism behind become too apparent. The game they play with their characters follows the rules set down by Broadway practice. A minor example, but nevertheless typical, is *The Heroine*, a recent comedy by Frank Tarloff. The wife of a Hollywood writer of TV commercials, disturbed by her husband's boredom with his work, hires a call girl to restore his confidence. The play becomes a contest between wife and mistress. Although there are far too many plays about bored Hollywood writers, or writers in general who live on lavish suburban estates, this particular play had a novel approach in exposing the weaknesses of monogamous marriage, which for the wife becomes habit and dull domesticity. The call girl wonders why any woman should want to be a wife when all the pleasures are enjoyed by the unmarried. When the wife attempts to instruct the sexually attractive young lady in how to approach her husband, she is mildly rebuked with, "Honey, I wouldn't tell you how to season a pot roast." The wife is preoccupied with redecorating the house, selecting a school for the children, and worrying about her husband's ego. The hired call girl is busy with love, sex, and a glamorous appearance. What a Shavian delight could have been achieved if the marriage institution had been subjected to ridicule. American girls rush into early marriage, get bogged down in the kitchen or with the children, then wonder where romance faded. The author, instead, dismisses the hired call girl and has the wife regain a more satisfying husband.

Equally disturbing is the glib use of popular clichés. Some writers touch on political and social issues, psychiatry, the search for love, and the loneliness of lost souls—never to explore them fully, but only to repeat what has become current knowledge. Audiences are given the impression of new insight, but it turns out to be the comforting reiteration of what they have already shared with their friends. Most disturbing is the popularization of Freudian analysis. Evil is clinically analyzed rather than dramatically presented. In *Dark at the Top of the Stairs*, for example, Lottie, the vulgar-mouthed sister of Cora, tells of her sexual difficulties with her husband Morris. Her confession is a self-analysis that presumably resolves the problem by unearthing it. Her coarse talk is a compensation for her unsatisfactory sex life, but no character change occurs, nor do relationships with her husband or sister move in new directions.

Psychiatry aims at a deeper understanding of motivations. Self-recognition presumably should lead to action. With popular playwrights, it becomes a device to resolve conflicts and cleanse guilt. In the old-fashioned melodrama, the hero discovered a treasure with which to pay off the mortgage; he now resolves everything by discovering he hated his parents. In *Detective Story*, Captain Macleod, in his unexplained generosity to his killer, says, "I built my whole life on hating my father, and all the time he was inside me laughing, or maybe he was crying." Characters once faced alternatives when events demanded action; now they pin Freudian labels on their deeds, and all is forgiven. Hamlet understands only too well, yet with all his reasoned knowledge he kills Polonius in a burst of passion. Elmer Rice, in *Cue for Passion*, reducing a Hamlet play to a psychiatric study, removed the human drama.

The failure to be true to the material does not preclude effective scenes, often brilliant dialogue, but results in reducing the power of the total work. Either the writer is afraid of ideas or he has none. He may have nothing to say and strive to say it well. Often he convinces himself that the play he really wants to write will not be accepted by audiences. He admits his compromises, and having placed the guilt elsewhere, plays the game with one eye on motion picture sales. The play that results is sought by most producers, a play which excites with its seeming daring but does not violate too many accepted patterns. Writing becomes a way of making a living. William Gibson expressed these misgivings when he wrote in *The Seesaw Log*,

> One might say many and enthusiastic things about the rewards of the professional theatre, such as the money and the comradeship, and the money and the self-espials and the money. But to me they all lay in the arms of the truth that the theatre in this country was primarily a place not in which to be serious but in which to be likeable.

William Inge, subdued after two failures, said recently, "The theatre, if it is to survive at all, must remember its entertainment function," an apology for his submission to the success convention, which eventually becomes sterile. Tennessee Williams too has commented on the extent to which the full dedication of a writer's calling has been at times betrayed by the pursuit of money.

Most plays by the emergent deans belong to the theatre of realism derived from the well-made play of Scribe and Sardou. Ibsen took the suspense-crisis structure and gave it content. Revolutionary for its time, it has become the dominant form from which playwrights deviate. With *A Clearing in the Woods*, Arthur Laurents attempts a foray into expressionism, but the form belies an essentially realistic content. Tricks are borrowed—direct addresses to the audience, use of a narrator, visualization of thoughts—but they are efforts to give an exhausted form new vitality. Actors and directors as well as stage designers are so trained in the realistic theatre that they achieve polished productions, which for the moment appear to be the real thing, but on second thought expose their spurious quality. Audiences are comfortable with straight realism, and playwrights hesitate to disturb them. *The Subject Was Roses*, Frank D. Gilroy's first effort on Broadway, was a three-character realistic drama of father-mother-son relationships. The play was old-fashioned theatre, common in the thirties, but cleverly arranged and well performed. Audiences loved it as a return to the easily understood family-problem play, which requires no stretching of the imagination and offers ready identification.

Second-line playwrights represent the solid corps of continuing workmen, busy writing and planning for the coming season. Occasional failures may drive them completely to the embrace of Hollywood, or may force them to a reassessment of what they consider to be popular. William Inge, after four successive hits, broke his record with two dismal failures. His comment was, "Maybe we have to improve life before we can hope to improve theatre." Greatness does not arrive often, but it never rises from submission to compromise. We are loath to attempt new frontiers. The members of the New Dramatists Committee, for example, an organization devoted to helping promising playwrights, are all working for a Broadway success modeled on the lines of what has already been successful. Mary K. Frank, a commercial producer who guides the organization, insists, in her appeals to other Broadway producers for financial support, that her charges are the professionals who will supply next year's marketable products.

This blanket criticism ignores individual differences. Among the writers under consideration as the emergent deans are Pulitzer Prize-winners who are steady and reliable performers. Sidney Kingsley, the ablest veteran of the group, is definitely part of Broadway's Establishment. His life is the theatre. His wife, Madge Evans, is an actress, and Kingsley produces and directs his own plays. With calculated timing, he returns regularly with a new work that threatens to deal with a major issue of our time, yet never breaks the barriers of the contrived play. His most recent works, *Lunatics and Lovers* (1954) and *Night Life* (1962), are evidences of his further retreat from the serious social themes that marked his earlier success. Neither was received with critical acclaim. The irony is that what he thought popular had already become hackneyed.

Men in White, produced by the Group Theatre in 1933, was a Pulitzer Prize-winning study of integrity versus corruption in hospital life. *Dead End*, which followed in 1935, a realistic picture of crime in the slums, was another indication of his response to the Depression era. *The Patriots*, sponsored by the Playwrights Company, was a retelling of the Thomas Jefferson story, and was produced during World War II to encourage renewed faith in American destiny. This was followed by the long-running *Detective Story* (1949) and the adaptation of Arthur Koestler's novel *Darkness at Noon* (1951).

In *Lunatics and Lovers*, Kingsley abandoned his high aim. It is a broad farce about the shady characters who frequent the back alleys of the Times Square area, a more developed story of the flotsam that paraded through the local precinct station in *Detective Story* and served as colorful background material; in the later play they are central characters in a medley of love, sex, adultery, and bubble baths. Dan Cupid, purveyor of pornographic postcards and cheap perfume, assisted by Joe, his tough, hard-spoken medicine man; Judge, a middle-aged Casanova making love to every pretty woman; and Sable and Désirée, two worldly floosies with few inhibitions, form a mad collection of offbeat stereotypes who find their shenanigans do not work with a naïve dentist and his middle-class wife. The dialogue is brittle, the scenes often hilarious, but the play is replete with obvious trickery and corny clichés. Instead of being all-out farce, it pulls its punches and the result is romantic dribble. When the gullible dentist is about to be trapped into marrying Désirée, and the Judge is at the point of plying the dentist's wife with enough liquor so that he can seduce her, Sable, as tough a tart as ever frequented a rundown Broadway hotel, exhibits her heart of gold. She foils the plan and pleads for the sanctity of the home. She tells her companions that, no matter how far they sink, they should never break up a respectable American home. She also turns over her lifelong savings of $17,000 to Dan Cupid, to help him out of a scrape with the Internal Revenue Department, because she too has fallen in love. What might have been a riotous travesty of con men conning themselves turns into a collection of gags and artificial situations in a fabricated play aimed at commercial success.

Night Life takes place in a key club, one of those recent after-hours spots where—theoretically, at least—people of importance gather. A labor racketeer and a disillusioned young lawyer are in love with a nightclub singer. The locale affords an opportunity, much as in *Dead End* or *Detective Story*, to bring in a wide range of diversified characters, including a middle-aged man and wife whose marriage is disintegrating, and a film star whose sexual appetite leans indiscriminately to both sexes. Vignettes of the main characters' past unfold as the others on stage freeze in the semidarkness, and the piano plays softly in the background as the unifying element. The development has a dramatic fascination, but the resolution is again the unexpected, poorly motivated, noble deed, as in *Lunatics and Lovers*. The unhappy husband is shot as he stands up to the mobster to defend the lawyer, an act of courage by the little man in defiance of rule by terror. The killer, who has always had plausible alibis for his past murders, will now be convicted for an obvious act of homicide. Everything fits in too smoothly. The labor racketeer, the center of Kingsley's attention, never becomes a full-fledged character, but is merely a straw figure on which the playwright can vent his ire. Lust, intrigue, family quarrels, are mingled in an apparently serious attempt to depict the rise of a small-time dictator.

The same is true of *Detective Story* and *Darkness at Noon*, Kingsley's other plays since World War II. In the first, Captain Macleod is too devoted to justice and honor and the law. He is a typical TV lawman, a Sir Galahad of a neighborhood precinct, which is overrun with addicts, petty criminals, and social misfits. His marriage is on the rocks because he will never bend when prescribed morality is questioned. He must break, but he does so only in death. The final scene lacks conviction and fails to prove Kingsley's point that overzealousness, whether for good or evil, can destroy the cause it serves. Kingsley's own fears are revealed. He holds aloof from commitment because to him the dedicated idealist is as destructive as the fanatic fascist. No wonder he turned to *Darkness at Noon*, in which Koestler had attempted to explore the psychological forces that make Rubashov put party goals above all human considerations. Kingsley is an excellent craftsman whose early plays, rising out of the social awareness of the thirties, gave hope of a developing talent. Reduced now to picturing Broadway's sideshow freaks, he offers form without content, and a reliance on pure theatricalism. His weakness is his desire to be safe.

After four successive hits—*Come Back, Little Sheba* (1950), *Picnic* (1953), which also won a Pulitzer Prize, *Bus Stop* (1955), and *Dark at the Top of the Stairs* (1957)—William Inge spoiled his record with *A Loss of Roses* (1959) and *Natural Affection* (1963). The playwright who had been hailed as a junior Tennessee Williams did not take his reverses gracefully. He accused the producers of miscasting, saying Bette Davis should have played the role in *A Loss of Roses* instead of Shirley Booth, and blamed the director for misinterpreting *Natural Affection*. He also turned on the theatre where he had won fame and money:

> I find that I'm not really interested in theatre anymore, and I wonder if many are. After all, it's a pretty antique institution that has lost its ability to reflect the contemporary scene.

Inge should have been more severe with himself.

Natural Affection deals with small people trapped uncomprehendingly by their neuroses, but unlike his other plays has no one warmed by natural affection. All the characters are filled with hate and ugliness. A son murders a girl who offers him love, when she unintentionally reminds him of his mother; a mother unintentionally resents her son when she is rejected by her lover; a homosexual parades the wife he has bought, as an exhibit of his triumph over his inclinations. The full Tennessee Williams galaxy is present, but to no evident purpose. Inge may have intended to portray ordinary people driven, by rejection, to despair and violence, but actually produced a clinical case study of sexual depravity, with none of Tennessee Williams' poetic expression and defense of emotional freedom.

Even *Come Back, Little Sheba*, the first and best of Inge's work, exhibits no particularly novel insight into human beings, and the final resolution—the recognition of mutual need—is unconsciously superimposed. But the play's tenderness and its knowledge of the sufferings of the neglected people evoke sympathy for two pathetic lost souls. Inge has exhausted his theme.

The recent failures were deserved, for the plays were weak repetitions of what was inherent and explicit in the earlier work. Repetition is hardly forgivable if on a diminished note. Inge is dependent on the naturalistic-type structure of crisis and impact, but is too prone to substitute elementary psychology for dramatic development. In *Natural Affection*, compassion is missing; instead of Inge's professed love for human beings, there is a resort to violence for its own sake.

William Gibson has been unusually fortunate, at least financially. His novel *The Cobweb* was an immediate success and was sold to motion pictures, as was his first play, *Two for the Seesaw* (1958). *The Miracle Worker* (1959), an expanded version of a television script, became an even more popular favorite on stage and screen. Both plays are further evidence of the sensitivity of a playwright who prefers the security of the small theme and the comfort of the contrived plot. Experience may have confirmed Gibson in the pursuit of money. His one poetically conceived play on an unusual subject, *Dinny and the Witches*, failed off-Broadway at the same time that both his conventional plays were enjoying packed houses on Broadway. Although somewhat pretentious, *Dinny* is Gibson's sole exploration of non-naturalistic form. Originally a one-act play first presented at the Topeka Community Theatre, it is a musical fantasy that gets lost in its own playfulness, "a frolic on grave matters," as its subtitle indicates.

Dinny, a minor Faust in search of knowledge, "stops the clock of eternal time," which is in the possession of the witches in Central Park. He assumes control of a timeless world, a defiance of death, and command of his own destiny, but he fails in the quest for perfection, by eliminating change. Power to mold the world as one wishes brings man no closer to happiness. Dinny turns to the pure love of Amy, as Zenobia, one of the witches, holds a clock up to the audience to indicate that our time still moves on and warns that each beat is ticking away that much of our lives. We had better hurry along with our "nuclear business," she advises, but at least "savor the world while it is still with us."

In his two better-known plays, Gibson confines himself to the suspense drama of psychological realism, with all the concessions that Broadway demands. *The Seesaw Log*, a diary of the agonies a neophyte experiences in a major production, is a record of out-of-town rewriting, conflicts with the director, producer, and star, and the slow crumbling-away of the author's original intention. This cathartic recital makes good reading as a revelation of behind-the-scenes activity, but it is also a confession of weakness. Putting on one's desk Emerson's slogan, "Nothing will bring you peace but the triumph of principle," may be a reminder to one's conscience, but is not a record of fact.

Two for the Seesaw suffers from the ills of two-character plays. The relations between the protagonists have to be endlessly fluctuating, to avoid boredom. An obviously one-act play was built around enough telephone calls to give it full-length status. The use of two bedrooms—angled toward each other, but in "different buildings a few miles apart in New York"—permitted each character to be alone in his room or together with the other person or in contact through the telephone. Jerry Ryan, lawyer from Nebraska, discards his despondency after his affair with the generous, warm-hearted Gittel Mosca, a Jewish girl from the Bronx—the now-customary lonely souls who thirst for understanding and resolve all problems with sex. They discover a redeeming love, but Jerry spurns it, and in the usual unconvincing ending, tears up his divorce papers. Returning to one's wife is understandable if the play has been built around that relationship, as in *Mary, Mary*. Gittel's passionate giving of herself suddenly becomes a sacrifice to marital readjustment. Jerry's final words,

"Love is having, having had, having had—so deeply, daily, year in and out, that a man and a woman exchange—guts, mind, memory, exchange—eyes. Love is seeing through the other's eyes."

He is referring to his wife, after which he pulls down the curtain with the lines, "I love you, Gittel." Jerry has *used* Gittel for his own therapeutic needs; his declaration of love is more like a self-justifying thank-you.

The painfully detailed log of Gibson's own sacrifice to commercial pressures is a corroboration of a major failing in contemporary playwrights. It is natural for a young writer to bow to the practical stage wisdom of Fred Coe, the producer, the suggestions of Arthur Penn, the director, and the petulant whim of a star like Henry Fonda. It is also conceivable that the play may have been improved in the process. The story of two suffering souls needing to be wanted is far from original; the most notable achievement of this play is the portrayal of the intense, life-loving girl who gives to others and will always be hurt by others.

James and William Goldman, a brother team who had two plays on Broadway in one season, recounted the heartbreak they endured in the dismembering of their first play, *Blood, Sweat, and Stanley Poole*, when they were forced to revise the script in hasty hotel-room conferences. Producers' demands were callous and commercial. Directors were hired and fired at weekly intervals. Internecine warfare destroyed morale. Above all, they protested that the integrity of their material had been tampered with, and that an innocuous conventional failure resulted. Such accusations are common in the theatre, but usually confined to cocktail post-mortems. *The Seesaw Log* is a public self-absolution.

Certainly changes in lines and scenes are readily admissible if wiser heads prevail, for the theatre is a collective enterprise, and all concerned contribute to the final result—a distinct art form. The writer may work in isolation, but once he joins in production, many forces are set in motion. The only crime is to give way on the theme of the play. Compromise on principles is corrosive. Writers have rejected the lure of financial gain and Broadway credit if they felt their creation was abused beyond recognition. Gibson's capitulation is well expressed in his own summation, "the rewards of the professional theatre, such as the money and the comradeship, and the money and the self-espials and the money . . ." The Goldmans' next effort, *A Family Affair*, was a thoroughly trite musical concoction, and they are now comfortably installed in the Hollywood hierarchy.

William Gibson's protestations were not vindicated by his next play, *The Miracle Worker*. Helen Keller is so well known to audiences that they bring sympathy in advance. Plays about historical figures have the disadvantage of having to overcome previously conceived images, but they gain from audience interest. *Dylan* and *Luther* added little to our knowledge of these men, but the scenes evoked memories of lines unsaid. In *The Miracle Worker*, Gibson concentrated on the struggle between a determined teacher and a recalcitrant, savage child. The opening of new worlds to a stricken human being lost in darkness, who later converted her hostilities into bringing light to others, was replaced by Ann Sullivan's seesaw battle to win the girl's confidence. An efficient, well-plotted, sentimental, tear-jerking melodrama overwhelmed the emergence of character. Brecht once said, in condemnation of the realistic theatre, that any playwright can bring tears to the eyes of an audience. Gibson does—but empathy, instead of arising from the depths of human compassion, is stirred by theatrical manipulation, as in the scene when the young Helen Keller drops the water pitcher and is being guided to the pump. The long walk to the discovery of the relation between words and objects is subservient to the outward physical excitement.

Dore Schary's play about Franklin D. Roosevelt, *Sunrise at Campobello*, had an equally tense scene in which Ralph Bellamy, who played the President, fought with every live nerve in his partially paralyzed body to cross the few feet from platform seat to lectern, as the audience waited breathlessly before breaking into wild applause as he stood up, smiled at the public, and began the opening words of his speech nominating Alfred E. Smith. In Arthur Laurents' *Home of the Brave*, to provoke the bedridden Coney, the psychiatrist shouts at him, "Get up and walk, Coney. Get up and walk! You lousy, yellow, Jew bastard! Get up and walk!" Coney rises in rage, walks toward the doctor, his hands outstretched with intent to kill. Anger overwhelms a psychosomatic sickness induced by unwillingness to be part of life. Such devices are effective when they are an outgrowth of structure, character, and developed conflict.

Another addition to the two-character bedroom boom is Robert Anderson's *Silent Night, Lonely Night* (1959). There are minor characters in the play, but the action centers on the man and woman in a New England inn on Christmas Eve. They are middle-aged, unhappy in their marriages, and terribly despondent. Katherine is opposed to adultery, for she comes of stern moral background. John Sparrow, guilt-laden about his wife's mental illness, has had previous affairs but has always remained coldly distant, unable to feel a sincere emotion. They circle back and forth in their preparation for the affair, with the telephone handy as a means of communication with the missing mates. Sex again is salvation, and the implicit approval of extramarital relations is mitigated by each one's returning to his marriage in the end, better prepared to endure his unhappiness. Henry Fonda, who is now type-cast as the man in such two-character plays, repeated his role of *Two for the Seesaw*. The Christmas background implied the religious approval of resurrection through adultery. The play is amazingly devoid of action, a subdued, nonviolent, and often graceful discussion of two people's quest for human warmth, but it falls into the trap of skirting the forbidden and restoring the accepted.

Tea and Sympathy (1953), Robert Anderson's first play, which has become a standard vehicle in summer stock, did indicate a delicacy of feeling and show skill in constructing a realistic suspense drama. Anderson intended to have Tom Lee a nonconformist, the young man who cannot bring himself to engage in the usual vulgarities of school life. The accusation of homosexuality dominates the play. The now-famous resolution in which Laura Reynolds, the housemaster's wife, unbuttons her blouse and invites Tom to the proof of his manhood has little relation to the logic of the plot, but is a nicely superimposed shock-ending. Anderson's other play, *All Summer Long* (1954), was based on Donald Wetzel's novel *A Reef and a Curse*, and is less concerned with sex. A boy builds a retaining wall to save the family house from the expected flood, while the adults are too busy with their petty bickering to become involved in anything beyond the self. Anderson has spent five years as a Hollywood screenwriter, but is now returning to the theatre. He is engaged in a musical version of the motion picture *Roman Holiday*, a reversal of the usual practice in which Broadway musicals become Hollywood pictures, and has completed another play about marital difficulty, *The Days Between*.

Robert Ardrey, on the other hand, has consciously resisted Broadway's compromises. His two most recent plays, presented off-Broadway, both deal with presumably unpopular political themes. Ardrey is a committed writer, but he has not varied from his only successful work, *Thunder Rock* (1939). The theatre is his forum where he persistently displays the problem of the disheartened liberal who finds unscrupulous extremists using the right to dissent for the destruction of that right. Danger lies, not in the fanaticism of reaction, but in the failure of men of balanced judgment to act. In *Thunder Rock* the disillusioned journalist retires to his lighthouse because a cynical world refuses to heed his warning. In his fantasy, he reviews the past history of man, then steps forward to fight once more for decency and justice. Ardrey is extremely sensitive to a senseless world, but believes that though madness may dominate for the moment, it will destroy itself in the end. Reason and integrity will ultimately triumph. These broad generalities, despite good intentions, are difficult to dramatize effectively.

In Ardrey's *Sing Me No Lullaby* (1954), Mike Hertzog, a brilliant mathematician, prepares to desert to the Chinese because he is hounded unjustly by the F.B.I. Ben Collinger, his University of Illinois classmate (1930), who has withdrawn from active politics and is now a successful businessman, returns to run for office, to do what he can to prevent the damage that has resulted from political extremists. He knows that Mike has contributed to his own plight by being too dogmatic in defense of Marxism, but he refuses with equal intolerance to condone the suppression of such views. Mike's scientific contribution and his right to dissent are worth preserving. *The Shadow of Heroes* (1958) is one of the few efforts to dramatize the Hungarian revolt of 1956. The play is a powerful documentation of historical events centering around Janos Kadar, who betrays his best friends when the needs of the party demand it. Once more, Ardrey is disturbed by "total commitments" that ignore human values. He wants the world to belong to the Collingers as well.

Like Odets, Hellman, and Irwin Shaw, Ardrey is a product of the Depression era. His ardent endorsement of social justice does not rise in positive and effective drama in his plays, for his position is undramatic—the best one can do is to fight with the knowledge of ultimate defeat. Because in *Thunder Rock* the intellectual steps out of his ivory tower, the play was well received in Britain during the bombings. For an American public in need of enthusiasm, Ardrey is too negative. He sounds like a character from *Heartbreak House* or S. N. Behrman's *Rain from Heaven*, repeating that the amoral intensity of fanatics will destroy reason but at least one can go down bravely. American leadership, as well as youth in search of positive goals, deserves more from Ardrey's unquestioned poetic gifts.

Whereas Ardrey is concerned, in broad philosophic terms, with dogmatism assuming the mask of righteousness, Arthur Laurents has consistently been a champion of specific victims of tyranny. His willingness, likewise, to think in social terms has been turned to good effect in musical plays which reach beyond personal adventure or private romance. *West Side Story* (1957) was his first big Broadway success, although his four previous plays, all nonmusical—*Home of the Brave* (1945), *The Bird Cage* (1950), *Time of the Cuckoo* (1952), *A Clearing in the Woods* (1957)—had firmly established his reputation as a serious writer.

Home of the Brave is one of the few good plays to come out of World War II, although it deals less with war than with racial or religious prejudice. In the original play, Coney is a Jew. In the motion picture, he became a Negro. The army and its use of narcosynthesis make up the background for a study of ingrown hates, which become more evident and cruel under the demanding conditions of war. The buildup is through flashbacks depicting the raw emotions of men under fire. Bigotry produces its ugliness and self-preservation, but it is juxtaposed with the strength of newfound comradeship. The letter from Mingo's wife, the "Dear Joe" letter, is integrated into the action of the play, for the theme that man must stand up and fight when pushed too far is well expressed in the lines of poetry she has written:

> "And frightened we are, everyone.
> Someone must take a stand.
> Coward, take my coward's hand."

Coney's recovery and his departure with his war buddies to open a bar together have the touch of the imposed resolution, but Laurents needed a positive ending for his social conviction.

In *The Bird Cage*, the employees finally stand up against the tyrannical nightclub owner, Wally, and walk out in defiance and solidarity. *Time of the Cuckoo*, among the first of the two-character seduction plays, has an American schoolteacher seeking romance abroad run full tilt against her own ingrained Puritanism and long-preserved chastity. *A Clearing in the Woods* was an indication of Laurents' continuing willingness to experiment in form. The mixture of fantasy and stream of consciousness helps a basically simple, naturalistic story of an American woman as sweetheart, wife, and mother in different stages of her dream world and actuality. Laurents again is concerned with "the loneliness afoot in this country" and the need for each one to recognize what "an imperfect human being he is," in order to make the adjustment to life.

West Side Story (1957) set Laurents on the path of writing librettos for musical plays. In the pattern set by Oklahoma! he participated in effecting a unity of plot, lyrics, and choreography that made this story of love and gang warfare one of the finest American productions. More and more, writers are turning to the musical play as Broadway increases its percentage of expensive musical productions. Gypsy, which followed in 1960, is the usual star vehicle. To the story of Gypsy Rose Lee, Laurents added the social implications of a demanding stage mother, too eager for fame and money. Most recently, togeethr with Stephen Sondheim, he attempted an avant-garde topical revue, Anyone Can Whistle, which failed to elicit critical approval despite its witty and abrasive skits on a world gone mad.

His only return to the straight dramatic play in recent years was Invitation to a March (1960), about which Celeste Holm, who played Camilla Jablonski, said:

> This play occurs on so many levels and with one's sympathy moving so constantly that it gives a bursting sense of life not often encountered in today's theatre.

The author should welcome such enthusiastic comments from his star, since he also directed the play, but Laurents, who has verged on escape from the success formula, slips into the conventional traps. The action of the play, which was originally entitled The Sleepwalker, takes place at a Long Island beach home. Norma, the heroine, constantly falls asleep as a secret protest against her forthcoming marriage to the conformist Schuyler Grogan, who stands for "martinis at seven, dinner at eight, breakfast at nine, beach at ten, lunch at one, tennis at three," which is enough to put more than Norma to sleep. The mothers are the customary status-seeking lost ladies, unhappily married. "All she wants," says Schuyler, "is a good marriage for her daughter, and all my mother wants is a conversation piece for her son." The plumber, who turns out to be the illegitimate son of the carefree, zany, independent nonconformist, Camilla Jablonski, kisses the sleeping princess, and away she runs with him, fully awake, to welcome love unregulated.

As in *A Clearing in the Woods*, the fairy overtones are solidly secured to a drawing-room-conversation, realistic family play. The theme—do what you really want—is hardly significant, and the characters rarely emerge beyond the cardboard stage, but the situations and the dialogue make a delightful comedy. The weakness lies in the over-obvious allegory and contrived ending. Schuyler's wealthy father turns out to be the father of Camilla's son, the poor plumber. The little boy, Cary, runs around beating a drum, presumably for the march to which we all fall in line. The young lovers dance off into the moonlight in joyous nonconformity, rather than accept the invitation to the march. Only Camilla has learned to be happy, for she ignores convention and lives by the love of nature and the dictates of the heart. One feels that Laurents himself would like to abandon Broadway's invitation to march and follow the example of Camilla Jablonski.

Brief mention should be made of other writers who fall somewhat arbitrarily into the category of emergent deans. N. Richard Nash belongs more properly to a later discussion of refugees from television, but is considered here because of his long association with the theatre. His work began with social comment in *The Young and the Fair* (1948), but has increasingly become bogged down by adherence to the taboos of the mass media. Like Laurents and Anderson, he has turned to writing musical librettos. *Wildcat* (1960) was his first futile foray in this direction, but *110 in the Shade* (1964) was an unexpected success. *The Rainmaker* (1954) was Nash's only popular play; its conversion six years later into a musical was proof of its inherent lyrical quality and its basically romantic theme. Obviously an *Oklahoma!* imitation, *110 in the Shade* has Western folk background and the opposition of good and evil in the most elementary terms. Starbuck, the con man, who is the American prototype of the picaro, lives by his wits and, like an itinerant Christ, awakens love and beauty in the hearts of those ready for his words. He is the plumber son of Camilla Jablonski, who awakens the sleeping princess. The original play spent too much time in personal confessions to reveal character. The lyrics and music move more effectively. Like politicians of all parties, who stand for progress and justice and democracy, Nash is for the fulness of life and the defiance of those who would still the heart. So much vacuity is more pleasant in song and dance.

Dore Schary likewise belongs with the writers whose intentions are serious. For years a screenwriter, and later chief executive in charge of major studios, Schary turned to the theatre in his mature years for freedom of expression. He not only writes but produces and directs his plays, an arrangement that gives him a unique position of independence. His four plays to date have been high-minded in purpose, but betray too many concessions to the commercial theatre. *Sunrise at Campobello* (1958) records the heroic struggles of Franklin D. Roosevelt to resume normal life after being stricken with poliomyelitis. Unlike *The Miracle Worker*, this play is the dramatic struggle of a man's will against forces that have crippled him, a struggle movingly portrayed in visual terms—the initial adjustment to crutches, the walk to the platform at a political convention—but too much of the play is devoted to irrelevant discussion of New Deal political philosophy that does not relate to Roosevelt's personal struggle. Government figures of a moment in American history walk in and out of the play, to the delight of the audience, but the different elements are not interrelated. A documentary was confused with a family picture; a personal struggle became a political debate. But the audience warmly welcomed the opportunity to live once more with a much-beloved man. A play about John F. Kennedy would arouse similar acclaim.

In 1961, Schary offered his dramatization of Morris L. West's *The Devil's Advocate*, which received little attention but was a more dignified play. Again he used the documentary or cinematic form, this time to present episodes in the life of Nerone, the Christ-like leader of the Italian countryside. Schary, profiting from West's superb material, came close to creating a peasant saint whose warm humanity triumphs in the fight against communism. With equal social concern, Schary continued with *The Highest Tree* (1961), one of the few plays concerned with the dangers of strontium 90 and the moral responsibilities of the scientist engaged in nuclear research. Excluding *A Majority of One*, Leonard Spigelgass' popular exploitation of East-West understanding, which Dore Schary directed and co-produced, Schary has striven to fulfill the function of the playwright and guide audiences to an awareness of contemporary man, but his noble intentions outdistance his ability to give them artistic form. *One by One,* Schary's fourth play, which opened in December, 1964, is concerned with paraplegics, who need not be handicapped in mind or heart. By implication, the physically sound may too often be more seriously handicapped by their failure to feel and think honestly. A valid theme was not accompanied by valid characters and situations, and a heartbreaking story was reduced to conventional formula.

More significant is Barrie Stavis, who for the last three decades has devoted himself to the serious drama of social meaning. In 1948, *Lamp at Midnight,* a play about Galileo, received more critical acclaim than did Brecht's *Galileo,* presented by Charles Laughton on Broadway the same year. Before that, New Stages had produced *The Sun and I,* a tale of Joseph and the pharaohs, which Stavis has rewritten many times. *The Man Who Never Died,* a play about Joe Hill, the martyred poet of the militant labor movement at the time of World War I, is Stavis' most successful work; it was performed off-Broadway in 1958. Since then, he has been at work on a monumental task, a series of historical dramas centering around the lives of key individuals who represent the development of democracy in the Western world—George Washington, Hidalgo, Simon Bolivar. He is a writer who believes in the dignity of man, the necessity of progress, and he reasserts his faith in man's ability to achieve a better world through knowledge and awareness. His carefully documented *Banners of Steel,* a play about John Brown, which raises the question of individual responsibility for social guilt, has been accepted as the first play for the college circuit organized by the American National Theatre and Academy.

Jerome Lawrence and Robert E. Lee are an enterprising team in the tradition of Kaufman and Hart, Chodorov and Fields, and—one is almost tempted to say—Gilbert and Sullivan, for their plays border on the circus extravaganza. Four plays to date are historical and documentary, with little evidence of original insight but an amazing adroitness in dramatic spectacle. *Inherit the Wind* (1955) was a re-enactment of the Scopes trial and the clash between Fundamentalism and Darwinism, brilliantly played in the original production by the late Paul Muni as the Clarence Darrow figure and by Ed Begley as William Jennings Bryan. An entire Tennessee community came to life in a picture of the many small people caught by forces that swept them on to bigotry or defiance. The usual devices of courtroom pyrotechnics were well exploited in the triumph of reason, intelligence, and liberalism over conformity. The efforts of the Lawrence-Lee team to dramatize the Warren G. Harding political corruption in *The Gang's All Here* (1959) and the Harry Golden story in *Only in America* (1960), as well as Soviet-American relations in *A Call on Kuprin* (1961), were less successful.

The emergent deans are all good technicians. They aim at serious theatre but too easily fall victim to success formulas. None is a pioneer. They move in after the trees are felled and the enemy routed, to cultivate fertile territory.

10

BROADWAY'S BOYS

It's got to be a comment on something. I don't want to write the little family comedy anymore. They've worn it out for theatre by doing so much of it on TV.

RONALD ALEXANDER

Unable to lick the new system, some artists join it; and we get commercialized art, judged as a commodity.

KENNETH TYNAN

"It isn't enough to be loved, sweetheart. You've got to know what to do with it."

WILLIAM HANLEY Mrs. Dally Has a Lover

THE LARGEST CONTINGENT of Broadway playwrights consists of the unpretentious professionals who, as a rule, are contemptuous of the serious playwright and are dedicated to the glory of pure entertainment. Few are ever considered in a critical work on the American theatre; yet they represent the common denominator of current taste. Like their predecessors in all ages, they regard the theatre as a place for laughs, thrills, and escape from boredom. Philosophic insights, new awareness of man's condition, probing in depth, man's need to move forward, experiments in technique, and flights into fancy are consciously ignored. Their eyes are not on posterity, but on their income tax bracket. But if the theatre encompasses all of life, if its range includes nightclub, skits, and Sophocles, the plays of these writers deserve recognition. They attract the largest audiences and preserve the myths of an established order. From a troupe of *commedia dell'arte* performers in a small Italian town, to Gertrude Berg at the Music Box Theatre, this category supplies the mainstream of popular entertainment and is closely allied to the material that pours out of Hollywood and is seen on the national networks.

Such entertainment should be displayed in separate theatres as well as to distinct audiences. There is no reason, of course, why an individual who, in his own complexity, is as varied as the theatre should not enjoy *Mother Courage* one evening, Shakespeare the next, and *Mary, Mary* the third. But he should know beforehand what lies in wait for him. In France, theatres are classified, and light entertainment is generously supplied by a professional corps of *boulevard* writers. In New York, plays of all descriptions are tossed onto the same stage and evaluated by the same standards. The American *boulevard* writer has no separate area in which to operate.

Among Broadway's showmen, there exists an acute craft-consciousness. They are proud of the well-turned phrase, the suspense-sustained second-act curtain, and their upper echelon status in the Dramatists Guild. There is something naïve and refreshing in their frank admission of being interested primarily in money and not in the sick condition of man. They readily confess to charges of catering to popular taste, for it is they who determine popular taste. Were their plays the only ones presented, critics would rightly bewail an uninspired season. Significant drama, however, is not always available, whereas Broadway's boys always have plays ready, not to storm great heights or redirect the course of history, but to "give the public what it wants." Tribute is long overdue the "honest hacks."

Most practitioners of this kind of writing commute between Hollywood and New York, for there is little variation in the product. The theatre affords them more freedom in language and

situation. Those who take themselves too seriously are either os-
tracized or graduated to the class of emergent deans. George
Abbott, better known as a director of such plays, and George S.
Kaufman, who has collaborated with many different playwrights,
are—together with Howard Lindsay and Russel Crouse—the recognized masters of the field. Abbott and Kaufman have pre-
empted the specialized profession of play doctor. They are called
in to pep up dialogue, add action scenes, rearrange crises, and
their services are eagerly sought and highly rewarded. Since the
material in most of these plays is interchangeable, the correct
combination is what works.

Though subject matter and topicality alter from generation
to generation, the continuing element is sex, with all its variations, from the problems of the newly married couple (*Barefoot in
the Park*) to tax-deductible adultery (*Any Wednesday*). The new
gimmick, a different angle, is what determines originality. In
Never Too Late, it was the emotional tailspin of a man who is
already a grandfather and discovers that his middle-aged wife is
pregnant again. Whatever the middle-class audience talks about
at canasta parties, golf clubs, or social affairs is grist for the mill.
Today, awareness of self, growing-up pains, relations between
parents and children, and problems with the analyst are good for
a laugh, or several topics can be combined, as in *Dear Me, the
Sky is Falling* by the present master of the quip, Leonard Spigelgass, who has a half-dozen new scripts available for producers'
choice each season.

Jerome Chodorov and Joseph Fields, another team of skillful
collaborators, who also produce and direct, displayed a brilliant
farce of life in Greenwich Village with *My Sister Eileen*, even
though the original material was supplied by Ruth McKenny's
novel. Garson Kanin was able to write a delightfully innocuous
combination of politics and romance in *Born Yesterday* (1946).
Though he has tried repeatedly to equal his early success, he has
fallen victim to the mediocrity of the mass media with which he
has been associated, and his later plays all sound like sophisticated daytime serials.

Once the popular theatre is recognized and given due credit,
its shortcomings should be pointed out. The aim of such theatre
is pure entertainment, but too often it is neither pure nor enter-

taining. Designed as box-office fare, such plays fail just as often as more serious drama. With investment costs so high today, production is—increasingly—limited to the most highly polished and the most ingenious work. Summer stock and community theatres are the ideal exhibition grounds for the unpretentious play, but it goes unheeded unless accompanied by a "Broadway success" label. The major shortcoming of the formula play is not that it fails to aim its sights higher, but that it fails within its own ground rules. Emphasis is on action, fast movement, dexterity in arranging situations. The result is obvious melodrama—the playwright's manipulation is apparent, and the situations so fabricated that credulity is destroyed and the suspension of disbelief becomes impossible.

In comedy, these plays depend on the rapid firing of gags and wisecracks, which usually come out of well-catalogued files and not out of character or events. When the playwright strains too hard for laughter, spontaneity vanishes. And since the plot is often merely a rack on which to hang jokes, once the jokes fail, little is left. *Mary, Mary,* so consciously laden with gags, produced fewer laughs than *Who's Afraid of Virginia Woolf?*

The third weakness is what is considered the greatest strength, the attitude toward sex. Basically, these tough Broadway boys are soft-hearted sentimentalists, outrageously righteous. Laughter derives, not from sex as an accepted fact of life, but from a nervous prurience in touching the forbidden. Lines are more outspoken, situations more daring, but when the scuffling is over, the good woman triumphs, the family is upheld, the libertine punished, and decency defended. Though they protest to the contrary, such writers do have something to say. They take pride in belonging to the theatre of no ideas, the answer to the public's cry, "I don't go to the theatre to think or to be reminded of everyday problems. I want to get away from it all and be entertained"; but they entertain by assuring the comfort-seeking public that the traditional way is the best. Most of the writers of Broadway's sophisticated comedies are secretly law-abiding citizens. A few examples will prove the point.

Mary, Mary by Jean Kerr, wife of the dramatic critic Walter Kerr, established long-run records at the Helen Hayes Theatre. Road companies have toured every part of the nation. Mrs. Kerr had already earned a reputation for amusing writing with her

books *Please Don't Eat the Daisies* and *The Snake Has All the
Lines*. She had co-operated with her husband on the book for
Goldilocks when that intrepid reviewer dared to expose his own
handiwork to the barbs of other critics. Together with Eleanor
Brooke, she wrote *The King of Hearts* (1954), a political comedy,
and she also had to her credit sketches for the musical revue
Touch and Go. Obviously, Jean Kerr came to the theatre with the
background and experience for light comedy.

Mary, Mary, however, is the perfection of the trite and the
banal, a perfect example of the overworked elements of the commodity formula play. The action takes place in a living room,
which also serves as an office away from the office for Bob Mc-
Kellaway. He is to be married to Tiffany, an attractive girl of
twenty-one, rich, and interested in wheat germ and health foods.
In view of her age and interests, she is obviously not the proper
mate for the literate publishing executive. In the opening scene,
Tiffany insists on serving to Oscar, the tax lawyer, a cocktail of
"raw milk, brewer's yeast, and wheat germ." How can she possibly be the woman for Bob? Who is? He has recently been divorced from Mary and is still in love with her, although he is unwilling to admit it. The situation is now set up. How does Mary
come back into the picture?

Oscar, who is both lawyer and friend, needs Mary to check
on several expense items in preparing Bob's tax return, and asked
her to be present. Oscar is the standard commentator, confessor,
and counselor who stands apart from the action but serves as an
author's instrument to manipulate others.

Preset are the elements of the triangle—the husband, the
wife that was, and the wife to be—with Oscar as the fourth member to whom each can tell his troubles. Needed is a fifth, so in
comes the movie star, Dirk, to arouse Bob's jealousy. Everything
has been nicely arranged by the playwright, and with a five-
character cast and one simple set, a producer's eyes water with
anticipated profits.

After Mary enters, it is perfectly clear that she and Bob deserve each other and ought to remarry. We are sure that, in spite
of all their petty squabbling, they will. Surprise lies only in watching how the playwright will bring it about. Mary, having difficulty
finding a hotel room, has Dirk bring her back to Bob's apartment.
They have had dinner together and Mary has had too much to

drink. Bob returns unexpectedly. The highways are snowed in, and he has been forced to cancel his trip out of town with Tiffany. Dirk has already made an effort to seduce Mary, and now Bob is available for the pajama scene. But since they are divorced, not even ex-husband and ex-wife will go to bed together.

The plot creaks and groans, the glue to hold it together a sticky mess of gag lines such as Oscar's "Let us not to the marriage of true impediments admit minds." Or Mary's line when Dirk tells her that he did not have a ghost writer for his novel, "I'm glad . . . I fully expect that any day now we're going to have The Confessions of St. Augustine as told to Gerold Frank." The conversation is sprinkled next with a few topical references to David Susskind, and to Eleanor Roosevelt's features. Bob and Mary end up in each other's arms, and love, family, and marriage are happily restored. Nothing has been disturbed, though always seemingly threatened. Sex is conversational, adult, and sophisticated, but except for a few kisses nothing happens. Dirk does not seduce Mary, who wavers only because she is slightly drunk. Temptation is always present, but everything is held within strict moral law.

The characters are all stereotypes. Mary and Bob are likable, witty, companionable, and comprehensible. There are no villains; all are nice people without even shadings of gray. If anyone deserves sympathy it is Tiffany, not as bright as the others, and much younger. She was trapped. As she explains it:

"I don't want to sound conceited, but when you're twenty-one, and you're sort of pretty and very rich, you get used to men falling in love with you."

Tiffany was attracted to Bob because he was the first man not attracted to her, but her suffering is mild. She'll get a more appropriate man, and Dirk will have no trouble finding other women. Every move is planned, even to there being no children of the marriage, to eliminate any unnecessary moral condemnation of divorce. It is pure soap opera, ready for a drawn-out daytime serial on television. What made the play so popular? Audiences, mostly middle-class, felt they were in on smart conversation and clean, healthy fun with a suggestion of the risqué.

Any Wednesday, which almost folded in its out-of-town try-outs after internecine disagreements and generally indifferent reviews, was brought to Broadway to comply with producer obligations. The playwright, Muriel Resnik, who had been knocking on the door for years, was immediately accepted into the ranks of the clever purveyors of light comedy. Sandy Dennis helped with her appealing portrayal of the youthful mistress of an executive who uses the suite, which he visits any Wednesday, as a tax-deductible entertainment item. Bring wife and young man into the picture, and a repetition of the same story is on its way. The play gets credit for being more adult, since adultery is accepted, as in George Axelrod's *The Seven Year Itch*; yet it is always clear that no one is hurt. The marriage is restored, all is forgiven, and the young ladies in question will go on to their own marriage problems.

Dear Me, the Sky is Falling, an example of family situation-comedy, brought Gertrude Berg and Leonard Spigelgass together for the second time. The actress has become a national institution, known for her fixed portrayal of the noble Jewish mother with the rising inflection whose good heart and common sense solve all problems. Singlehanded, she attempted better East-West relations with her understanding of a Japanese widower in *A Majority of One*. Spigelgass, on the other hand, is on his way to becoming a modern Scribe, with more open sex and psychiatry added. His plays reflect the prevailing culture. In Clifford Odets' more serious works, the Jewish middle class faced loss of status and wealth by falling into the working class during the Depression. With Spigelgass, they have moved out of the Bronx into Westchester County. The father plays golf and wants to retire to Florida; the daughter is about to be married to a stuffy young man bound to be a big-business executive. The mother, dominant and demanding, but unlike Albee's emasculating, sterile females, is all heart, pure love, self-sacrificing and misunderstood. Everything goes wrong as Mom's interference brings everyone to the point of disaster and the psychiatrist's couch. In the end, Mom's common sense prevails, the family is restored, the girl marries the man she loves, and the psychiatrist ends on the couch telling his problems to Gertrude Berg.

The technique is the same as in adultery plays. Open with a nicely arranged situation, let it become increasingly complicated, surround the action with fast gags, find a clever way to restore harmony, and end with the sanctity of the home and motherhood. The playwright's hand is seen manipulating the puppets. Molière, in *Le Bourgeois Gentilhomme*, did not hesitate to use burlesque antics and obvious artifice, but he mocked the social roots which forced the characters into ludicrous situations. The present family comedies give the impression of laughing at established institutions, but skim the surface merrily, to offend no one.

The action melodrama often eliminates comedy and concentrates on the gunplay and daredevil heroics of the television Western. *The Desperate Hours* (1955) by Joseph Hayes is a combination of suspense-thriller and family involvement. The killers hide out in a good American home, and the contrast between good and evil is neatly balanced. Emphasis is on the mounting tension as the lives of innocent people are in danger. The multiple set shows two levels of the Hilliard home, a sheriff's office off left, and the window of a neighbor's house, off right. Radio calls, police messages, and the arrival of the F.B.I. announce the prison break of three armed and desperate men. The escaped convicts take over the home of the Hilliards, and for two days and three acts all the variations of possible terror are employed. The Hilliards meet the situation with courage, sacrifice for loved ones, and gathering strength. The desperadoes crumble with inner strife, self-protection, and cowardice. In the end, the sheriff renews confidence in the human race by saying the comforting last lines of the play, "The world's full of Hilliards . . ."

The situation is pregnant with dramatic possibility. Plays in which a group of people face almost certain death can become a test of values, a forced re-examination of long-held beliefs. *The Petrified Forest*, Robert Sherwood's earlier melodrama of a killer holding people hostage in a desert inn, used the tricks of melodrama, but did make an effort to pit direct action and contempt for human life, as represented by the outlaw Mantee, against the detached, nonviolent cynical humanity of Alan Squire. In *The Desperate Hours*, no character changes, no one emerges from crisis different from what he was before. Normal American life has been disrupted by the sudden intrusion of danger. The way in which the Hilliards respond presumes that their values are unquestionably superior. They emerge victorious and evil is destroyed. Society, as presently constituted, is able to face any threat to its existence.

Hayes wants the audience to go home exhilarated by the tri-
umph of virtue, which is equated to a good American family.
When he criticized much of present-day theatre for being "sick,"
Edward Albee answered,

> Mr. Hayes . . . and a lot of other men who get their livelihood by
> constructing pieces of escapist commercialism for our stage, are all
> of one mind to certain points: that the status quo must be main-
> tained; that the theatre must be a dream palace of escape and never
> an arena of involvement; that any question raised must be given (by
> the fall of the third-act curtain) a pat answer; that our people do
> not have the fiber to withstand an attack on the most questionable of
> their values.

Since the popular entertainment plays never seek to disturb
but only to entertain, the search is always on, as in TV commercials, for some unexpected twist that will shock, amuse, and re-
assure. Howard Teichman with *The Girls in 509* (1958) overworked the novel idea of two rock-ribbed Republican ladies
locked in a hotel room ever since Roosevelt was elected, fearful
of venturing forth into a changed society. The opportunity for
political satire was lost because the emphasis was on time gags
and the ladies' eccentricities. His earlier play, *The Solid Gold
Cadillac* (1953), has a whimsical old lady attend a stockholders'
meeting and disrupt the procedures with the honesty of her questions. What could have been a farce about big business petered
out in labored wisecracks and too obviously contrived situations.
George S. Kaufman's last-minute doctoring of the play increased
its pace but added little content.

Harry Kurnitz, one of the most adept hands among the entertainment pros, turned to the arts for new material and mocked
the pretensions of *nouveau riche* art collectors (probably Albert
C. Barnes) in *Reclining Figure* (1954) and the world of sym-
phony conductors in *Once More with Feeling* (1958), but
satirizing the nonsense so common in the arts today became the
usual boy-meets-girl plot under new circumstances. Kurnitz' kinship with the French *boulevard* writers was emphasized by his
adaptation of Marcel Achard's *A Shot in the Dark* (1962), an in-
tricate "who-dunnit"; Julie Harris as the maid tried desperately
to overcome the weaknesses of the script.

Howard Lindsay and Russel Crouse, the grand old showmen

whose personal charm and interest in the theatre have made them recognized leaders of playwrights' organizations, are masters of the innocuous who constantly strive to be funny and always in good taste. Over the years, they have collaborated on dozens of plays and musicals, and produced and directed an equal number, until they have become a Broadway success legend. *Life with Father* (1939), based on the Clarence Day novel, and its sequel ten years later, *Life with Mother,* put them four-square behind family love, clean sex, and tear-jerking sentimentality. In *State of the Union* (1945), they flirted with politics and won a Pulitzer Prize. More recently, they dramatized Howard Nemerov's novel of the basketball scandal in the colleges, *Tall Story* (1955), and replaced the quiet satire of the original with vapid romance. In *The Sound of Music* (1959), they gave a wholesome picture of religious simplicity in the story of the Trapp family. Their musical play *Mr. President* (1962), with score and lyrics by Irving Berlin, was a Hollywood-bound flag-waving tribute to patriotism, honoring our hallowed institutions while recognizing the unfortunate presence of corruption and chicanery. *Mr. President* was advertised as wholesome entertainment, but failed to attract even a gullible public. Lindsay and Crouse know better, and there is an unconscious air of condescension in their plays. Villains parade unceremoniously in Washington or Czechoslovakia (*The Great Sebastians,* 1956), but are always defeated by defenders of virtue and honest politics. The virgin comes close to seduction, but ends in the arms of the plumed knight. Serious topics become saccharine melodrama and adult fairy tales.

Most of the writers of the entertainment school follow the patterns already described. A word should be said about a newcomer in the field, Sidney Michaels, who together with Spigelgass gives strong indication of being able to keep every theatre on Broadway from going dark. Five plays are optioned for future production. His *Tchin-Tchin* (1963) was a gay romp showing two different approaches to adultery, the outward, coarse vulgarity but inner sensitivity of the man, and the precious elegance of the woman. In the New York production, Anthony Quinn and Margaret Leighton used the commonplace text for a display of amazing virtuosity in the contrast of two social levels, with bedroom capers as the meeting ground. The French refuse to make sex a religious rite. Michaels tried his best but became virtuous.

For *Dylan* (1964), he was fortunate in having Alec Guinness play the lead. The play departs from the well-made realistic formula and uses the now-popular episodic technique of the Epic theatre. The Welsh poet, Dylan Thomas, is shown unhappy with Caitlin, running to liquor and women in his wild drive toward self-destruction during his two visits to the United States. What lay within the poet's heart, why his creative fire was drowned in despair and exhibitionism, was passed over for drinking bouts and seduction scenes. The only vignette that approached the dignity of the poet's personal tragedy was the one in which the audience at the "Y" waits while Thomas hastily scribbles the final line of "In my craft and sullen art."

Writers whose intentions are insufficient to "prove the validity of their work" and who never pretend to achieve more than a marketable commodity aimed at the pleasure-seeking businessman and women's theatre parties have a difficult time fulfilling the possibilities of a minor art. The form is definite, the ingredients established, but the old gags are overstrained; the rowdy, fast-paced, unadulterated high-jinks of a George S. Kaufman and Moss Hart are gone. For the moment, until a success comes along which alters the trend, the writers confine themselves to sexual titillation, off-color banter, and situations with good people at the point of immorality but eventually saved. The novitiate can hardly compete in this highly professional field. The skilled craftsmen turn out a glittering, polished product. Neil Simon, a graduate of the Sergeant Bilko and Garry Moore shows, is the current leader in the field of comedy, the successor to Norman Krasna, Harry Kurnitz, and George Axelrod.

Barefoot in the Park is a TV writer's dream, a chance to let loose with all the bromides about sex prohibited on the home screen. The play is a refreshing retelling of the marital difficulties of newlyweds. They live in a fifth-floor walk-up apartment. There is no room to move about. They climb over the bed to get into the closet, they experience the usual sex embarrassments, and the mood is sustained in rapid tempo. The battery of gags keeps pounding away with such lines as, "Let's discuss it," and her retort, "Not with you in the room." The play marks Simon's third successive hit. *Come Blow Your Horn* (1961), about a Jewish manufacturer and his playboy son, has been made into a motion picture with Frank Sinatra. *Little Me* (1962), based on Patrick

Dennis' original work, had Sid Caesar playing all seven male roles. With *Barefoot in the Park,* Neil Simon redeemed Broadway's boys.

Lighter fare occasionally achieves comic excellence that is original and honest. Two examples of men who write in the popular vein and do not demean their craft are Samuel Taylor in high comedy and Ronald Alexander in broad satire. Taylor, though he writes polished drawing-room comedies with elegance and wit, may belong with S. N. Behrman and Philip Barry to an earlier era. He won deserved recognition for *The Happy Time* (1950), a dramatization of Robert Fontaine's stories of a waggish French-Canadian family, and further enhanced his reputation with *Sabrina Fair* (1955), a modern Cinderella story, and *The Pleasure of His Company* (1958). *Beekman Place* (1964) has the neatly prepared epigrams, the opulent living room overlooking the East River, the artfully contrived situations, but the glitter and gloss no longer seem worth the effort. The invitation to laugh at the clever banter of the cocktail set got lost in the delivery after World War II.

A famous violinist with the unbelievable name of Christian Bach-Nielsen has retreated from the world to live in isolation with his devoted wife, his beloved sonatas, and an excellent cook who plays Bach. The visit of Lady Piper, his wife's best friend, introduces the usual complications of adultery, which the sophisticated upper class face with bristling innuendoes. They never panic in the face of disaster but go down bravely with a pursed lip or a polite retort. Samuel Taylor senses that times have changed, for he introduces two young lovers who are ardent advocates of nuclear disarmament and have participated in demonstrations to ban the bomb (British, of course). The serious subject weighed down the comedy too heavily. Domestic problems were crudely out of place alongside possible atomic annihilation. The violinist returns to active participation in the affairs of the world and all the couples are happily united. But the current decade may be too removed from Samuel Taylor's drawing-room comedy.

Ronald Alexander, who had previously written *The Grand Prize* and *Holiday for Lovers,* both well-fashioned comedies, appeared in 1963 with *Nobody Loves an Albatross,* a caustic satire on television production. The rapid-fire gags never cease, but the play is consistent with its theme and dares to say something. Characters are again the usual types—the trapped Hollywood writers complaining of the loss of integrity, the cynical producer, the pretty secretary who falls in love with the attractive heel; the situations are prefabricated, save for the appearance of a zany character with a laugh meter; but the play does not superimpose a forced ending and assert the triumph of conventional morality.

Nat Bentley, a fast-talking television writer and producer, completely without talent, lives off the work of friends, lies, cheats, plays one against the other, has no scruples or loyalty, and is always defending scruples and loyalty—an utterly charming rogue of the *What Makes Sammy Run?* school. He is a monster, polished and successful, and those who surround him are equally corrupt and self-seeking. These are the creators of the beautiful myths that appear on television screens in millions of homes. Bentley is the perfection of emptiness, a modern picaro who lives by his wits. The play is plausible because the world in which he lives accepts his values. All who surround him are cut of the same cloth. Bentley triumphs because he is a greater liar and knows it. There is no self-deception, no nobler self crushed by a rotten world. Rather, there is a recognition that Bentley's morality is more durable. When the attractive secretary, like most women on television who are in love, urges her man to go straight, accept honesty and devotion to others, he does not fall into her arms in an embrace of true love, but rejects her nonsense and goes on to greater success. To accept, for him, would mean defeat and failure. He never wavers in his Napoleonic rise to be the greatest phony in a phony world. The barbs and gags have special Hollywood overtones, but the satire is broadly meaningful in its reference to our general cultural pattern. The sharp edge cuts beyond the confines of a raucous Beverly Hills living room.

Alexander wryly complains that comedy is rarely given its rightful prestige and that all critics rate *Mourning Becomes Electra* higher than *Ah, Wilderness!* He ignores the fact that the trilogy explores the nature of the human psyche with shattering dramatic power, whereas the family comedy is one of O'Neill's weakest plays. Too many writers of comedy settle for a laugh. George Bernard Shaw, the last great master of comedy, did not lack recognition, but he wrote from a point of view which did not hesitate to hold up an entire society to view, as Molière and Aristophanes had before him.

Alexander takes the limited case of a television writer, and ridicules his values, but behind the laughter lies an implicit admiration. Getting to the top is more important than preserving integrity. Moreover, the public generally accepts TV production as a rallying point for petty minds, as the output clearly corroborates. Alexander does not affirm that accepted values are false, but rather that their defense is faulty. Bentley invites sympathy, not for his courage, but for his honesty in knowing how thoroughly dishonest he is. He confirms the public's opinion of television programs. Alexander's hero is in the right place for his talents.

Brecht once said, discussing contemporary playwrights, that the reason "money is not the subject of their plays may well indicate that it is the object." Broadway's boys avoid unexplored areas for they prefer things as they are. They are part of what they mock, protecting a vested interest. They re-establish the status quo because it is the world at which they can laugh, yet the school of reassurance can turn out imaginative and inventive plays, as it has with the works of Thornton Wilder. There is no need for reaffirmation to be dull.

Were only "pure entertainment" playwrights to exist, the theatre would jog merrily along to boredom and extinction. The dialectic of art is such that their presence magnifies the work of the few who rise in protest.

11

THE REFUGEES FROM TELEVISION

But of course it violates history. If the revolution had been carried out by Equity, it would have involved a few million less people . . . I'm saying . . . that we . . . as human beings have no relationship to the eternal truth.

PADDY CHAYEFSKY, *The New York Times* Interview, Feb. 9, 1964

". . . one of the many who trot so merrily through the marketplace . . . in the inconsequential shadow world of the theatre." GORE VIDAL

FEW AMERICAN WRITERS are able to devote themselves exclusively to writing for the theatre. Financial rewards are too hazardous, even for those who have had one or two plays on Broadway. A smash hit plus a sale to motion pictures can make a writer independent, and this is what all aim for but few achieve. Most professional playwrights, to earn a living, are compelled to turn to television or motion pictures. On the other hand, a phenomenon of this decade is the number of writers who have devoted their energies exclusively to television and then sought new outlets on

Broadway, or adapted or expanded their television scripts into stage plays. By and large, their efforts have not added to their stature as writers or to the prestige of the American theatre.

In 1954, a co-operative organization was formed under the leadership of Fred Coe, the producer, to write serious television drama. Among the members were Tad Mosel, Horton Foote, Robert Alan Aurthur, David Shaw, N. Richard Nash, and Paddy Chayefsky. Out of this effort, sponsored mainly by the Philco–Goodyear TV Playhouse, came such plays as Paddy Chayefsky's *Middle of the Night*, Robert Alan Aurthur's *A Very Special Baby*, and Tad Mosel's *Other People's Houses*. In addition to this group, many others such as James Costigan, Reginald Rose, Rod Serling, and Gore Vidal were finding opportunities to improve the general low level of television programs. With their names known to millions through the mass medium, they even went so far as to publish their work in book form, a presumption that it deserved more than a one-shot viewing and was entitled to a degree of permanence. The boom did not last long. Networks reduced the amount of time devoted to original plays, and writers returned to filling assignments for the regular formula situation comedies and adventure serials.

The television writer today is rarely heard defending the high-mindedness of his craft; he turns, instead, to competing in the Broadway mart. In 1964, the two most successful comedies, Neil Simon's *Barefoot in the Park* and Ronald Alexander's *Nobody Loves an Albatross*, were written by men whose apprenticeship had been served in television.

For writers, the theatre means fame rather than fortune, and a sense of literary prestige—an escape from the anonymity and wholesale production of television. The networks, discarding original drama, have turned to some extent to well-known plays of the past, and reshaped them to conform to the time limits of programming. Shakespeare or Ibsen is cut to size, implying that much of the play was useless froth and hence unnecessary, and that all can be adjusted to the Procrustean bed of television. In reverse, writers have expanded their original one-hour TV dramas to full-length stage productions. In most cases, the blowing up and the thinning down have not improved the work. Philip Reisman, Jr., defending his putting into capsule form the work of others, said, ". . . the so-called 'barbarism' committed on plays for television isn't 'barbarism' at all. It is a trimming of over-statement, of what would come out on TV as fatty tissue."

The dangers in making the transition from television to the theatre are only too apparent if one weighs the total contribution made by video writers to the American theatre. Mechanical substitution from one medium to another ignores the separate disciplines of distinct art forms. Television drama requires precision of timing, and regularly interspersed commercial or station breaks. The theatre, too, has its intermissions, but these can be eliminated or spaced at varying time intervals. The television program is competing with the other stations on the dial, and each section of the script must end on high suspense to insure a return to the program. Character development or truthfulness of situation give way to devices to sustain interest. As a result, characters are usually preset and there is little opportunity for development of personal relations or variations in reactions. The camera rather than the human eye becomes the instrument of observation, and its power lies in the use of the closeup. Emphasis is on the expression on the actor's face, thereby permitting a minimum of dialogue and group relationships. The camera can fill gaps by focusing on background or specific objects. The writer relies on quickly developed situations, and the actor as well must establish identification immediately. The result is instant drama.

Television may appeal to a large audience, but for one performance only. Video tape has now made reruns possible, but except for summer programs television demands the endlessly new. Everything is geared to the nervous pressure of a single take. The theatre, on the other hand, is based on group relationships and developing conflicts. It is the most demanding of all writing forms, and its audience the most difficult to please. Slickness triumphs occasionally, but it has to be bulwarked by the perfection of pretense.

There are still other factors that affect television production. If the show is "live," then it is severely restricted by lack of space and a minimum of expensive rehearsal time. If filmed, the technique belongs to motion pictures. Television is designed to sell a product, and the play is part of a sales campaign. A great deal of money is involved, and the advertising agency or the commercial sponsor exercises censorship over content. Certain subjects and language are forbidden. Writers turn to the theatre for freedom of expression. Gore Vidal, not too upset by television's taboos, points out that, under the Czars, Russian writers learned to express themselves by indirection. His assumption is that television writers have as much to say. For the most part, they are not unhappy, and voluntarily sell their talent by the same rules that regulate the sale of a commodity. They merrily conform for a price. The result is the perpetuation of stereotypes, the reliance on trickery, and the retarded development of an art form which has as yet failed to grow up. The introduction from time to time of documentary realism raises cries of courageous truth, and a dash of fantasy hails the arrival of a lyric poet. But the television viewer is rescued by that awesome dial. He can switch to another channel and watch wrestling or football. The theatre audience is not so fortunate and therefore demands more.

When television-trained playwrights attempt to transpose alien techniques to the theatre, the damaging effects can be seen in their work. Paddy Chayefsky is video's most celebrated graduate. *Marty*, his best-known work, was the first television script to be made into a motion picture. *Middle of the Night* (1958), his first Broadway play, was an expansion of an original television drama. (*The Tenth Man* [1959] and *Gideon* [1961] were written as original plays for the theatre and are discussed in the chapter on the religious theatre.) *The Passion of Joseph D* (1964) well illustrates the problems of the television writer now dedicated to the theatre. The play deals with the Russian Revolution and the role played by Stalin, whose real name was Joseph Dzhugashvili. Influenced by the expressionists, and Bertolt Brecht in particular, Chayefsky attempted a political burlesque comparable to those frequently seen in German nightclubs.

The play is in the form of historical episodes, often unrelated; actors address the audience directly, and songs and comedy routines interrupt the action. The most successful scenes are those played in the manner of a nightclub revue. The opening moments show the exiled revolutionaries returning in freight cars after the overthrow of the Czar. Each one defends his personal political theories, and acrimonious debate among splinter groups finally erupts into a hilarious musical number in Gilbert and Sullivan style about deviationists, counter-revolutionary imperialists, and

socioeconomic collaborationists. Another scene in a similar vein
shows Trotsky as an orchestra leader conducting the Revolution.
In a garish form-fitting suit, Ascot tie, and a pince-nez, he addresses the audience as though he were a stand-up comedian,
then directs the patient peasants in the background when to
droop, when to sing, or when to fall into a martial tableau.

Had the play maintained this broad satiric tone, it might
have been a bright new form. Chayefsky, however, turns serious
and realistic in the scenes with Stalin, who is pictured as a grim,
tough, unsmiling bullyboy whose participation in the Revolution
satisfies a religious craving. Christ's passion on the Cross and
his love of mankind are converted into the bloody passion of
Joseph D. Once a seminary student who rejected the Christian
God, Stalin finds a new god in Lenin, with himself as prophet.
His fanaticism for the future welfare of man includes murdering
a stupid police guard to get a pair of boots and driving his own
wife to insanity. Stalin is a one-dimensional wooden figure, a
ruthless despot in love, sex, or politics. Lenin the Saviour is seen
as a political conservative, who, in the final confrontation of the
two, regrets the direction the Revolution has taken and talks
like a New Deal liberal. Such historical distortions and political
inaccuracies, certainly not borne out by any evidence, might be
condoned if the entire play was a high-jinks parody. But the
realistic scenes, the essential core of the play, do not merge with
the burlesque antics.

After the seizure of power, Lenin, who is ill following two
paralytic strokes, regrets that nothing has really been accom-
plished, and fears it never will be. Stalin demands immediate
electrification of industry and collectivization of the farms. Fearing Stalin's excesses, Lenin decides to remove him from party
leadership, but before he can give the orders he dies in Stalin's
arms, a nicely arranged television ending. The scene, moreover,
instead of re-creating history, which in itself had dramatic power,
has two men engage in a political debate. Chayefsky said that
he purposefully distorted events in accordance with a writer's
privilege, but he violated the demand of his art as well, and
the theatre does not forgive easily. *Joseph D* oscillates between
high comedy, musical parody, and dead seriousness. Occasional
insights into character have little relationship to what follows.
Stalin's political brutality is presumably complemented by his

brutality to his wife, but no explanation is offered. The play has no spine to hold its diverse elements together.

Brecht's narrative realism is not mastered as easily as the television writer assumes. Bursts of song pointing a moral at the end of a scene, confidences to the audience, and a series of burlesque skits do not add up to Brecht's vitriolic poetry, dramatic power, command of documentation, and essential irony. Chayefsky defended his work, saying,

> But of course it violates history. If the revolution had been carried out by Equity it would have involved a few million less people. I'm saying in this play that we as persons, as human beings, have no relationship to the eternal truth. That is God's province and we've got to stop horsing around with it.

Whatever that last phrase means, and it sounds like utter nonsense, it is no excuse for simplifying history on Madison Avenue terms. The exaggerated caricature of the Russians is as puerile as the Russians' poking broad fun at Western imperialists.

Chayefsky likes the sound of his own words. Long-winded sentences with pretentious imagery are broken by sudden incursions into prosaic everyday speech. The language has no unity of style, as it did in *Marty*. Chayefsky enjoys writing on big themes. With *Gideon* he tackled God, with *The Passion of Joseph D* he takes on the Russian Revolution. But big themes need a big point of view. One line in *Joseph D* says, "What a terrible noise the splitting of hairs makes!" It is an excellent comment on the play.

In addition to his television work, and such motion pictures as *Marty* and his original screen play *The Goddess*, Paddy Chayefsky has now had four plays on Broadway. *The Middle of the Night* is about middle-class Jewish people on New York's West Side. Like *Marty*, it is a tender treatment of the search for love by lonely people, not physically attractive and for the most part inarticulate, who discover happiness in the dullness of their lives. A widower seeks companionship with a young girl no older than his own daughter. Though he sentimentalizes them, Chayefsky is more relaxed and comfortable with the ordinary people he knows. In the final scene, the girl says,

> "I'm confused, very confused, and yet I feel very sure. There are so many things I wanted to tell you that I never said."

The widower's sister interrupts with, "The coffee is on. It will be ready in a couple of minutes." This is Chayefsky's repeated device—an intimate revelation, a disclosure from the heart, followed immediately by some everyday practicality.

Before the curtain comes down, the girl adds,

"This much I know, I love you. I told my husband. Maybe there's something wrong with loving an older man, but any love is better than none."

Jerry Kingsley, the widower, in overcoming the objection of his children and his relatives, which is the substance of the play, asserts the need for small concessions from life when he says, "Even a few years of happiness you don't throw away. We'll get married." And immediately adds, "Do you want to go outside? I feel like walking forty blocks in the snow." Everything is neatly pieced together, a few sympathetic tears are shed, and the joy of belonging to the human race has once more been affirmed.

Gore Vidal has established a reputation as a wit, political satirist, and commentator on today's manners. Essentially a novelist, he turned to a new "trade" (his own word), television writing, in order to earn money. He frankly admits it and is fully aware of the pitfalls, but urbane admission does not eliminate capitulation. His three plays to date are political comedies, a refreshing relief from the personal problems and the excursions into adultery. He comes from a family that has been active in politics, and he himself was an unsuccessful candidate for Congress from New York. Vidal is the grandson of the late Senator Gore and lived for a while in the nation's capital.

Visit to a Small Planet (1957), his first Broadway play, was an expanded TV script. Vidal had accused the advertising agencies of trying to blunt the political barbs, but for the Broadway production, as he admits in the published preface to the play, he himself meekly and "deliberately dulled the edge of satire" to insure a Broadway hit. Under pressure from producers, he

obscured meanings, softened blows, humbly turned wrath aside, emerging . . . with a successful play which represents me very little . . . the play that might have been . . . was far more interesting and true . . . I played the game stolidly according to the rules I abhor.

Kreton lands from another planet and proceeds to turn the cold war into a hot war because that's the thing we twentieth-century people seem to do really well. He plans to take over the world, as is usual in science fiction—but not in order to establish a dictatorship; merely because he enjoys war. It is his hobby. On his own "superior" planet there is no war; work has been eliminated, and food, sex, marriage, and birth no longer exist because there is no death. Kreton is escaping from this ideal world, which he finds unalterably dull. He envies us "for being so violent, so loving, so beautifully imperfect, and so much happier than we know." In the end, Ellen, the young girl in the American family he visits, prevents him from starting war; in the television script, war starts as the result of an accident.

On stage, Vidal evidently intended to show that man can alter his destiny. The situation lends itself to comments on military leaders, TV commentators, patriotic slogans, and the divided world of today. Vidal pokes fun, as well, at writers of science fiction, who always make visitors from other planets either creatures superior to man or weird, horrifying monsters. Kreton is just like us, but bored, and rather retarded emotionally and morally. Amusing as the play is in spots, the satire is forced. Vidal labeled it "a comedy akin to vaudeville," but as such, the characters are too broad and most of the comedy slapstick. The "teeth" that Vidal pulled during the tryouts removed everything too sharp to prevent a hit and kept the work "a play that might have been."

The Best Man, which followed in 1960, is a cleverly constructed play on presidential politics. The motion picture version was released in time for the 1964 election campaign. The action takes place in the hotel rooms of the two leading candidates for nomination during the party convention. The three acts, in the tradition of the well-made play, are evenly divided into two scenes each, one taking place in Secretary Russell's room and the other in Senator Cantwell's. The balanced construction is matched by balanced opponents. Russell is a statesman, intelligent, abhorring mud-slinging politics. He is a charming gentleman, but his marriage is a failure and he has turned to affairs with other women. At one time in the past, he had suffered a severe mental breakdown. Cantwell is a coarse illiterate boor, but has a happy marriage and is a devoted father and husband.

He is completely unscrupulous in his efforts to get the nomination. His hidden weakness is that he is a former homosexual. Russell can win if he releases the scandal about his opponent, but if he does so, he will be contaminated by the evil he is trying to uproot. The play ends with neither candidate getting the nomination. Russell turns over his delegates to a dark horse.

The many comments on our political foibles are penetrating, but the major theme is evaded. Russell's idealism is unconvincing, for the fight between the two men is not on principle or a compromise on political issues, but on permitting knowledge of a scandal to be broadcast. Russell could easily have turned over the matter to his campaign manager or to anyone else. What salvages the theme is Russell's fear of turning into the opposite of what he is, of becoming Cantwell. Again the teeth are removed. There are suggestions that, with all his excellence, Russell might have been too unyielding and intolerant as President. So our crude political machinery works out for the best—neither a liberal nor a conservative wins, but a middle-of-the-road nonentity. Russell doesn't lose everything; he regains his wife.

The gags, however, do arise out of situation. An ex-President in the Harry Truman tradition says, about those who are backing Rockefeller:

> "In the back of their minds they think if they make him President, he might decide to pay off the national debt out of his own pocket. If he would, I'd vote for him."

And in an anticipation of the Goldwater campaign, he remarks later, "In those days you had to pour God over everything like ketchup." Russell, as he walks out to address a delegation, says, "For those whom we are about to deceive, Oh, Lord, make us truly compassionate."

Vidal's best play and his only failure is *Romulus*, which he adapted from Duerrenmatt's work. The fall of the Roman Empire is given contemporary meaning by using the invading Goths as Nazis. Romulus, named after the legendary founder of the city, is the last of the Roman emperors. He is willing to assist in the destruction of Rome because it is too effete to survive. The leader of the barbarians is just as worried about extremists as is Romulus. The two sit and talk about raising chickens and gardening. Our Western civilization has lost its will to live because it no longer has values that offer crusading vitality. Vidal took credit for the play, but Duerrenmatt's original work was more worldly, more imaginative, and uncompromisingly satirical.

Vidal was so fascinated by the material that his latest novel, *Julian*, deals with another emperor of the Roman decline. Dudley Fitts, in reviewing the book, praises the "beguiling power of his wit, his craftsman's sleight of hand," but goes on to say that when Vidal gets into the more serious discussions on Roman civilization, "his failure is what ultimately keeps the novel from rising above the level of high entertainment." The same is true of his plays.

Tad Mosel's *All the Way Home* (1960) won many awards, including the Pulitzer Prize, for its depiction of the painful growing up of a young boy in Tennessee, his experiences with death, and his discovery of the comfort of love. The play, an adaptation of the excellent autobiographical novel *A Death in the Family* by the late James Agee, avoids the clichés of television, but lacks dramatic action. It relies on the quiet revelation of honest and poignant human feelings. The production in New York was noteworthy in that critics and audience joined in an effort to keep it running when it seemed doomed at the box office.

James Costigan's *Little Moon of Alban* (1960) resisted expansion from its TV length to theatre size. It is a confusion of Irish melodrama and pietistic homilies in which a girl aids the English soldier who killed her fiancé. *Baby Want a Kiss* (1964), his second play and the first written directly for the theatre, was a success in its Actors Studio production, but more because of the appearance of Paul Newman and his wife, Joanne Woodward, in the parts of a husband-wife team of motion picture stars who visit a well-known writer, played by James Costigan himself—a field day for type-casting. The fourth character, a fuzzy sheepdog, made a brief appearance and was played by a fuzzy sheepdog which was given full credit.

Baby Want a Kiss has little plot, a great deal of talk, and attempts to rise above the naturalistic set and dialogue to a symbolic representation of cultural distortions in American life today. The writer lives alone, surrounded by his Gothic antiques, and occupies himself dusting the furniture, emptying ashtrays, and fluffing pillows, presumably to represent order, simplicity, and the natural man of Rousseau. The Hollywood stars boast of their ideal marital relationship, their fabulous careers, and their high tax bracket, presumably to represent the emptiness of the pursuit of glamour and material gains. The play flutters off into a mystifying intermingling of appearance and reality. Each of the actors reveals to the writer his underlying personal unhappiness and sexual frustrations, and each in turn makes love to the host. They all play a game of telling a dream while the others act it out. Much of it sounds like a parody of Edward Albee and Tennessee Williams, but the parodies become more important than the point of the play. The satire slips into self-conscious laughter.

If James Costigan gave evidence of exploring a nonrealistic form, Dale Wasserman gives promise of writing more significant drama. After many years in motion pictures and television, he made his Broadway debut with *One Flew Over the Cuckoo's Nest* (1963). Though not greeted too enthusiastically by the critics, even with Kirk Douglas in the lead, the play was a worthy effort to dramatize Ken Kesey's allegorical novel. In a mental health institution, Nurse Ratched, with the outward pretense of psychiatric understanding, demands complete conformity and submission to her will. Randle P. McMurphy, the last of the individualists, becomes an inmate to avoid working with the road crew. His main interest is in people, and in the tradition of the poor man's Christ he does more to cure the sick and the disheartened than the nurse's calculated regimen. His defiance enlists the co-operation of even the most submissive, and in the best scene of the play the inmates shatter the clinical coldness of the institution with a wild orgy, aided by liquor and women smuggled in from the outside. McMurphy's individual rebellion is no match for a despot's power. The nurse conspires to have a prefrontal lobotomy performed to reduce him to a complacent idiot. Wasserman's use of a mental institution to represent the world of conformity probably antagonized the psychiatrically minded public, and the good and evil figures were too extreme. Nor was there need to explain the nurse's Hitler complex as the result of sexual repression, nor to have an American Indian kill McMurphy in a merciful gesture to save him from perpetual humiliation. Though the symbols got out of hand, the play was a noble effort in the manner of Giraudoux to treat the world's ills in a comic vein. With greater control, it might have earned more respect. Dale Wasserman should not permit an initial failure to keep him from the theatre.

Ronald Alexander once remarked,

In the theatre you are guaranteed nothing. You write for yourself. You don't have to think of an idea that would appeal to Camel cigarettes.

The theatre has resisted efforts to reduce it to an appendage of television. It would warmly embrace a more determined effort to master it as a separate art. The refugees can well afford to leave their clichés on Madison Avenue. For those who abuse the increased liberty the theatre affords by smugly adding words and phrases barred from the air, the theatre has had little tolerance. Its greatest rewards may yet go to those who, like Paddy Chayefsky, James Costigan, or Ronald Alexander, accept the freedom as a challenge in a separate art.

12

NEW-PLAY MADNESS AND SOME
NEW VOICES

*It did become evident that conditions were not favorable to distin-
guished playwrighting at home, and that we had reason to be grateful
for the availability of plays discovered and seasoned abroad.*

JOHN GASSNER

*The artist must prophesy, not in the sense that he fortells things to
come, but in the sense that he tells his audience, at risk of their dis-
pleasure, the secrets of their own hearts.*

R. G. COLLINGWOOD

*". . . the people who worry so much about the next dollar . . . these
people are hooked worse than me."*

JACK GELBER, The Connection

BROADWAY IS DEVOTED almost exclusively to the production of
new plays. On the surface, this would appear to be the ideal
situation for the playwright, and indeed more new plays are
presented in New York each season than in any other major
theatre center, but Broadway has developed special character-

istics which discourage rather than stimulate the fullest freedom of expression.

Each production is a separate commercial venture. There exists no relationship of one play to another, no balance of programming, no variation in style or content, no overall planning. As a matter of fact, as a direct result of this situation there are no theatres on Broadway in the sense of continuing production organizations. There are houses for rent, owned by real estate operators. Frequently producers do own theatres also, but as separate operations to reduce dependence on other realtors.

The production of new plays is a costly and speculative business. A straight dramatic play with one set and a small cast involves a minimum investment of $100,000. A musical play may cost more than a half-million dollars before the curtain rises on opening night. These sums of money are raised mostly from investors or "angels," who buy a piece of the *property* (strange term for a work of art). All necessary personnel from director and cast to technician and press agent is hired for one production. A theatre is rented and a vast operation moves into high gear. If the opening night results in unanimous critical approval, fabulous profits are assured. The play runs until the players and the demand for tickets are exhausted. Motion picture sales, national and international companies, follow, and the final return on the investment exceeds that of any glamour stock in a bull market.

If the reviews are unfavorable, the play closes immediately. The investment is a total loss, and the talent and energy wasted. Rarely does a play with bad reviews last more than one week, often no more than one night. In the 1963–64 season, nine plays closed after a single performance. The playwright, if a newcomer, is forgotten, the play retired to the archives, and the financial loss reduced to deductions on personal income tax returns. The entire maneuver reconstitutes itself for the next play.

The widespread repercussions of this "hit or flop" psychology affect every aspect of the theatre. Broadway's unique coloration derives from this frenetic exploitation of the new play. Everyone involved, artist or entrepreneur, becomes a gambler in a game of high stakes in which the odds are against the player. Of the fifty productions on Broadway and a greater number off-Broadway in one season, few triumph. No other business would permit such a percentage of failure. But to demand superior products of an art every year is to impose a generative power and a timetable foreign to its nature.

From Shakespeare to Shaw, a period of three centuries in the English theatre, there were certainly not three hundred significant plays. And even in the days of the glory of the Elizabethan and Jacobean drama, a period of four decades at most, not every year witnessed a major work. Nor did Shakespeare himself write a masterpiece with annual regularity. It is certainly unreasonable to ask more of the New York theatre. Yet the new-play business demands a score of successful plays with clocklike regularity. Admirable as such a result would be, the Broadway syndrome hinders its realization. The demand is profit-inspired and not the outgrowth of creative necessity. Show business has become big business, and the values of the marketplace conflict with those of the world of art. Box office success and excellence of material are not incompatible, but the Broadway setup is self-contradictory and eventually self-destructive.

Fear of financial loss to investors curtails experimental boldness. The new production cannot stray too far from the familiar, and high costs bar technical innovations. Actors and directors, contracted for a single production, have little opportunity for artistic growth or radical departure in style. Investment anxieties become a self-imposed and arbitrary censorship. Broadway is forced to import its best work. The balance of trade is unfavorable.

The theatre, however, does not conform easily. "Every age projects its own image of man in its art," André Malraux has said, and the theatre, as an art, pursues a reckless life of its own, often at variance with established economics. Those producers in whom the spirit of the artist remains unquenchable may be inspired to risk a noble failure. In the past few years, *Moby Dick*, a dramatization of the Melville novel, Bertolt Brecht's *Mother Courage* and *Arturo Ui*, as well as Jack Richardson's *Lorenzo*, were financial disasters. Any of these productions would have been proudly included in a European repertory theatre. Audiences received them warmly, but the operating budget was so high that capacity audiences were necessary to sustain them, and after a great expenditure of talent, energy, and money, all of them passed from the scene, to be forgotten or to survive largely as warnings to the ambivalent producer.

Concentration on the new play deprives the audience of its heritage and tradition. Plays of the past, or even those of the previous season, are rarely performed, for they no longer have possibilities of motion picture sales. Occasionally, a revival is ventured, and in recent years the public has seen *Strange Interlude, School for Scandal*, and *Heartbreak House*, as well as the Burton *Hamlet* and the Scofield *King Lear*. The O'Neill play was the first production of the newly formed Actors Studio Theatre, which is subsidized by the talent of its membership; the others were all-star revivals for limited runs and national tours or were presentations by visiting foreign companies. Even industry plans a market for its used models. For the theatre, the market exists away from New York, in summer stock or regional houses. Built-in obsolescence is immediate and decisive.

Off-Broadway more frequently presents plays of the past, and in the 1963–64 season, works by Ibsen, Chekhov, Pirandello, Molière, and Euripides were offered alongside revivals of more recent works by Beckett, Pinter, and Ghelderode. Audiences should be grateful for the opportunity to see the classics or "near-classics" of the theatre, even though the motivating reason for production is the director's or actor's preference for a sure-fire piece as a showcase for his talents. The gratitude is diminished when these productions, at least those not presented by a permanent theatre, are shoddy and suffer from the ills of commercial thinking. They, too, are one-shot enterprises and fail to offer criteria for the continuing comparison of the old with the new. The theatre as the unfolding process of a culture, as a many-sided revelation of the times, exists only in haphazard planlessness.

For the money investor, the entire process can be hectic, but he may at least have enjoyed his association with show business, and he can recoup his losses in the other business enterprises that constitute his major interest. For those who invest their talent, the situation is indeed serious, for they have no sense of security or of belonging to an age that is security-conscious.

The critic, too, is affected by Broadway's spirit. His judgments, like those of Ibsen's Brand, derive from an "all or nothing" situation. He refuses to be deterred from what are assumed to be the postulates of an uncompromising god. He holds thumbs up or down in obedience to the Broadway gods of the long run and the high price of tickets. Nor can he avoid his predicament. He is not watching the work of an established institution whose audience is assured. He cannot judge on the basis of a playwright's potential or appeal to a special public. A play is something to be recommended to *all* his readers, who want their money's worth when they make an occasional visit to the theatre. The critic is subject to the pressures of a middle-class audience that can afford high prices for tickets, has little tolerance for the nonconformist, and discriminates in favor of the "successful plays." A new work is either headed for the long run or relegated to the discard heap.

This situation was clearly evidenced in the attacks on the Lincoln Center Repertory Theatre during its initial season. The daily critics judged each play by Broadway standards. They remained conditioned by the "hit" psychology. The directors of Lincoln Center had made mistakes, mistakes which were the outgrowth of thinking in Broadway's terms, but despite obvious weaknesses a repertory theatre with a permanent company had been established—a step of great importance in eventually overcoming the domination of the commercial theatre. Where repertory and permanence already existed in the Lincoln Center complex, as in dance, music, or opera, the same criteria did not apply. Long-held values give way grudgingly.

Most serious is the effect on the playwright. Since there are no established theatres on Broadway, he is denied the opportunity of being associated with a practical working group such as Molière and Shakespeare had, or in our own time, Eugene O'Neill and Clifford Odets. This deficiency is being met on a minor scale by the Actors Studio playwrighting unit and Ford Foundation grants to playwrights in residence at new repertory theatres.

The playwright cannot disassociate himself from the rules of the game. Unconsciously, he conforms to the demands of the market and strives for the next smash hit, rather than giving voice to that which must be said and finding the form the content demands. He is drawn to a formula product which is more acceptable to producers and audiences. He needs to be seen and heard and he follows the path with fewest heartaches and fastest rewards. The new play becomes a refurbished model of the old, with staple component parts rearranged to disturb no one and to preserve the myths of the day.

Paradoxically, the contrived commodity play offers no easy road to success. The percentage of casualties is high. The skilled craftsmen of the synthetic work turn out such a glittering product that the novitiate is hard put to it to compete. The play which braves the tide and charts a new direction achieves, in the long run, greater fame and financial rewards. The adventurous writer who disregards the formula is more likely to be the next hero of Broadway, for he brings in his wake a new formula for the professionals to imitate.

Yet most playwrights prefer to follow in the path of Muriel Resnik, whose *Any Wednesday*, a neatly contrived tale of adultery, was sold to Warner Brothers for $750,000. Her success encourages the playwright to conform to established procedures, rearranging clichés in pursuit of equal financial glory. Even in the original selection of material and the approach to his characters, the writer is subtly influenced by Broadway's demands. Tennessee Williams admits changing *Cat on a Hot Tin Roof* to take advantage of the box-office appeal of sex, violence, depravity, and the happy ending. Maggie touches Brick's cheek as she "gently, with love," hands his life back to him. Arthur Miller altered scenes and dialogue in *Death of a Salesman* at Elia Kazan's request, to soften the attack on success myths. Gore Vidal removed the "wrath" and "softened the blows" of *Visit to a Small Planet* to have a play with greater popular appeal.

Since the producer has to sell a property, he trusts in name brands. He offers to investors a package deal which includes stars and established directors and writers. Little opportunity is offered to younger, less known talent. Yet there are no guarantees in the Broadway lottery. Within the last five years new plays by Tennessee Williams, Lillian Hellman, Sidney Kingsley, and William Inge have been greeted with thumbs down. Not only the first play, but every succeeding play, must be box-office-proof. There is no room for failure. The writer must start with perfection and maintain that level. He cannot develop into a playwright. He must *be* one full-blown. So disastrous are the consequences of rejection that the playwright turns to the less precarious fields of television and motion pictures. The theatre succeeds in shunting its potential talent elsewhere. The history of Broadway is the history of one-shot playwrights who never reappeared.

If the writer is determined to reject the standards of the marketplace and pursue his art truthfully, he must reconcile himself to isolation, loneliness, and suffering, knowing that if he joins the crowd, he will eventually succumb to the commercial rule that audiences are infinitely more amused by what reassures them. If he is willing to accept the theatre as the most demanding of all arts, as the opportunity for contributing to man's awareness of the world in which he lives, then, in the words of R. G. Collingwood, he must assume the role of a prophet,

> not in the sense that he foretells things to come, but in the sense that he tells his audience, at the risk of their displeasure, the secrets of their own hearts.

James Baldwin, whose first play, *Blues for Mister Charlie*, reached Broadway in 1964, pictures himself as the astute guerilla fighter in the war against complacency, and says of the American writer that

> he must tell other Americans the tragic and therefore beautiful truth, even if at variance with what they wish to do. . . . The war of an artist with his society is a lover's war, and he does at his best, what lovers do, which is to reveal the beloved to himself, and with that revelation, make freedom real.

Few playwrights are willing or able to do so.

We turn to a consideration of those who have made the effort. Though the total achievement of the promising new voices is not overly impressive, the future of the American theatre lies in their hands.

The 1962 season was enlivened by speculations as to whether Jack Richardson or Edward Albee would be the first to repeat the example of O'Neill, who in 1920 moved from an avant-garde reputation off-Broadway to national fame on Broadway. Albee was the winner and was catapulted into leadership and unbelievable financial gain. An honorable failure left Richardson in oblivion. The plays of both were eagerly anticipated, and were presented on Broadway even though they were departures from the commodity output. Albee's was the better constructed, Richardson's the more poetic; Albee's the more sensational, Richardson's the more ambitious.

Jack Richardson deserves extended comment. His experience is an excellent example of the difficulties facing a talented playwright. A native New Yorker and a graduate of Columbia University, *summa cum laude* in philosophy, Richardson received a scholarship for graduate work at the University of Munich, where he not only met his wife but wrote his first play. He is now completely preoccupied with the theatre. He had published several short stories and a first novel, *The Prison Life of Harris Filmore*, but his first play, *The Prodigal*, in 1960, turned his efforts toward the stage.

The Prodigal is a retelling of the Orestes legend, and herein lies Richardson's initial problem. He writes in the tradition of the established French playwright from Racine to Anouilh. Almost every serious French writer turns to Greek drama for source material. French audiences are familiar with classical legends, which are deeply ingrained in their culture. For American audiences, such a play must stand on its own merits, and the meaningful association with the past is lost.

Richardson's play is more a philosophical dissertation than a dramatic experience. Orestes refuses to be part of a cause, to be a committed human being. He is symbolic of the cynical intellect which questions the role of avenger. He has no desire to become a hero from either traditional or political demand. Agamemnon represents liberal social thinking, and Aegisthus stands for return to a reactionary past. In a discussion with his son, Agamemnon says,

> "My life and your contentment are minor things. I have begun the building of the best possible temple for man to live in. And Aegisthus could destroy and replace it with a lightless cave."

Orestes answers,

> "I kill Aegisthus for the coming world? . . . Your death will never force me so far past myself. Let the world drag me through its self-made judicial mud. I will let you die and do nothing."

Orestes does stand aside and dispassionately watches his father's murder.

Six months later, he is to be married. He hopes to live a normal family life, to have children, and, as he says, "watch conception," but his mission calls and he is drawn "past himself." He rejects his role as liberator, but says,

"The world demands that we inherit the pretensions of our fathers. That we go on killing in the name of ancient illusions about ourselves. That we assume the right to punish order and invent philosophies, to make our worst enemies seem inspired. Who am I to contradict all this any longer?"

He returns to Argos, kills Aegisthus, and becomes a victim of forces he now understands. Murder is never justified, but society has evolved rational explanations for myths it cannot ignore. Orestes' act of awareness renders him lost and lonely, dedicated to what he knows is irrational.

Richardson, like so many contemporary writers, depends on an existentialist point of view. The play is written in highly literate prose often rising to nobility, but remains essentially static, for Richardson has not learned, as has Sartre, to express ideas through actions.

Gallows Humor, Richardson's second play, was his first attempt at comedy. It consists of two companion one-act pieces, with a man and woman as the main characters and the warden as the third character who appears in both plays. In the first a man is to be executed. The warden supplies him with a prostitute to make his final hours endurable. He spurns her advances, for he has rejected the disturbing violence of physical passion and achieved a sense of order on which he can depend. The doomed man had been a lawyer who saw lives unbalanced by excessive passion. He seeks a rigid formalism, a classic harmony, to restore his faith in things. What results is a comic order of keeping himself tidy, performing his household chores in the cell, not putting ashes on the floor. He can thus face death unafraid because he has reached the point of willed control.

The prostitute feels that her reputation is at stake. Her goal is to give men their final comfort through the means of which she is mistress. She is an intelligent and capable prostitute who advocates, out of necessity, a life that flows from passion and irrational order. She wants him to accept death through indulgence in life. She tosses ashes all over the floor. Her triumph means his death on a more human level, of little consequence in any event, since he is to be hanged in a few minutes. In the bout between logic and passion, the curtain comes down as the two embrace passionately.

The second play is a dissolve to the other side of the coin. The executioner is at home with his unfaithful wife. The warden, who had supplied the prostitute in the first play, is the man with whom the wife is having an affair. The executioner is trying to rebel against the discipline, order, and precision of daily life, which have dulled his existence. He longs to travel, to run away, leave his wife, have adventure, wildness, disorder, and not to have to put the rope methodically around men's necks. His protest takes the form of leaving ashes in his slippers, a thing he has never done before. In the end, his wife brings him back to order, domesticity, the cleaning of the dishes, and executions. The warden is in both plays, for he is the keeper of the rules and he too violates them, as all men must. The plays are an example of wry humor, but much too conversational. All the characters, including the prostitute, sound like Richardson. Both plays need a bit of the wildness he advocates, but Richardson managed to make philosophic discussion implicit in *Gallows Humor* rather than overtly stated, as in *The Prodigal*.

Lorenzo, which failed on Broadway, belongs in a repertory theatre. The production was on a grand scale with a distinguished cast. Alfred Drake played Lorenzo, the head of a mobile acting company which is caught between two factions in the mountains near Milan during "a small war of the Renaissance." Lorenzo's son and daughter are drawn, by the excitement, toward involvement in actual living. The son wants to participate in the struggle against the cruel duke, for the welfare of humanity. The daughter, who has played the great courtesans of drama but is still virginal, wants the experience of sex. The mother longs for a last romantic fling in Clytemnestra style. Lorenzo rebukes them all, remains aloof, insisting that the world of art is universal and beyond the petty machinations of temporary political issues. But life is demanding and all get involved, including Lorenzo, who dies defending the honor of his daughter. Passion and personal dignity sweep aside logical conviction. And the irony is that each man justifies his acts with his own logic. The cruel duke destroys human life for the eventual betterment of man. When his army is defeated, he joins the actor's company and pulls the wagon in place of Lorenzo.

The play is reminiscent of Brecht's *Mother Courage*, but Richardson writes a tighter plot sequence. However, he repeats his earlier themes that commitment is essential, and man, lacking directives, can only fall back on the false values of the past. Though Richardson evokes a cynical emptiness, he does assert an ultimate dignity. His inexperience as a playwright leads him to compress too many ideas into one play. With *Lorenzo*, he rejected the pruning of classical simplicity he had exercised in *The Prodigal*. Scenes grind to a halt in elaborate and often worthy discussions of politics, war, and religion. Not knowing how to resolve his problems theatrically, Richardson falls back on declamation. He is, however, a playwright who almost alone among the new voices tackles major themes on a scale beyond that of our present diminished theatre.

Arthur Kopit, a recent Harvard graduate, created a sensation with his first play *Oh Dad, Poor Dad, Mamma's Hung You in the Closet, and I'm Feeling So Sad*, which is subtitled "A Pseudoclassical Tragifarce in a Bastard French Tradition." A fortunate combination of circumstances also helped in the success of his first venture. Jerome Robbins, well-known choreographer, directed the play and achieved movement close to modern ballet, which the play required. Josephine Van Fleet, a resourceful actress, romped through the leading role with bravura vindictiveness, ably assisted by Barbara Harris, a rising talent in the American stage and the most successful of the recent graduates from the little theatres.

The play is unique for many reasons. It is a grotesque, surrealist attack on sex, mother, and the devouring female. The characters are comic-strip exaggerations, symbolic and ludicrous on the level of a grand hoax or a sophomoric parody of Tennessee Williams, Ionesco, and all avant-garde writers. On stage, it is a technician's delight, with its Venus's-flytraps that grow larger and the piranha fish which has spoken lines, doors that open and close on their own power, chairs that slide away or remain fixed, and a corpse that embraces the young Rosalie as she attempts her seduction of Jonathan.

Kopit's titles for his earlier student plays were preparations for the long-winded nonsense of this fantasy of cannibalism and mockery of romance. The names of many of the characters begin with the prefix Rose. Madame Rosepettle says she wanted her husband to be "Mine, all mine—mine to love, mine to live with, mine to kill; my husband my lover my own . . . *my very own.*" She achieved her purpose by murdering him, and now drags his corpse around with her on her travels as a physical symbol of her triumph. She keeps her son Jonathan at the perpetual age of ten, warding off the destroying problems of growing up. She amuses herself by kicking sand in lovers' faces on the beach, and lures Commodore Roseabove into a disillusioning and embarrassing tête-a-tête. Rosalie, a constant teen-ager, tries to win possession of men by being all sex. She would seduce Jonathan and free him from his mother's hold so that she can possess him completely. The women do not always triumph. In the end, as Rosalie manages to get Jonathan on his mother's bed, the father's corpse hops out of the closet, falls between them, and raises a dead hand in warning to Jonathan. Rosalie is suffocated under the stamp and coin collection.

The form of the play is a single conceit developed in multiple ramifications, a succession of tricks which grow thin and repetitious. Madame Rosepettle essays a serious explanatory note, which sounds hollow when surrounded by the high jinks that keep the play bubbling. Instead of confessing on a couch to her analyst, Madame Rosepettle confesses on her feet to her captive lover:

> ". . . it is I who have saved him [her son]. Saved him from the world beyond that door. . . . A world waiting to devour those who trust in it . . . A world vicious under the hypocrisy of kindness, ruthless under the falseness of a smile. . . . Leave my room and enter your world again, Mr. Roseabove—your sex-driven, dirt-washed waste of cannibals eating each other up while they pretend they're kissing. Go, Mr. Roseabove, enter your blind world of darkness."

The play is far too discursive, and incompatible with Rosalie's more direct, "Take off your clothes. . . . Drop your pants on top of him [your father], then you won't see his face."

As a first play, *Oh Dad, Poor Dad* was a lighthearted contribution on a much overworked theme. It perhaps would have been better as a long, concentrated, one-act play. A college-boy hoax on the present trend of being anti-woman, anti-sex, and anti-life can be amusing for a short time. Kopit now faces the tensions imposed on the writer of a first-play success. He wrote two short one-acters, *The Day the Whores Came Out to Play Tennis* and *Mhil'daiim*, which were scheduled for production at the University of Minnesota but withdrawn when the issue of obscenity was raised. When presented at the Actors Studio, they elicited little enthusiasm. Another full-length play, *Asylum or What the Gentlemen Are Up To Not to Mention the Ladies*, which he describes as a sinister comedy dealing with the transformation of a man from sanity to insanity, has had production problems and has been withdrawn by the author for further revisions.

Kopit's first efforts are insufficient for definitive judgment. If he can sustain the macabre laughter at the expense of our sacred cows, he may become a valued demonic clown, but he is too preoccupied with his personal and seemingly sensational rebellion.

Jack Gelber's *The Connection* is a play of dubious merit that made off-Broadway theatre history. The daily critics dismissed it ruthlessly, and it would have folded if not for the repertory system of the Living Theatre and the amazing ability of Judith Malina and Julian Beck to ignore the financial demands of the box office. The play held on until the weekly critics had an opportunity to publish their reviews. Howard Hughes called it "the most original piece of new American playwriting in a long, long time." Equally fervent were Harold Clurman and Kenneth Tynan. The response to the play emphasized the deep gap between the daily journalistic reviewers with their immediate reactions to performance and those critics who pride themselves on a more comprehensive theory of dramatic criticism.

Around *The Connection* a vociferous debate developed. Admirers of the play went overboard about the assumed philosophic implications, which, to say the least, are highly problematical. *The Connection* is an ultrarealistic demonstration of uncensored vulgarity and the repeated use of four-letter words, which, with *Ubu Roi*, aroused a united puritanical opposition to the Living Theatre. When *The Connection* was made into a motion-picture with Shirley Clarke as director and Lewis Allen as an independent producer, a legal battle had to be waged for permission to show it in art theatres. But the stage production proved that a play, if kept alive beyond the blows of the daily press, can sustain itself and give audiences an independent opportunity to judge. The play also sustained the Living Theatre and kept it momentarily from bankruptcy.

The Connection is another "waiting" play, of which so many have appeared in this decade. A group of junkies await the connection who will bring them their fix. They engage in introspective improvisations, as does the jazz combo which is on stage all the time. Unlike Godot, Cowboy (the connection) does arrive in the second part of the play. Each of the addicts retires to the toilet, which is placed upstage center, seat and all visible, gets his shot, and achieves his temporary euphoria. Leach, in whose pad the action occurs, takes an overdose and almost dies from the effect.

The form of the play is a mixture of extreme naturalism and Pirandello. A producer and a director, with two cameramen, at work on a documentary, walk in and out of the audience, leap on stage, try to create the impression of different levels of reality and appearance, and generate the improvisational character of the dialogue. Such devices are meaningful when related to the theme. In *The Connection* they were unnecessary and had little value other than to show that squares can also be hooked by heroin. Presumably, Gelber was trying to show that the boundaries between the two worlds are erased by common experiences, but this conclusion was not functional in the play, which is essentially the revelation of a slice of life. Audiences were held by the fascination of watching dope addicts, and entertained by an excellent jazz combo, which improvised musically between the verbal improvisations of the characters.

The play moves with a sense of expectancy, of awaiting the connection. It then becomes individual reactions to the fix. The most intense moment was one not written in the original script. When Leach takes his dose, he does so downstage center, and for six minutes goes through the actual process of heating the heroin, fixing the syringe, and inserting it in his vein. The sordid hipster surroundings have a fascination of their own, and the play gives an insight into a world of social outcasts, but critics found philosophical implications behind the physical reality. At one point, Sam, the more educated junkie, says:

> "I used to think that the people who walk the street, the people who work every day, the people who worry so much about the next dollar, the next new coat, the chlorophyll addicts, the aspirin addicts, the vitamin addicts, those people are hooked worse than me."

These remarks were built up into a theory of Leach's pad as a microcosm, a symbolic reflection of American culture. Cowboy, the connection, commenting on working for wages, says:

> "What's wrong with day jobs? Or being square? Man, I haven't anything against them. There are lousy hipsters and lousy squares."

Certainly, no single observation made by a character can give the entire play a universal significance. In Gorki's *Lower Depths*, a grim picture of derelicts rises to an affirmation of man's ultimate dignity, which is central to the entire work. In O'Neill's *The Iceman Cometh*, marginal characters, given to drink and hopelessness, regain a moment of dignity by clinging to their pipe dreams. O'Neill asserts the need for illusion. In *The Connection*, Jack Gelber supplies nothing more than a detailed exhibition of an aspect of life that few people see in the normal course of events. The remarks quoted here are merely casual observations by characters who are nonsymbolic. Four-letter words may be needed for explosive power or expressive vehemence, or may be justified when essential to the meaning of the play. In *The Connection*, their repetition became a scatological perversion. Ibsen once said of "slice of life" plays: "Zola enters the sewer to bathe in it; I, to scour it."

Jack Gelber went all-out in derivative avant-garde extremes and wound up in a dead end, much in the fashion of contemporary painters, who are Johnny-come-latelies on the bandwagon of abstract expressionism. His next play, *The Apple*, produced the following year, could not be sustained even by friendly critics. Actors use their own names as characters in *The Apple*. An artist who splashes paint haphazardly on a canvas auctions it off during intermission to anyone in the audience who cares to buy it. Every type of irrelevancy and incongruity and illogicality mount to a confusion from which form and meaning have vanished. Jack

Gelber is a playwright whose next play cannot afford to repeat the sterile emptiness of mere engagement in technique.

More positive achievements may be expected of Murray Schisgal, Lewis John Carlino, and William Hanley. Schisgal was fortunate with his one-act plays *The Typists* and *The Tiger* in having Eli Wallach and his wife, Anne Jackson, perform the two characters in both plays. It may well be a case in which the actors carried the plays beyond their actual merit.

The Tiger takes place in the loft bedroom of a simple mail clerk, who reads a great deal but whose life is timid and unadventurous. He carries a woman into his bedroom and attempts to play the role of the dangerous seducer. It is a battle of the sexes in reverse, for the woman, far more clever, becomes his willing accomplice, encourages him to study for his promotional examination, and assures him that she will return frequently. Middle-class and married, she too needs the romance of adventure.

The Typists is more in the Ionesco tradition. Two office employees, sitting at their typewriters, reveal the dullness of their lives, their attraction for one another, and their inability to burst loose and enjoy the fulness of life their passions indicate. The theme is, again, the oft-repeated mechanization of American lives.

Schisgal has pioneered no new paths, but he does indicate a command of dialogue, a compassion for people, a tenderness that gives promise of more sustained later work. Like many young writers, he was first recognized abroad. *The Typists* and *The Tiger* were first performed in London, and *The Typists* was repeated at the Edinburgh Festival in 1960. Two full-length plays, *Ducks and Lovers* and *Luv*, have been shown at the Arts Theatre in London. English critics were mildly enthusiastic.

In November, 1964, Murray Schisgal was catapulted to national fame and financial security when *Luv*, his first play to be offered on Broadway, was greeted with unanimous enthusiasm by the daily critics. The script did not merit the unstinted praise; the production did. Mike Nichols, a master of improvisational satire and a proven director of comedy (*Barefoot in the Park, The Knack*), transformed Schisgal's repetitive devices and labored conceits into brilliantly stylized antic routines. The slim plot encouraged the director's freedom, for the play is essentially an extended vaudeville skit—a series of parodies on the romantic triangle. "L-u-v," says Schisgal, "is the perversion of l-o-v-e. I don't have the authority to define the other." He contents himself with projecting three characters, who are puppets, into a commodity world which standardizes emotional reactions—characters whose predictable responses replace the purity of feeling.

In *Luv*, the technique employed is that of inverted polarity. Whatever a character says or does at the beginning of a scene turns into its opposite at the end of the scene. If he is happy, he ends up by bewailing his unhappiness, or vice versa. Lies and deception apply to both extremes of a man's self-analysis. Any person may assume the role of another, for none is a specific individual; each is a composite caricature of psychological labels.

Milt Manville, outwardly prosperous but actually a scavenger of refuse cans, saves Harry Berlin, a former classmate at Poly-Arts U., from jumping off a bridge. Harry is the lost and defeated intellectual who has embraced despair ever since a dog urinated on his trouser leg. Milt urges Harry to regain hope and "luv" by marrying Ellen, Milt's own wife, from whom he is seeking a divorce. In the second act, four months later, Milt and Ellen, after unsuccessful second marriages, want to return to their original conjugal unhappiness. Having once saved Harry from suicide, Milt must now try to get rid of him by throwing him off the bridge.

The situations are sustained by comments on psychiatry, Freudianism, sex charts, homosexuality, success myths, and avant-garde plays. The weakness of the development is that the parody takes itself seriously and becomes the thing parodied. No new statement is made, other than that all previous statements are absurd. Mike Nichols skillfully combined precise timing, economy of gesture, and slapstick novelties into a polished example of present-day *commedia dell'arte*. Schisgal may not be so lucky with his next play. He will have to go beyond obvious imitation of Ionesco. Mockery of what society *is* implies belief in what society should be, and laughter at human inadequacy presupposes ideals that have been breached. Schisgal should assume the authority to define both sides of the equation.

Lewis John Carlino, after writing many one-act plays, such as *Objective Case* and *Mr. Flannery's Ocean*, which were produced in summer stock and experimental theatres, made his New York debut with *Cages*, two one-act plays, the first of which was called *Snowangel* and the second, *Epiphany*. Indicative of a trend in the off-Broadway theatre, again, as with Schisgal's first work, two highly skilled professional actors performed the roles in both plays—this time, Shelley Winters and Jack Warden. Carlino's appearance had been long awaited, for much had been written about his poetic sensitivity and concern with form. But *Cages*, which was well received by the New York critics, did little to build his reputation. The same material and the same devices have been endlessly repeated. Much of *Cages* is immature thinking masquerading as new theatre.

Snowangel takes place in the run-down room of a cheap prostitute. The man enters but hesitates to complete the transaction despite the tired and bored insistence of the woman. He has paid thirty dollars to spend a few hours, and he longs for "affection" in addition to sex. He insists she act out the part of the girl with whom he was once in love, particularly the time they met in the Chinese Room at the Metropolitan Museum of Art. She fails to do so, and rebukes him for trying to relive his life and not realizing that she too has memories of love never fulfilled. As she relates her tale, he crawls to her side, repeats the words of the man she had been dreaming of, and gives her the "affection" he had originally demanded.

The meeting of two lonely souls, usually with a bed stage-center, who disclose heartache and rejection in order to come to some mutual recognition of something bigger than themselves, some humanity over and beyond the reality of thirty dollars for the evening, has become unendurably tiresome. A few weeks before *Cages* opened, *The Rattle of a Simple Man*, a play by Charles Dyer, portrayed a latent homosexual trying to function in a virile fashion with a prostitute. As she understands his anxieties, she reveals her own, and the two social outcasts find a moment of forgetfulness in compassion for another. How can two such trivial plays, within such a short span, be produced in a theatre demanding revelation? Such plays can be salvaged only if they are written with poetry and tenderness. *Snowangel* is sentimental and mawkish.

Epiphany tries to portray domestic relations by erupting into weird avant-garde fantasy. An ornithologist imitates the noises of a rooster because he resents his domestic chores; his wife, a successful career woman, supports him. The two play games, much in the Albee fashion of *Who's Afraid of Virginia Woolf?* When the wife becomes superior in all their harmless games, the husband locks the doors, pulls the telephone from the wall, brings out the trappings for a chicken roost, puts on a sharp razor-edged rooster beak, and reverts to an animal existence. With Albee, the fun of contrived games is an element in the savage battle to dominate. With Carlino, the device seems like a paltry copy of what is now considered acceptable. Too many critics today fear they will be accused of being unreceptive to new forms, and so they lavish excessive praise on what is derivative. Unquestionably, there should be critical tolerance for seedling playwrights, but riding the new bandwagon should not elicit indiscriminate hosannas. The avant-garde writer can be as dishonest as his commercial colleague on Broadway.

Telemachus Clay, which appeared off-Broadway later in the same season, did much to restore Carlino's reputation. It is an earlier work in the form of a "collage for voices," and was ably directed by Cyril Simon. Eleven actors seated on high stools face the audience and act out some seventy different parts in the life of the young man, Telemachus Clay, who seeks his father and his fortune. Clay, the young writer, caught in the dullness of a small town and a compromising love affair, runs off to Hollywood; in the end he is still seeking, still searching, still hoping to find himself and the values by which he can live. The interplay of voices, the overlapping of scenes, the lyric interludes, achieved at times an orchestration of sound and meaning that were a unique experience.

Carlino has a talent for words. He handles them joyously. They bubble all over the stage, but he repeats the platitudes of small-town existence and Hollywood hypocrisy so that the story never grows beyond that of the personal adventures of a young man. The conceit of having Telemachus Clay spawned in the cornfield by four field-workers and Clay's search to find his real father could have been developed into an original treatment of the Telemachus complex. Carlino held himself in check, and the result was technically brilliant but limited in meaning.

Carlino's one-act plays, such as *The Brick and the Rose* and *Used Car for Sale*, are among the eight already published by Dramatists Play Service. He is another of the members of the Actors Studio playwrights' unit who have been given unusual opportunities, but he hesitates to explore his full potential. His first play for Broadway, *The Exercise*, has been announced. Unquestionably a talented writer, Carlino must face the problem of completely divorcing himself from the commercial elements which taint the experimental.

William Hanley likewise appeared for the first time off-Broadway with a pair of two-character one-act plays. The first, *Whisper into My Good Ear*, has two old men, who plan to commit suicide, meeting in a public park. Instead, they talk, reveal their lives, their warped dreams, their fears. The older man, Max, more the philosopher, calmly discusses his latent homosexuality. In the end, under Charlie's persuasion—"What are ya gonna prove by blowing your brains out?"—they decide to wait another day. Charlie's final line is, "Is one more day gonna kill you, Max?" They go off restored to a knowledge of the little things that can make life tolerable.

The second one-act play, *Mrs. Dally Has a Lover*, takes place in the kitchen of a railroad apartment in New York City, where a married woman is having an affair with an eighteen-year-old boy, Frankie. As they sit and drink coffee, they too reveal their hungers, their longings, their need for love. Mrs. Dally is married to a coarse man who scoffs at her love of poetry; Frankie is simple, accepting, and uninformed. The two have found in each other something that can sustain them. Mrs. Dally says, "It isn't enough just to be loved, sweetheart. You have to know what to do with it." And when Frankie questions what he has to do with it, she says, "You have to pass it on to others." The adulterous relationship is never sordid, but again an effort to find what being alive means, and discovering it in the joy of a line of poetry, in the touching of a man's arm, in words unsaid and moods reciprocated, in a determination to "listen to the sweet music and pass it on."

Slow Dance on the Killing Ground marked Hanley's introduction to Broadway. This warm, tender, and humorous three-character play is in line with the current trend of nonplotted dramas in which people meet, expose their inner fears, their outward arrogance, their protective, unconvincing self-deceptions, and their desperate need for compassion.

The three characters are the hunted and wounded victims of an insensitive society: Glas, a non-Jewish refugee from Nazi Germany; Randall, a lithe young Negro with a high I.Q., flowery phrases, and fears of persecution; Rosie, a homely eighteen-year-old girl who is seeking an abortionist. Each finds momentary protection in the shabby luncheonette that Glas runs in the Brooklyn warehouse district. Each goes through the motions of preparing the slow dance before wandering out into the killing ground of the world beyond—strangely enough, on the night that Eichman was hanged.

Although plays of tortured self-revelation have become the repeated pattern of recent playwrighting, Hanley is distinguished by his sensitivity to the secrets of the heart and his joy in understanding people. His language is often overluxuriant, and the structure of his plays in need of discipline, but he is a welcome newcomer to the theatre.

Although the work of new playwrights of the present decade does not evoke much enthusiasm, there are many writers who have come close to achievement, any one of whom, given the opportunity for production and growth, may produce more significant plays. Arnold Weinstein, whose *The 25-Cent White Hat* was performed experimentally for special matinees, and whose *The Red Eye of Love* was well received off-Broadway, fell victim to the claustrophobia engendered by the Actors Studio, of which he is a member. He wrote the book for *Dynamite Tonight*, which spoofed atomic warfare and closed after one performance. *The Red Eye of Love* was a lively satirical treatment of the Hollywood hero and a delightful exposé of the American success myth. Weinstein knows the theatre, has been flirting with experimental techniques, but he needs to harness his wild exuberance.

Theodore Apstein indicated unusual promise in *Come Share My House*, but his energies have been devoted to television, both as writer and producer. Michael Shurtleff, whose highly original *Call Me by My Rightful Name* created a small furor in its off-Broadway presentation, is another pliable talent diverted by success to other media.

There are a host of others who have had at least one play off-Broadway and never gone beyond that, writers who have retreated to the better-paying fields of television or motion pictures or who refuse to engage in the difficulties and heartaches of theatre production. Many of them have provided a bright moment in the theatre and vanished. Many of them are still writing plays and may reappear on the New York scene. One can do no more than list some of them. Oliver Hailey showed a quick sense of laughter and satire in *Hey, You, Light Man*; Josh Greenfield had a momentary success with *Clandestine in the Morning Line*; Joseph Caldwell displayed wit and humanity in *The Cockeyed Kite*, and David Rayfiel showed a more serious turn toward awareness of social dislocation in *P.S. 193*, as did William Archibald in *The Cantilevered Terrace* and Val Coleman in *The Jackhammer*. With *Shout from the Rooftops* and *A Secret Hiding Place*, both presented in the 1964–65 season, Jess Gregg made a belated bid for recognition. Among the older voices, Molly Kazan will be remembered more for her encouragement of young writers than for her own plays, such as *Of Rosemarie and the Alligators*. Her unfortunate death in 1963 was a severe loss to the writers' unit of the Actors Studio.

A playwright who created a minor sensation is Kenneth H. Brown. *The Brig*, put on by the Living Theatre, is a return to grim realism in which the barbarism and brutality of a Marine Corps prison stockade are re-enacted. There is practically no dialogue in the script. The prisoners and their guards go through their daily routines with mounting tension until the savage explosion in an attempted escape, and the resulting sadistic retaliation. Critics saw in *The Brig* a symbolic exposé of the world at large and its present-day absorption with violence and inhumanity. The Living Theatre, which had advocated new techniques and the theatre of Artaud, returned in this document to the utmost in representationalism. Judith Malina and Julian Beck, who in addition to being devoted theatre workers and artists are also active in the peace movement, may have used *The Brig* as an opportunity to horrify people at the bestiality which corrodes men in general and the Armed Forces in particular. But all that resulted, despite the general acclaim, was a monotonously repetitive, undramatic recording of the life behind barbed wire, and a theatre of "cruelty" without imagination.

13

THE MUSICAL THEATRE —
Heirs to Richard Rodgers

*I have tried to express that winsome forbearance that my own heart
is seeking . . . In a modest way, I have endeavored to rediscover the
nobility of gracefulness and the pleasure of sweetness.*

GIAN-CARLO MENOTTI

*The musical has been elected by default to serve in the absence of a
poetic theatre, a romantic theatre, a heroic theatre, a moral theatre,
and a theatrical theatre.*

ALAN JAY LERNER

THE DRAMA REVEALS man's condition in words and actions; the
musical play, in song and dance—a language that is universal
and exportable. *How to Succeed in Business Without Really Trying*, the Abe Burrows–Frank Loesser musical, thoroughly American in theme, was a triumph in Tokyo, an indication possibly,
not of the universality of Tin Pan Alley so much as of the growing
Westernization of Japan.

The straight dramatic play may attempt to bridge man's loneliness and isolation; the musical does so. The play may reach for the unknown, the disturbing, the nature of discontent; the musical reinforces the joy of living, the escape from realism, no matter how realistic it may strive to be. It has been said that if children are not present in the matinee audiences, no musical has a chance of success. The dramatic play remains, even today, confined largely to naturalism and verisimilitude, a portrayal of the drabness of life with all its anxieties. The musical opens onto the world of opulence, fantasy, and make-believe.

Alan Jay Lerner, who as a lyricist has *Brigadoon, My Fair Lady*, and *Camelot* to his credit, has called for an end to "the drama of eavesdropping and amateur psychiatry" and a return to a theatre of "eloquence, humor and poetry." He goes on to say that in the absence of "a poetic theatre, a romantic theatre, a heroic theatre, a moral theatre, and a theatrical theatre," the musical has been elected by default. Whether the musical succeeds on Lerner's terms is another question, but there is no doubt that it can be a glorious achievement of all the theatre arts, the last stronghold of spectacle and extravaganza.

Musical theatre is a generic term that includes everything from burlesque and the variety show to grand opera. In all its aspects, it constitutes a major part of theatrical vitality. Opera has become separated from the main stream, even to having separate buildings and institutions and a social protocol which surrounds it. Variety shows have moved over to elaborate television programs surrounding a single personality like Andy Williams or Danny Kaye. Theatre forms, however, refuse to be confined to rigid compartments, and even the words are lacking to make sharp distinctions. The drama often uses music and song, and the musical should certainly be dramatic. The straight play can rise to flights of poetic fancy, and the musical be prosaic. A broad division might be between musical drama and nonmusical drama, but that would give overemphasis to one aspect. The term "musical *comedy*" no longer always applies, as witness *West Side Story* or *Regina* or even *No Strings*, all of which have unhappy endings in which boy does not get girl, if that is the basis for determining comedy. Broadway with its usual indifference to definitions prefers the word "musical," an adjective without a noun, to indicate the one common denominator and cover a multitude of sins. Opera has moved onto Broadway with the work of Gian-Carlo Menotti—*The Medium* in 1947 and *Maria Golovin* in 1958—called "opera" because Menotti places emphasis on unity achieved through music. He has said, "The artistic strength of an opera bouffa is measured by the laughter inherent in the music itself." His meager success on Broadway and his popularity with music audiences elevated him to the Metropolitan Opera, which commissioned his most recent work, *The Last Savage* (1964).

Burlesque, which now belongs more to sociological research, continues to crop up, usually off-Broadway, and is visited by curious youth and nostalgic old-timers as a relic of the past. Ann Corio, veteran queen of the "bump and grind school," keeps a burlesque show running at the Casino East Theatre year in and year out, but other efforts at revival have floundered. Burlesque stays alive by creeping into the regular Broadway play. In *A Funny Thing Happened on the Way to the Forum*, Zero Mostel engaged in burlesque antics far beyond the dictates of the script, and even in a serious play like *Dylan*, a scene occurs in which the Welsh poet has a brawl with a performing stripteaser.

Since there are no clear-cut categories, the musical theatre for present purposes will be divided into the musical play, which follows a story line, and the musical revue, which does not.

Music has been part of the theatre since its earliest days. Before the development of Western civilization, dance and chant arose as essential elements in the survival of the community. In the execution of more effective war policy, propitiation of the gods, or initiation of the young into religious rites, music preceded spoken theatre. In ancient Greece, not only in the broad farces of Aristophanes but in the tragedies as well, music and dance were used extensively. Movement to musical accompaniment was part of a total experience.

Most plays would be enhanced by the addition of music. The separation occurred mostly for economic reasons and on account of union demands, but also as a result of the austere hand that naturalism placed on the stage. Tennessee Williams and Arthur Miller do incorporate music (the flute in *Death of a Salesman*, the jukebox in *The Glass Menagerie*) though mainly for mood or for an extension of relationships beyond the reach of words. To express our own times music has been a powerful force, whether it be popular songs, jazz lyrics, folk tunes, or the choral outbursts of the civil rights movement. In the last few years, a rash of plays dealing with Negro problems have combined message with music, in the free use of gospel singing and freedom lyrics, as in *Trumpets of the Lord, Tambourines to Glory*, and *Jerico-Jim Crow.*

The musical theatre is Broadway's proudest boast, and the legend has been fostered that it is a unique American contribution. Facts do not support this claim, for Europe has a long history of light opera and musical comedy that includes such diverse elements as the eighteenth-century John Gay's *The Beggars' Opera*, Franz Lehar's *The Merry Widow*, Gilbert and Sullivan, *The Folies Bergère*, and the nightclubs of Berlin. Moreover, in 1964, of the ten musical productions still running at midseason, three were of British origin: *Oliver, Stop the World, I Want to Get Off*, and *The Girl Who Came to Supper*, and the fourth, *Rugantino*, was, of all things, an import from Italy. But Broadway does engineer more productions with a higher degree of efficiency. Popular music and urban jazz, as Leonard Bernstein calls it, have been most intensely perfected on this side of the ocean. Yet even in our own history, *Blossom Time*, the perennial success of the Shubert era, was written by Sigmund Romberg, a native of Vienna, and *My Fair Lady* is based on a play by the Anglo-Irish George Bernard Shaw, and has music composed by Frederick Loewe, an Austrian. The tough sentimentality of the tunesmiths and the frenzy of acrobatic choreography have achieved a technical excellence, a sense of timing and rhythm, a choral precision, and jazz pacing that is uniquely American.

The two most significant developments in the musical theatre have been the rise in the cost of production and the "integrated" musical play. The two are not disconnected. Musical plays have become the giant corporate enterprise of show business. A production now is capitalized at a half-million dollars, all of which may go down the drain after a run of one week. The investment is a highly speculative gamble. *Jenny* with the magic name of Mary Martin was a financial failure, whereas *Funny Girl*, which seemed hopeless out of town, was a hit when Barbra Streisand, a newcomer, caught the public's fancy. Both plays, strangely enough, deal with the lives of stage personalities—the first with Laurette

Taylor, and the second with Fanny Brice. Though the risks are greater than in a South American oil company on the eve of revolution, money keeps pouring in. Obviously, angels enjoy the glamour of Broadway, but few businessmen would call enjoyment a worthy justification for investing repeatedly, even if done on emotional rather than financial grounds. Annual audits indicate that most musicals never recoup the initial capitalization. Add the present disclosures about the producers' bookkeeping methods, and even with projected reform no sane person would get involved. But the total picture has a more pleasant side. New ways have been developed to cushion losses, particularly by prior sales to recording companies and motion pictures, and the investor's eyes are on the astronomical profits that can be achieved if the show is a success.

My Fair Lady broke all records and is the rare exception, but a few figures are significant. The New York box office receipts of the seven-year run were over twenty million dollars. Almost four million people saw the musical on Broadway; an even larger number bought tickets for the many road companies. Foreign sales brought in another forty million dollars, and the State Department thought enough of the show to sponsor its tour of the Soviet Union for two months. Warner Brothers bought the motion picture rights for the unbelievable price of five million dollars. The original cast album has sold four million copies to date. No wonder producers, and even the most wary investors, are frantically searching for a successor. Occasionally, one pops up. *Hello, Dolly!* and *Fiddler on the Roof* are now on their merry way.

The *My Fair Lady* figures are not intended to be a statistical account of show business, or to offer encouragement to hesitant angels, but rather to point out the artistic implications. The musical play has become a mass medium aimed at all the people and subject to the forces which beset any art of this character. The once intimate opening night within the confines of Shubert Alley now reaches to every corner of the globe. The stakes are high, and the pressure is on to protect a huge investment, reap the greatest profit, perfect the product, and avoid any dangers.

Despite the uncertainty of success and the amount of money involved, musicals are slowly taking over Broadway. In the past five years, 1960–64, over sixty musical plays have been produced, and the number is growing. In the 1962 season, of a total of fifty-eight productions, eleven were musicals; in 1963, of a similar total number, fifteen were musicals.

My Fair Lady blended the varied artistic components into a unified production which made money. Other musicals are therefore expected to follow the trend. The old musical was a disconnected sequence of scenes, with lavish pageantry, leg shows, costume parades, and, above all, the antics of a comedian. *The Ziegfeld Follies* and George White's *Scandals* were the epitome of the extravaganza which centered around a distinctive comic personality. W. C. Fields, Ed Wynn, Groucho Marx, Jimmy Durante, Bobby Clark, and Bert Lahr are some of the names which highlighted the era of the grand clown, who, surrounded by a chorus of beautiful girls, lampooned pretense, performed pratfalls, was buffeted by circumstance, but managed to get in the last word for explosive destruction of the commonplace.

Two world wars, a depression, and international problems have deprived our age of unfettered laughter. The broad gesture, obvious slapstick, with its implicit social overtones, has become an anachronism. On a lesser scale the comedian is still with us. Zero Mostel, out of the Borscht Circuit, could have rivaled the best of the boys of another day, but present-day material offers him little scope. He turned to serious drama and played Leopold Bloom in *Ulysses in Nighttown,* an off-Broadway dramatization of James Joyce. On Broadway, he played Jean in Ionesco's *Rhinoceros* and Tevye in *Fiddler on the Roof.*

Bert Lahr, the last of the vanishing comedians, played in Beckett's *Waiting for Godot,* a stroke of genius by the casting director. Lahr continued with a bit of Shakespeare and then starred in *The Beauty Part,* which failed because S. J. Perelman's subtle verbal humor no longer found an appreciative audience. In what Broadway calls a "book" musical, he finally returned as Foxy in 1964, twenty-five years after he had co-starred with Ethel Merman in *DuBarry Was a Lady.* The plot, which places Ben Jonson's *Volpone* in the gold rush days of Alaska, gave Lahr an opportunity to exercise his talents. The book by Ian Hunter and Ring Lardner, Jr., is the old-fashioned sketchy outline avoiding overrefinements of characterization; the score by Robert Emmett Dolan, with lyrics by Johnny Mercer, recaptures the rowdy horseplay of the twenties. Bert Lahr was back in his heyday. He followed the story line but had full play for his personal style: the rolling eyes, the weeping in pretended agony, chasing girls all over Brandy's Saloon, changing costumes from a raccoon coat to a nightgown to an English hunting outfit, singing "Bon Vivant," and scampering up the proscenium arch when chased by a jealous lover—creating the onstage chaos which can be set right by a sudden shift of mood. *Foxy* was twenty years too late; it failed on Broadway.

The sixties have witnessed the rise of the stand-up comedian, attempting to follow in the tradition of Will Rogers, who, with his gum-chewing, lariat-tossing understatement created an essentially American comic character, the dry humor of the down-to-earth realist, cynical of pomp and power. This tradition, smaller in scope, is carried on by Mort Sahl and Dick Gregory. Gifted pantomime, clever imitations, and skits spoofing topical events on a more sophisticated level brought *An Evening with Mike Nichols and Elaine May* to Broadway. So successful were they that Mike Nichols was assigned to direct *Barefoot in the Park* and provide the tempo, the movement, and the hilarity that an able comedian could impart to a rather trivial situation comedy. But the big, brash, individually styled, zany comedian of the past is a disappearing phenomenon.

The "book" musical, which is the musical play, began with *Oklahoma!* (1943), which also popularized the superfluous exclamation mark after the title (*Oliver!, Fiorello!*) and started the Rodgers–Hammerstein dynasty. *South Pacific, My Fair Lady, West Side Story,* and *Hello, Dolly!* followed the new pattern. A musical play is a composite of all the theatre arts: acting, plot or libretto, music, music arrangement, song, lyrics, choreography, costumes, lighting, and set. Each is a belligerent art form seeking to assert itself. Both in creation and in performance, each strives to dominate with its own inherent power. Though there had been scattered examples in the past, *Oklahoma!* was the first major success to achieve subordination of all the elements to an overall point of view. Gian-Carlo Menotti has said, "No art can achieve that Apollonian serenity so essential to great comedy unless it clearly reflects the solid symmetry of its inner architecture." A sentimental musical cream-puff like *She Loves Me* (with lyrics by Sheldon Harnick and music by Jerry Bock) succeeded because the various components were brilliantly integrated—a perfection of colorful nostalgia in the Franz Lehar tradition. No longer is the hastily pieced-together, mechanically arranged combination of standard ingredients looked upon favorably. The philosophy of the revue is giving way to the art of the musical play, but old methods die slowly. A hit like *A Funny Thing Happened on the Way to the Forum* or *Funny Girl* was being pieced together the week before its arrival, but Zero Mostel and Plautus saved *A Funny Thing*, and Barbra Streisand, *Funny Girl*.

For the integrated musical play, a total unified dramatic experience in song and dance and lyrics must arise out of situation and character. Again, *My Fair Lady* with lyrics by Alan Jay Lerner and music by Frederick Loewe is an outstanding example. Shaw's *Pygmalion* was considered unlikely story material and counter to the accepted tradition. It was rejected by a dozen librettists before Lerner and Moss Hart started work on the adaptation. But the biting social satire was deftly blunted. Shaw, who believed in environment over heredity as the determinant of personality, had a Cockney flower girl, given the training and opportunity, outshine the Ascot set. He was gleefully rebuking the upper class for its presumed superiority. *My Fair Lady* concentrates on the romantic angle and the outcome of a gentleman's wager, but the story moves as a developing plot, and out of it rise the music, the lyrics, and choral arrangements. "With a Little Bit of Luck" tells more of Doolittle's philosophy than all his speeches, and Professor Higgins' attitude toward women is revealed in "I'm an Ordinary Man." Eliza's longings are expressed in "Wouldn't It Be Loverly."

Sparkling dialogue (mostly Shaw), story, character, and Loewe's music achieve a common goal, flowing in and out of one another, strengthening the general line, and reaching a multiple impact of sound, color, and dance, in the complex, delicately balanced unity of a musical play. No sparsely dressed girls dash in for a rousing choral number and a choreographer's dream. No display of period costumes engulfs the stage for a designer's delight. No comedian takes stage center to halt proceedings with his personal routine. The result is not Shaw's *Pygmalion*, but a distinct work growing out of it, which stands in its own right. Lerner and Loewe, combining again on *Camelot*, were unable to repeat their success, and the partnership was dissolved.

Hello, Dolly! is an improvement over Thornton Wilder's *The Matchmaker.* Wilder had written a regional period-comedy of Yonkers at the turn of the century, which is hardly his best work. Its insistence that love conquers all, that life is beautiful, and that a persistent woman can soften the heart of a miserly half-million-aire is sufficiently sentimental for Michael Stewart's adaptation. Dolly's availability as a meddler in human affairs is summed up in "I Put My Hand In." Vandergelder's search for a wife is neatly expressed in "It Takes a Woman," and the sanctity of the home is defended in "Motherhood." The untrammeled exuberance of Wilder is better realized in *Hello, Dolly!* Jerry Herman, who wrote both music and lyrics, did not equal the work of Lerner and Loewe, but he had a superior director. The integrated musi-cal demands a strong personality who commands the respect of all artists and imposes a single will. Like Jerome Robbins in the case of *West Side Story* and Joseph Layton with *The Girl Who Came to Supper,* Gower Champion, also an ex-choreographer, im-parted to *Hello, Dolly!* unity, wit, and imagination.

Fiddler on the Roof, brilliantly directed and supervised by Jerome Robbins, with book by Joseph Stein, music by Jerry Bock, and lyrics by Sheldon Harnick, is an example of the integrated musical that becomes a deeply moving human document. This tale of the orthodox Jews in the village of Anatevka during the days of the Czars employs music, song, and dance to intensify the spirit of Sholom Aleichem's original stories. The entire community comes to life—the matchmaker, the butcher, the rabbi, the tailor, and mainly Tevye the dairyman, his scolding wife, and their five growing daughters. The people, peaceful and order-loving, cher-ish and preserve their traditions—the opening song with the en-tire company is "Tradition," performed as a ritual of chant and dance in the manner of the past. Equally evocative is "Sabbath Prayer," sung by different families gathered around the devotional candles, to show the village held together by the strength of common beliefs.

Tradition is upset when the three older daughters fall in love with men of their own choice. Tevye sees his traditional world shattered but he accepts with dignity and understanding. In the end, the village is uprooted and the Jews disperse to different parts of the world. Tevye packs his cart and pulls what is left of the family and his possessions with him—a lost and noble figure, a Jewish "Father Courage." All the elements of the musical play combine to point up the courage of man and his need for love. *Fiddler on the Roof* is the musical play's answer to the theatre of the absurd.

Zero Mostel, who plays the central role of Tevye, gave the theatre a memorable portrayal. The shifting of the eyes, the shuffling gait, the intimate talks with God, the flailing of the hands, and the raising of the shoulders are parts of a total characterization. The great clown became the most human figure.

The triumph of these integrated musical plays has strengthened the trend. Leonard Bernstein is at work with the veteran team of Betty Comden and Adolph Green on a musical based on Thornton Wilder's *The Skin of Our Teeth*. Richard Rodgers, largely responsible for the present movement, has remarked that there is a demand today for subject matter "that is less superficial than it used to be and that asks for more emotionality in the relationship between subject and score." Harold Rome, whose music goes back to the pro-labor revue *Pins and Needles* and who also wrote the score for S. N. Behrman's libretto of *Fanny*, agrees that today more is required than "putting attractive music and lyrics together." "Songs," he says, "have to carry character and plot interest in addition to a much more sophisticated musical taste." Stephen Sondheim, always experimental, holds the opposite point of view: "The 'integrated' story-musical has become a tired formula and new approaches are needed."

Extremism in pursuit of integration is no virtue. The separate parts need an excellence of their own. *Fade Out—Fade In,* by the Betty Comden–Adolph Green–Jule Styne combination, had a feeble book and derivative music, but was rescued by the robust direction of the old doctor, George Abbott, and the zestful impudence of the star, Carol Burnett. Her performance as a girl who rises to film stardom by mistake is closer to that of the clowns of the thirties, this time played by a woman. *Funny Girl*, again with music by Jule Styne, and a sentimental book by Isobel Lennart, had nothing working in its favor a week before it opened on Broadway, even to the changing of directors at the last minute, but became a hit when the public took a fancy to the new star, Barbra Streisand, whose raucous singing and strutting and clowning resurrected Fanny Brice. Perhaps the ungainly comedienne who also plays the romantic lead has replaced the old-time clown.

The book has assumed increased importance. Playwrights with established reputations have become librettists—Arthur Laurents (*West Side Story*), Maxwell Anderson (*Lost in the Stars*), Lillian Hellman (*Candide*), S. N. Behrman (*Fanny*), William Gibson (*Golden Boy*). Alan Jay Lerner and Abe Burrows, expert professional craftsmen, say that writers should be cautioned not to take a story which does not lend itself to the fullness of musical expression. This advice is not only vague, but not borne out by facts. Looking over the successful musicals of the past decade, and particularly those with integrated structure, makes it apparent that there is no set law for the derivation of musical stories. They have ranged from the silliest nonsense to the most serious literary works. The essential thing is not the source, but the way in which the librettist is able to develop a sufficiently meaningful story line which will give full play to other elements.

West Side Story, an up-to-date version of *Romeo and Juliet*, was an idea of Jerome Robbins', which he confided to Arthur Laurents. *Candide*, the Voltaire novel, seemingly perfect material for contemporary satire, failed on Broadway, whereas *The Pajama Game*, which gave little promise as musical material, was successful. The book may be derived from any source—a headline in the newspapers about a naïve member of the Peace Corps (*Hot Spot*), or biographies of public figures (*Fiorello!*). Lives of stage personalities are always popular, and overdone, *Sophie* (Sophie Tucker), *Jennie* (Laurette Taylor), *Gypsy* (Gypsy Rose Lee). Novels have been used—Edna Ferber's *Saratoga Trunk*, Budd Schulberg's *What Makes Sammy Run?*—and the short stories of James Thurber (*A Thurber Carnival*) and Damon Runyon (*Guys and Dolls*).

The most consistently reliable source has been successful stage plays, from Aristophanes, *The Happiest Girl in the World* (*Lysistrata*), and Plautus, *A Funny Thing Happened on the Way to the Forum*, to Shakespeare, *Kiss Me, Kate* (*The Taming of the Shrew*) and *The Boys from Syracuse* (*Comedy of Errors*), to Eugene O'Neill, *New Girl in Town* (*Anna Christie*) and *Take Me Along* (*Ah, Wilderness!*). The play is a more attractive source, for it already has dialogue and is arranged in dramatic sequence, but there is no guarantee of success. *110 in the Shade*, which N. Richard Nash rewrote from *The Rainmaker*—in an effort to recapture the regional flavor and folksy background of *Oklahoma!*—was both overplotted and nonunified. This flabby version of his own play suffered also from the too easily predictable style of Agnes de Mille Americana choreography. *Juno* by the late Marc Blitzstein was based on Sean O'Casey's *Juno and the Paycock,* an almost impossible task, for it meant distortion of the original material to unrecognizable limits. How much wiser it would have been if the gifted Blitzstein had taken instead O'Casey's *Red Roses for Me,* in which the third act cries aloud for dance and music. Of the Big Four among integrated musicals, *Oklahoma!* was based on Lynn Riggs's play *Green Grow the Lilacs, South Pacific* on the prose tales of James A. Michener, *My Fair Lady* on Shaw's *Pygmalion,* and *West Side Story* indirectly on Shakespeare.

The common thread that runs through all stories is, of course, boy meets girl. Musicals have explored the entire gamut from the usual ending to efforts at mature romance and social realism. Meredith Willson, for one, can always be counted on to continue the nostalgic sentimental tradition; music and story are sweet and heartwarming. *The Music Man,* an American fast-talker with a heart of gold, is really Billy Graham with a trumpet. *Here's Love* reverses the usual process and takes its story from the motion picture *The Miracle on Thirty-fourth Street.* Meredith Willson is the miracle of Broadway, for almost singlehanded he put together this exploitation of Santa Claus and Macy's in a comforting "glamour of innocence" production. Rick Besoyan, another one-man operation (he writes book, music, and lyrics in the style of the English trio, Noel Coward, Lionel Bart, and Anthony Newley), spoofed the Western melodrama successfully in his long-run off-Broadway show *Little Mary Sunshine,* but when he attempted to ridicule the romantic *schmaltz* of the Viennese operetta in *Student Gypsy,* he failed on Broadway. Meredith Willson treated Santa Claus and love with the utter reverence and Midwestern simplicity essential for capturing the hearts of millions of Americans. *She Loves Me* (music by Jerry Bock and lyrics by Sheldon Harnick), only slightly tongue-in-cheek, delicately touched all heartstrings with a pastel romance in a Viennese perfume shop. *No Strings,* on the other hand, for which Richard Rodgers attempted both lyrics and music, deals with the serious theme of the love between a Negro model and a white American writer in Paris. Like *Fiddler on the Roof* and *West Side Story*, it does not end on a happy note.

Musicals today relate more closely to contemporary events, and the search for subject matter has led to political and social issues. Not only *No Strings*, but *Kwamina*, attempts the theme of race relations. Robert Alan Aurthur's story of a village in West Africa has a romance between the ...ite girl who is the doctor and the young Negro leader of his people. It had all the possibilities of an explosive story, but instead of portraying the emergence of new nations and the social conflicts with the West, the musical became all girl-meets-boy. The same is true of *Milk and Honey* (book by Don Appell, music and lyrics by Jerry Herman), in which the enthusiasm, spirit, and hope of Israel become the search by three widows for husbands in a kibbutz. New themes have included a satire on business, *I Can Get It for You Wholesale;* even psychiatry may come into the picture with S. N. Behrman's promised libretto for Lillian Ross's *Vertical and Horizontal*. As always on Broadway, themes run in cycles. The year of *Flower Drum Song* produced a flurry of oriental musicals. The future may belong to Thornton Wilder or, more likely, James Baldwin.

With all the present trends, the musical remains a form that changes slowly. Off-Broadway, from which much has been expected, has become a little Broadway, concentrating on revivals performed by aspiring talents, and usually showcase productions. Little originality has been demonstrated. *Once Upon a Mattress*, a Cinderella story, was a chance for young Mary Rodgers as composer. *The Streets of New York*, a spoof of the nineteenth-century melodrama, was worthy of a college varsity show. *Jo* (music by William Dyer, book and lyrics by Don Parks) was a tiresome reenactment of *Little Women*. The intimate revue is the one development that belongs more properly to off-Broadway, for with a few actors and a piano, every coffeehouse can have its own musical production. The little theatres of the back alleys, which have pioneered in presenting Genet, Pinter, and Beckett, have now given rise to equally bold avant-garde musical forms. *Waiting for Godot* or *The American Dream* has not as yet found a parallel in musical expression.

Gian-Carlo Menotti has carved out a place of his own. The Metropolitan Opera produced *The Last Savage* (1964), a comic opera, which except for its recitative sounds like a slick, pretentious Broadway musical, but its seductive simplicity and musical satire captured the most critical audience. This opera bouffa is almost like an avant-garde play on the possessive female. Abdul from India poses as "the last savage" to please Kitty, a Vassar anthropologist. He is captivated by her charm but horrified by her civilization that contains action painting, beat poetry, and electronic music, all of which are parodied in the work. He runs off to the jungle and is trapped by the pursuing Kitty with television sets, refrigerator, and modern plumbing, which she installs in their honeymoon cave. The serious quality gets ponderous, and the literate references too pretentious, but it is an opera intended to mock both opera and contemporary civilization at the same time.

Musically, there has been little variation in recent years. The Irving Berlin–George Gershwin era passed over to Cole Porter and Richard Rodgers, and most composers today sound like heirs-apparent to the Rodgers throne. Kurt Weill, who had worked with Brecht in Germany, provided one of the few instances of a possible radical departure. *The Threepenny Opera* is a sharp, incisive, satirical musical with social commentary. In his American work, Weill was influenced too much by adjustment to Broadway. *Lost in the Stars,* with a book by Maxwell Anderson based on Alan Paton's *Cry, the Beloved Country,* and *Street Scene,* based on Elmer Rice's play with lyrics by Langston Hughes, are "serious" musicals, but too close to conventional forms. Frank Loesser, and Harold Rome in such work as *Fanny,* together with Harold Arlen (*Saratoga*), have approached at times the tradition Weill sought to establish.

Leonard Bernstein belongs to this group, but the most impressive contribution was that of the late Marc Blitzstein. He had given musical expression to the Depression era with *The Cradle Will Rock,* which also made theatre history when it was forced to move to another theatre at the last minute because of political pressure and was played without orchestra, scenery, or costumes, but with Blitzstein at the piano and the actors seated in the audience. He attempted operatic breadth for a popular musical in *Regina,* and was at work on a Sacco-Vanzetti opera when his unfortunate death occurred. He fought against the axiom that if a musical "gives pleasure it cannot be serious," but he may well have been fighting for a lost cause.

The musical play changes slowly. A Broadway axiom says, "Don't criticize musicals. After all, they're entertainment. Laugh and enjoy yourself." Few dare disturb what has become a hallowed institution. Richard Rodgers makes everyone feel comfortable. His songs are easily sung at home. When Weill or Blitzstein or Stephen Sondheim or Arthur Laurents attempt different musicals, they are regarded as unholy rebels violating the sacred code of show business. Musicals are for nonthinking joy. Despite the high cost of tickets they are considered a big dollar value as well as a welcome relief from the dull two-character play.

All theatre is entertainment, and the musical can well afford to exert itself to avoid repetition and exhaustion of the standard patterns. The integrated musical play can be fantasy and dream and magic and mystery not available in the ordinary drama. At its best, it provides, through the full combination of all the theatre arts, an awareness, an insight into modern man which, even in the comic vein, can be more penetrating than that of the serious play.

14

THE OFF-BROADWAY THEATRE
AND THE TOPICAL REVUE

*I turned my back on Broadway because it had nothing to give me but
money and I had nothing to give it.*

EVA LE GALLIENNE

*A performance is an act of love in which the playwright, actor, and
theatre artist expose themselves, body and spirit, under ordeal, at
great risk, to produce catharsis and enlightenment for an anonymous
audience.*

The Living Theatre Brochure

WHEN EUGENE O'NEILL of the Provincetown company invaded
Broadway in 1920, a revolution followed. Realism and psychological truth replaced the conventional melodrama. The little
theatre movement was recognized as the needed impetus for
change. Four decades later, the family psychological drama is
entrenched and tired. Rumblings of discontent are heard, but on
Broadway as well as off. The commercial theatre is no longer a

completely closed society preserving outworn forms. It will produce anything for a profit, including Ionesco, Beckett, Pinter, or Brecht.

The off-Broadway theatre has gained increased recognition and complacency. Rare are fighting manifestoes issued from Macdougal Alley, or dedicated Eva LeGalliennes forsaking money for the glory of art. To a large extent, off-Broadway has become a minor Broadway, a financial not an aesthetic rebellion. The number of shows presented annually has increased, from seventy in 1960 to eighty-six in 1964, far more than on Broadway. Most were *vanity* productions, but no single word can characterize off-Broadway. It is not one, but many, a shifting complex of differing goals and contradictory enthusiasms.

Even the name off-Broadway is a misnomer. The Martinique Theatre is *on* Broadway within hailing distance of Times Square, and the New Theatre, latest and best-equipped of the converted lofts, is a stone's throw from Shubert Alley. Once dotting the low-rent area in the bohemian concentration of Greenwich Village, the little theatres have lost even their geographical unity. Now that the Village is expensive and increasingly middle class, theatres appear wherever a reburbished barn or church cellar permits 199 seats to be installed. To understand this varied activity, consideration should first be given to the few producing organizations that have attempted continuity and permanence.

The Phoenix Theatre is the most venerable and most durable. Its purpose, under the leadership of its founding directors T. Edward Hambleton and Norris Houghton, was to fill the gap left by Broadway's preoccupation with new plays and to present worthy plays of the past. Since 1953, offerings have ranged from Aristophanes to Marlowe and Ibsen, even including a cycle of Shakespeare's works. Though the performances have been of uneven quality, they have become an invaluable addition to New York's theatrical life. As a nonprofit organization, the Phoenix has valiantly striven to build a subscription audience, but with disheartening results. They have championed no cause, fought for no ideas, but have been content to present good plays at reasonable prices. From their ranks have come such actors as Fritz Weaver, and directors like Stuart Vaughan. The Phoenix has failed, however, to build a permanent company and a definite style, and in the absence of an overall guiding philosophy has grown eclectic and traditional.

Unsuccessful in gaining a faithful audience for the production of established plays, the Phoenix Theatre has turned to competition with Broadway in the new-play field. In 1963, *The Dragon* by Eugene Schwarz was offered with the well-known Broadway director Joseph Anthony staging the work. This gay fairy tale, an allegory of good and evil with the eventual triumph of initiative over stupid bureaucracy, provided one of the few opportunities to see the work of a playwright from the Communist world. Norris Houghton brought it back from a European trip and stole a march on Broadway's play-hunters. However, it took Roger Stevens, a commercial producer, to induce the Phoenix Theatre to present *Oh Dad, Poor Dad, Mamma's Hung You in the Closet and I'm Feeling So Sad,* their first production of a play by an unknown American playwright. (Kermit Bloomgarden, another Broadway producer, likewise ventured off-Broadway to present Errol John's *Moon on a Rainbow Shawl.*) Kopit's play proved to be the most outstanding success in Phoenix history and saved them temporarily from financial disaster. It also overcame their reluctance to present new writers. They were sufficiently encouraged to follow it with Frank D. Gilroy's *Who'll Save the Plowboy?* (also a first play by an American writer). This work aroused favorable comment for its deeply moving tale of a returning soldier who discovers the life he saved on the battlefield may not have been worth saving.

Further efforts to discover new plays were not rewarding. Bert Shevelove, a writer of slick Broadway comedy, was permitted to offer his rewrite of William Gillette's farce *Too Much Johnson,* which proved a dismal failure and an indication of the Phoenix's lack of well-defined theatrical philosophy in the selection of plays. The two new writers who were discovered did not remain associated with the organization. Gilroy's next play, *The Subject Was Roses,* went directly to Broadway. It is a traditional family drama out of the Ibsen school. *Oh Dad, Poor Dad,* after a two-year run at the Phoenix, was moved to Broadway for a limited engagement. It did not repeat its triumph. Gilroy's realistic play about the members of a family alternately needing and rejecting one another was more welcome to Broadway's audiences than a wild fantasy mocking family relations.

The Phoenix Theatre has changed its character since its fortunate alliance in 1964 with the Association of Producing Artists, an independent repertory company. A full season for subscribers is assured, but the move underscores the failure of the Phoenix to develop a program out of its own resources.

The Circle in the Square on Bleecker Street has had an enviable record since it was launched in 1951 by Theodore Mann and José Quintero. In addition to presenting unusual plays of the contemporary scene worthy of revival, such as *Yerma* or *The Cradle Song*, it has presented recent works by playwrights Broadway would ordinarily ignore, such as Brendan Behan's *The Quare Fellow* and Jean Genet's *The Balcony*. Through O'Neill and Wilder, the Circle in the Square achieved a unique distinction rarely accorded a little theatre. *Our Town* (1958), previously done everywhere save in New York, was so ably directed by José Quintero that Thornton Wilder dedicated his *Plays for Bleecker Street* to the theatre and gave them sole production rights. *The Iceman Cometh* (1956) initiated the O'Neill resurgence and further enhanced Quintero's reputation. Carlotta O'Neill regards Quintero as the official director for future productions of her husband's work.

In 1962, *Under Milk Wood*, Dylan Thomas' evocation of the life of a community, inspired William Ball, an imaginative new director, to arrange the verse drama with stylized movement, choral chant, and plastic design, which stimulated the trend toward more effective use of the arena stage. In 1964, Michael Cacoyannis, the Greek motion picture director, staged Euripides' *The Trojan Women* with austere grandeur, using the chorus, so often an obstacle for lesser directors of classic tragedy, as a powerful protagonist.

The Circle in the Square discovered such actors as Colleen Dewhurst, Geraldine Page, Jason Robards, Jr., and George C. Scott. It is the only off-Broadway theatre that operates an acting school in conjunction with its work. As the name implies, all productions are in the three-quarter round. The future of the organization is now uncertain, however. José Quintero has left, and Theodore Mann is in complete command. He is a combination of astute businessman and theatrical producer, the David Merrick of off-Broadway. Almost alone of little theatres, the Circle in the

Square has been financially profitable. Taste has been catholic, and though an overall style was never generated, the theatre has understood what off-Broadway can do and has done it exceedingly well.

The Living Theatre, guided by Julian Beck and his wife Judith Malina, is the last stronghold of the bohemian theatre. Despite insurmountable financial difficulties and the artistic differences imposed upon them by the middle-class world they are determined to enlighten, they survived for fourteen years, attempting to build a permanent company and investigate uncharted avenues of dramatic expression. A subsidy could have saved them, but it was always too little and available too late. In 1964, after years of continuous struggle, the doors of the theatre were padlocked for failure to pay taxes. The Becks defied the injunction and were hauled off to court, where they condemned the uncultured Internal Revenue agents and stoutly maintained that art is above the law.

All the productions were under the supervision of the Becks, so that theirs was the only theatre that forged a personal style, an international reputation, and a preciosity that alienated audiences. Close to the theatre of Artaud, of imagery, magic, and cruelty, the Becks issued high-sounding manifestoes, talked of revelation and "universal experience," and defied all existing rules of production. A miracle of the spirit kept the theatre going. The Becks announce undauntedly that on the stage "light is shed, truth is spoken, the dream interpreted." The first play, presented in 1951, was significantly Gertrude Stein's *Doctor Faustus Lights the Lights*, and in succeeding years their effort to buttress the contemporary poetic theatre witnessed William Carlos Williams' *Many Loves* and Paul Goodman's *The Young Disciple*. Flirting with the dangerous and the untried, the shocking and often the obscene, their repertory included the first production in the United States of Alfred Jarry's *Ubu Roi*. The play that brought them the greatest notoriety was *The Connection* by Jack Gelber, with which they later toured Europe as representatives of American experimental theatre.

There is something inspiring and magnificent about the Becks, and something awkward and embarrassing. They protest their devotion to the poetic, the adventurous, and offer *The Brig*, an ultra-naturalistic portrayal of cruelty and sadism in a Marine Corps stockade. They talk of ritual and communication, and present Jack Gelber's *The Apple*, a disjointed, distasteful, and discordant failure to communicate with anyone. Their well-intentioned *Man Is Man* by Bertolt Brecht was not superior to a rival production by less pretentious producers. Contemptuous of other theatres and dogmatic about their own, the Becks' overconscious desire to be avant-garde may keep them running so far ahead that they trail behind, a development of style without substance, a theatre to shock rather than to reveal, a rebellion unfocused. Opposition to what *is*, becomes an obsession; when a foundation once offered support, Julian Beck was perturbed by the possibility that the Living Theatre had become too acceptable. Their irrational contempt for conformity grew into a special conformity of their own, something precious rather than provocative, a cult rather than a challenge. Though their holy crusade became too private, their insistence on the new is admirable. They are needed gadflies to complacency.

David Ross, who directs and produces, has confined his efforts to Ibsen and Chekhov. His work is uneven, ranging from a competent production of *Uncle Vanya* to a sadly misinterpreted *The Three Sisters*. Keeping the masters of the modern drama available is indeed admirable, but David Ross has not as yet evolved a directorial style. At considerable expense, he remodeled a West Side church as a permanent home for his theatre, and opened with *The Three Sisters*. Critical condemnation would have resulted in immediate bankruptcy, had he not turned landlord and rented the theatre to *The Boys from Syracuse*, a sparkling revival of the Rodgers–Hart musical. It ran so long that David Ross was able to recoup his losses, again proving that off-Broadway audiences are becoming more like those farther uptown.

Theatre 60 (it changes its numerals to conform to the current year) opened with *Krapp's Last Tape* and *The Zoo Story*, coupling Beckett and Albee in the latter's introduction to the United States. Alan Schneider directed, and together with the playwright and the producer formed a combination that remained together and finally reached Broadway with *Who's Afraid of Virginia Woolf?* Albee has now joined Clinton Wilder and Richard Barr as a partner in a long-term occupancy of the Cherry Lane Theatre, which has become the recognized center of the theatre of the absurd. In addition to Samuel Beckett, foreign playwrights rounding out the program are Ionesco, Pinter, Arrabel, and Ugo Betti. With the profits from *Who's Afraid of Virginia Woolf?* a studio workshop has been set up for new writers, and in 1964, Adrienne Kennedy's *Funnyhouse of a Negro* and LeRoi Jones's *Dutchman* brought attention to the work of young Negro playwrights.

These groups, in existence for several years, were suddenly joined in 1964 by a newcomer, well financed, as well as high-minded in purpose, calling itself The New Theatre. Ivor Balding, an experienced manager, and Peter Cook of *Beyond the Fringe* joined with Joseph E. Levine, the motion picture producer, to open an excellently designed, elegantly equipped, and conveniently located theatre, which presented Ann Jellicoe's *The Knack,* directed by Mike Nichols. It was an ingeniously staged production of the most original comedy of the year.

With few exceptions, all other productions are one-shot deals presented at any of the available theatres for rent, just as on Broadway. Unlike Broadway, few of the ventures return a profit, nor can they, under present conditions. Off-Broadway is the only business that people go into knowing beforehand that they are almost certain to lose the entire investment—and do so eagerly. A brief review of the off-Broadway financial structure is enlightening. (The late-1964 Equity contract raised minimum salaries and may drastically curtail future operations.) The following figures are based on the 1963-64 season: Pre-production costs run about $20,000. Maximum weekly income at a 199-seat house is about $7,000, depending on variations in the price of seats. Operating expenses average $3,500. A potential weekly profit of $3,500 seems attractive, but one-half goes to the producer. More than eleven weeks of capacity operation would, therefore, be required to repay the original investment. With the house only half-filled, operating costs would be covered and the show could run forever, but the investors would never recoup one cent. Most new offerings run from four to six weeks, and result in a total loss of the money involved. Of the eighty-two productions in the 1963–64 season, twenty-one closed after less than ten performances. It is true that a few have made money in recent years, among them the long-running *The Threepenny Opera, Little*

Mary Sunshine, and *The Fantasticks,* but generally the only profit is garnered by the real estate owner. Theatre rentals are exorbitant.

Who, then, would be foolhardy enough to engage in so precarious an undertaking? The answer is simple—anyone who considers the investment necessary for a future career. An actor, director, or playwright with $20,000 raised from family or friends will put on a play so that his work can be seen in what is known today as a "vanity" or "showcase" production. The donors feel they have advanced the cause of art and helped a worthy relative. The production is not aimed at the entertainment of the public but at gaining a personal credit. As long as thousands of aspirants flock to New York and find no other way to gain recognition, this practice will continue, and as long as an off-Broadway theatre is a taxi ride from a producer's office, New York City will remain the showcase center. It is an expensive way to reach the limelight. A well-known authority to whom drama school graduates come for advice tells them bluntly that the requirements for success are talent, five years of unstinting sacrifice, and a rich uncle—in reverse order of importance.

For these productions, a director or an actor, anxious to be seen, usually chooses a well-known play. The result, quite tangentially, is that excellent plays of the past can be seen. Unfortunately, most are poorly done by inexperienced hands in dirty theatres, since the entire operation is a one-shot speculation. Such ventures could be tolerated if the public were not invited to pay. The show could comfortably close after agents, producers and critics had attended. All such productions could then be treated in a specialized category, thereby erasing the unsavory reputation they have given the off-Broadway theatre.

The playwright is in a different position. Both Broadway and off-Broadway producers are constantly searching for good scripts, but a vanity production is almost a guarantee of a play's inadequacy. The Writers Stage Company, organized in 1962 for "the discovery and production of works for the theatre by new American writers," lasted two seasons. The plays they would have liked to produce were already optioned, and those that were available had been rejected by equally willing producers. The company discovered that it was getting only second-rate material—David

Rayfiel's *P.S. 193* was an exception. The increased number of vanity productions is alarming, for it encourages most wasteful procedures for sifting talent.

The few permanent theatres and the showcase trial balloons are but two phases of off-Broadway's activities. Dedicated idealists still gather to produce a play about which they feel strongly, whether it be *The Night of the Auk* by Arch Oboler or *The Burning* by Wallace Hamilton, the latter a drama of a fourteenth-century monk who joins the lepers to demonstrate the continuing need of Christ on earth. This play preceded *The Deputy* and dealt with the same theme.

Independent producers account for most of what remains. They do not have permanent theatres and sometimes not even an office, but they do present plays periodically. Like all producers, their interest is in making a profit. With sound business management and astute selection of plays, they frequently do. Some are sensitive to the nature of off-Broadway and concentrate on appeals to special audiences. Three women have been outstanding. Judith Marechal, Vassar-trained and a graduate from David Merrick's office, has been successful in discovering new playwrights. Her productions include plays by Michael Shurtleff (*Call Me by My Rightful Name*), William Snyder (*The Days and Nights of Beebee Fenstermaker*), and Lewis John Carlino (*Cages*). The other two women are Clare Nichtern, formerly with the Phoenix Theatre, who presented Murray Schisgal's *The Typists* and *The Tiger*, and Lucille Lortel, who, in addition to the White Barn in Westport, Connecticut, operates the Theatre de Lys, one of the more attractive off-Broadway houses.

It becomes apparent that the off-Broadway theatre is a haphazard, multi-faceted chaos lacking any organized philosophy to give direction to the theatre of the future. Yet it is an essential complement to Broadway. In recent years, writers with established reputations have had off-Broadway productions of plays that could not meet the long-run requirements of commercial production, among them Robert Ardrey's *Sing Me No Lullaby*, Maxwell Anderson's *The Golden Six*, and William Gibson's *Dinny and the Witches*. Tennessee Williams chose a little theatre for *The Garden District* in 1957, saying:

I have suffered from a [audience] reaction of ethical bias and . . .
imposed morality . . . I couldn't cope at this time with doing another controversial play on Broadway.

Leading actors have chosen off-Broadway production as an oppor-
tunity to create a role they enjoyed, among them Henry Fonda in
Uncle Vanya, Eli Wallach and Anne Jackson in *The Typists* and
The Tiger, and Shelley Winters in *Cages.*

New forms, as well, do emerge. The most developed and most
widespread innovation is the topical revue.

THE TOPICAL REVUE

Both the Berlin nightclub and the London music hall have
a long, vitriolic history of lancing social humbug and political
pretense. When *Beyond the Fringe,* an import from the West
End of London, opened in New York in 1962, enough encouragement was given this type of show to promote its widespread development throughout the nation. Almost simultaneously, *Second
City Revue* opened in Chicago. It struck a popular chord, moved
to New York, and held on for two years. A multitude of imitators
of the topical revue have sprung up everywhere.

These small companies engage in spoken and acted skits
and monologues with very little music, as in *Beyond the Fringe,*
or almost exclusively in song and dance, as in Julius Monk's
Plaza 9. The Living Premise opened as an improvisational revue,
acting out any topic suggested by a member of the audience,
and was soon joined by *The Premise* and *The Establishment.* The
improvisational aspects were soon eliminated, as it became apparent that the prepared material was far superior to the rather
amateurish efforts to comment on audience suggestions. *The Committee,* a San Francisco contribution to the theatre of topical
skits and an offshoot of *Second City,* still preserves the outward
facade of improvising for each audience, but it is a hollow pretense, for their best numbers are those with precise timing and
careful rehearsal. To be endlessly inventive requires far too much
mental agility and wit.

The movement is a healthy effort to clear the decks for
sanity, or at least to offer a fresh look at established institutions.
It is a return to theatre as education, to a form of intellectual
as well as emotional delight. To a great extent, it is a by-product

of the enormous influence of the theatre of Bertolt Brecht. The popularity of the movement in England and the rise of many talented young actors and writers brought "That Was the Week That Was" to television, where the program startled and amused a tolerant nation with its no-holds-barred news commentary, taking pot shots at the sanctity of Parliament, the Royal Family, the class system, the Common Market, and American foreign policy. "TW3," as it is commonly known, was imitated in the United States and presented on the NBC network, with David Frost, one of the originators of the British group, brought over to develop an American counterpart, but in the transplanting the wit lost its bite.

The theatre is most effective when fearless, and the ground is fertile for nourishing fearlessness when the playwright is free to express his vision. The effects of the McCarthy era have lain subtly on the American stage, creating a hidden atmosphere of fear, which has been too lightly dismissed as a passing aberration, yet which has remained to prevent the American playwright from being as outspoken as his British contemporary. Political satire may well be the opening break in restoring the fullness of the right to dissent and exposing the absurdity of our prejudices. Required, however, is the rarest of talents—wit—and too often these programs degenerate into adolescent pranks or sophomoric nose-thumbing.

Off-Broadway is the natural habitat for the coffeehouse revue. The intellectual climate is more friendly to the rebellion against false heroes. *The Establishment*, now ensconced at the Strollers Club in midtown Manhattan, offers literate satire and has become a pleasurable retreat from the lavish splendor of Shubert Alley a few doors away. The skits and songs are devastating when they lampoon personal, domestic, or business relations; naïve when they hit fundamental political and social forces.

Second City takes its name from A. J. Liebling's column about Chicago in *The New Yorker* magazine. This theatre of improvised buffoonery had its beginning at the Compass Tavern, near the University of Chicago, in 1955, where David Shepherd and Paul Sills organized the Cabaret Theatre. Much in the style of "That Was the Week That Was," this local group comments not only on the daily newspaper headlines but on neighborhood situations. It has its own theatre cabaret, maintains a permanent

company as well as a training school for actors, and has initiated
a children's theatre of improvisation. After a short run on Broadway in 1961, the New York troupe moved to Square East, a more
intimate and informal location in Greenwich Village, where such
actors as Severn Darden, Paul Dooley, and Barbara Harris became skillful executioners in their commentary on "the popular,
the immediate, the localized."

Open Season, the second edition of *Second City,* failed to
achieve the buoyancy of the first show. Topical references gave
way to standard routines. A weary long-haul truck-driver, trying
to keep awake, says, "My eyes are O.K. It's the lids that are
tired." A customer in a southern restaurant tells the waitress that
he would like a bowl of alphabet soup "without the O's. I can't
eat O's, they don't agree with me." This is ransacking the file
of old jokes in the manner of the comedians at whom *Second
City* is trying to poke fun.

The astute Julius Monk, a nightclub operator, took the
Greenwich Village intimate revue, adapted it for his own purposes, gave it distinction and elegance, and brought it to the
Hotel Plaza, where he offers what he himself terms "a post-
prandial prank." He has reduced the old-time revue to cleverness
rather than extravagance, and provides a superior evening of
political banter. The point of view is apparently impartial. No
one is exempt from the tongue-in-cheek hilarity. President Johnson, De Gaulle, Nelson Rockefeller, all come in for their share,
as do suburban living, Mary McCarthy, co-operative dwellings,
and Edward Albee.

Most political satires are, of necessity, liberal in their point
of view, but there is no implied advocacy of anything from which
an attack can gather momentum. The intimate revue has become
an island of presumed superiority looking askance at humanity
rather than working with it. Open season on everyone means
respect for no one. Lacking a point of view, these revues find
that the easy road is toward pornography. Lenny Bruce, a devastating commentator who draws blood, has attracted attention
and a jail sentence for his use of "obscenity." To Lenny, vulgarity
is part of his act, integrated with his comments; others, particularly the college-bred women performing the skits, sound like
maiden aunts trying with considerable trepidation to join the
longshoremen's set.

True satire is based on belief, preferably held in common by a willing audience, which delights in seeing the balloons of pretense punctured or the high and mighty leveled to the common plane. Bernard Hollowood, editor of *Punch*, put his finger on the weakness when he said that "TW3" really was a family fight—upper-class Cambridge kidding the Establishment—and taken without rancor by the old fogies in their clubs on Pall Mall, who say to one another, "Bit near the knuckle, what, that bit about the Queen falling into the river!" And add, "This stuff does take people's minds off the real issues, eh what!" In a healthy climate, the topical revue can well be a social safety valve.

The best of off-Broadway is a response to appetites that Broadway does not satisfy. Very likely, different criteria are needed, for the theatre should have a place where failure is possible, where an honest work is not judged by demands for perfection, where experiments in form and content can be tried, and where plays by Yeats and Lorca, as well as those by Genet and Beckett, can be seen.

15

TRENDS OF THE DECADE

We seem to feel, at bottom, that the truth about white and black men in America is so terrible that it cannot really be told. But the truth about the past is really all we have to guide us in the present.
                                                                JAMES BALDWIN

The modern world paradoxically tends to throw man back upon himself while at the same time it increasingly tends to destroy the individual sense of his own selfhood. This creates an impasse which the modern dramatist, for the most part, has been unable to overcome.
                                                                ROBERT W. CORRIGAN

We feel we have an absolute right to errors. No one is on trial. No one is in danger.   ELIA KAZAN

THE THEATRE, like the society which nourishes it, is constantly changing. The past decade has witnessed no violent breaks with traditional structure, but important developments have occurred in theatre organization, thematic materials, and dramatic techniques.

THE REPERTORY THEATRE

The most significant change is the rise of repertory theatres in different sections of the country. True repertory is not to be confused with permanent organizations which engage in new productions each year. Like its European model, repertory demands rotation of plays and retention of productions as part of the company's reserve. Alternating plays may appear to be an innocuous requirement, but it has far-reaching implications. For the actor, accustomed to the monotony of repeating a single role, it offers the challenge of variety and differing characterizations. For the theatre, it provides the chance to sustain an experimental, daring, or even nonpopular work. Failure can be absorbed, and the growth of a writer or director need not be judged by box-office receipts. A playwright can be encouraged to explore new avenues of expression.

Few actual repertory companies are in existence in the United States. Opera and Shakespeare festivals have, to varying degrees, followed a repertory system, but the success philosophy of Broadway, the either-or approach which determines status by overnight achievement, has resisted the development of permanent theatre institutions. The great theatres of the world, however, are repertory. These include the Old Vic and the Bristol rep in England, the Comédie Française and Roget Planchon's Regional Theatre in France, the Berliner Ensemble in Germany, and the Moscow Art Theatre in Russia.

The Lincoln Center Repertory Theatre is an effort to achieve a comparable theatre on American soil. Its initial season indicated the problems involved. It has been the most widely publicized, the most heavily subsidized, and the most severely criticized of any theatre. After years of patient preparation, fifty thousand subscribers were obtained, huge sums of money donated, a new theatre built, and a season launched in early 1964 with Arthur Miller's *After the Fall*, Eugene O'Neill's *Marco Millions*, and S. N. Behrman's *But for Whom Charlie*. (The plays are discussed in the chapters devoted to their respective authors. The significance of repertory and an evaluation of the initial season concern us here.)

The choice of three plays by American writers was a welcome tribute to our own achievements and a recognition of a deserved pride in the American theatre. O'Neill certainly merited a place. The cry was raised that *Marco Millions* is not representative of his work. No play really is, for he was constantly groping, changing, and striving in new directions. The earlier realistic plays had been revived and were unsuited to a huge, projecting platform stage. The later works and even the posthumous plays were well known and sought by other producers. *Marco Millions*, which had not been seen since its original production by the Theatre Guild, is an excellent vehicle for pageantry and scenic beauty, and has a theme of contemporary relevance. It presents O'Neill in a more buoyant and poetic mood and was well worth doing. José Quintero's direction, however, did not reveal the play's dynamic interrelationship of Western materialism and Oriental delicacy, but concentrated on the mechanics of staging.

But for Whom Charlie, a rather innocuous play, more appropriate for a proscenium stage, was poorly cast, and the company was unable to recreate the brittle style of a comedy of manners.

After the Fall, despite unfavorable reviews, drew the largest audiences; this play, in the spirit of repertory, will be retained for future seasons. Miller's continued association with the group is an act of faith and one worthy of commendation. A playwright as an active member of a repertory company is its greatest asset. No other repertory company in the United States has been able to attract new plays by established writers.

Miracles had been expected. Hopes had been so high and publicity so strenuous that the Lincoln Center was a vulnerable target for attack. Objections were raised that a subsidized theatre had done no better than Broadway producers, that the choice of plays was unworthy of an experimental approach, that the last-minute addition of stars was a submission to commercial values, and that the theatre was too much influenced by the forces it was created to combat. In violation of its aims, the Lincoln Center presented only the Miller play during the summer, after the subscription list had expired. Thus, in its first season, it became a repertory theatre with one play. Successful theatres bear the imprint of a strong personality with artistic conviction, a Jouvet, a Brecht, or a Stanislavski, but the Lincoln Center has made little effort to unearth one.

Our concern is not to defend or to justify, but to understand the difficulties and to answer unwarranted and unduly hostile criticisms. An effective ensemble and a distinctive style cannot be achieved instantaneously. It is a developing process that takes time, patience, and trial and error. Robert Whitehead and Elia Kazan, the original directors of the Lincoln Center were aware of errors committed. In a *New York Times* article on August 9, 1964, Kazan said, "Failure is part of process . . . but we've done it—started, that is." The Moscow Art Theatre almost did not survive its first two productions and was acclaimed only with Chekhov's *The Sea Gull*, which had proved unsuccessful in its world premiere at St. Petersburg.

The second season began in October, 1964, with an ill-advised production of *The Changeling* by Thomas Middleton and William Rowley. This post-Shakespearean drama of corruption and licentiousness proved to be beyond the capabilities of a youthful company with little sense of period or style. To compensate for the weaknesses of the cast, Elia Kazan flooded the stage with an excess of theatrical effects—detailed re-enactments of bloody murder, walking ghosts, and tests of chastity that left little to the imagination of the audience. The result, unintentionally, was a caricature of the play and did little to restore the prestige of the organization.

Arthur Miller's second play in two years, *Incident at Vichy*, followed *The Changeling* and did much to regain public support, but the production emphasized continuing misconceptions as to the nature of repertory. New actors were hired for this play —much in the manner of Broadway. The director, Harold Clurman, showed amazingly little knowledge of the resources offered him by an open thrust stage.

Debate as to whether the Lincoln Center has fulfilled the contract with the public is less pertinent than the importance of having an established company in the heart of New York. Such a development marks the first major break in recent years with Broadway's commercial orientation—not that Broadway is all business and repertory all art. Well-intentioned producers do offer unusual plays, and repertory, as shown, can be commercially minded, but the necessity of returning a profit on an investment has not provided the most favorable climate for creative theatre. The Lincoln Center, with a subscription audience and assured financial support, can be free of the "hit or flop" code of Broadway. Under such a system, long rehearsals and thorough preparation are possible. Actors are secure in long-term contractual commitments. The big gamble—of money, art, talent, and script—is eliminated in favor of planned growth and long-range multiple perspectives. A theatre with all its manifold activities is in the process of rooting itself as a permanent member of the community. Weaknesses are manifest, reorganization may be necessary, the present Broadway-oriented leadership may be changed, but the project is of such historic importance that it merits recommendations for improvement rather than demands for dissolution.

Of other repertory companies, the two which are on a comparable grandiose scale are those founded by Tyrone Guthrie—the Festival Theatre of Stratford, Ontario, and the Minneapolis Theatre, which bears his name. Mr. Guthrie, a Johnny Appleseed planting theatres all over the world, used his international prestige and amazing resourcefulness to set the theatres in motion, and then with characteristic restlessness moved on elsewhere. The Canadian theatre, since its opening in 1953 when Alec Guinness starred in the first production, *Richard III*, in an outdoor tent, has become one of the world's finest theatrical centers. Today, with two permanent buildings, numerous peripheral activities in music and art, as well as an associated acting school, the Festival is an example of the possible achievements of a sound repertory system. Originally planned as the American version of the Royal Shakespeare Company at Stratford-upon-Avon, the Canadian group has presented most of the canon and is now offering the history plays in chronological order, but under pressure to widen audience appeal and give actors greater variety of style, has added the works of other playwrights.

Tyrone Guthrie, in the second year of the theatre's existence, experimented with a production of Sophocles' *Oedipus Rex*, and Michael Langham, his successor as artistic director, roamed far afield in the romantic theatre to present *Cyrano de Bergerac* in a glamorous swashbuckling production. The two non-Shakespearean plays were the only ones carried over into successive seasons. In 1964, ambitious programming incorporated Gilbert and Sullivan's *Yeomen of the Guard*, directed by William Ball, and the first effort at opera, *Le Mariage de Figaro*, directed by Jean Gascon, both presented at the newly acquired and refurbished Avon Theatre. At the main Festival Theatre, *Richard II* and

King Lear were joined by Molière's *Le Bourgeois Gentilhomme* and Wycherly's bawdy Restoration comedy *The Country Wife.*

The abandonment of an exclusively Shakespearean repertoire may have been necessary, but is regrettable at a time when the company, having worked together for many years under intelligent leadership, gave every indication of mastering a style worthy of the plays. The peaceful industrial town in the low hills of Ontario has become famous because of Shakespeare, its streets have been renamed after Shakespearean characters, and people from all over the world have flocked to see superior productions of Shakespeare's plays. Now even the name of the organization has dropped the word "Shakespeare."

Lack of confidence in Shakespeare may presage a weakening of intent and a preference for the immediately spectacular. Shakespeare has always triumphed in the long run. He is worthy of persistent devotion. A great Shakespearean theatre will survive. Michael Langham contends that Shakespeare will remain as the hard core of the repertory, but he welcomes the opportunity to become a more comprehensive theatre, now that the season extends to eight months of the year. He would add plays by contemporary writers as well, although the only effort in that direction was not successful. *The Canvas Barricade*, a comedy by the Canadian playwright Donald Lamont Jack, was presented less for the play's merits than out of patriotic motives.

The theatre has been notable for not limiting itself to one mode of expression. *Cyrano de Bergerac*, both with Christopher Plummer and, later, John Colicos in the title role, was a tour de force of unexcelled beauty and resplendent staging. *Timon of Athens* was an experiment in updating the play to modern times. *The Comedy of Errors* was embroidered with dance and pantomime and comic burlesque in *commedia dell'arte* style. *King Lear* was played against a background of primitive simplicity, with leather costumes in changing earth colors, in an attempt at an austere intellectual approach in contrast to the wild barbaric emotionalism of the past. A high degree of ensemble work has been manifested. At times, overemphasis has been given to physical pomp and technical trickery at the expense of insight, but this is unavoidable on a stage which calls for grandeur.

The architecture of the Festival Theatre deserves special mention. Its stately proportions combine austerity with elegance and invoke a feeling of awe and reverence, a return to the theatre as temple with ritual and ceremony, without excluding flamboyance, frivolity, and exultation. The pillared, porticoed stage, designed by Tyrone Guthrie and Tanya Moisewitsch, has become a model for new theatres, including those in Chichester, Minneapolis, and New York. The large playing area, with exits and entrances in all directions, including downstage, is not well adapted to intimate dramas, yet Michael Langham, who has attained remarkable subtlety in handling space relationships on the multi-level platform, was able in *The Country Wife*, a drawing-room comedy, to combine intimacy and spectacle. Mistakes have been made, always the price of growth and activity, particularly in *Timon of Athens*, in which Alcibiades' followers were dressed as Castro guerrillas, adding little to meaning and concentrating attention on mechanical innovations, but in all deference to the Stratford Festival, it has regained for the theatre some of its historic glory.

The Minnesota Theatre Company has been far less impressive, although at the present writing only two seasons have been completed. Tyrone Guthrie selected the twin cities as the preferred location away from New York when local support, aided by a Ford Foundation grant, permitted construction of a new theatre and recruitment of a professional company. Difficulties of organization and the task of unifying different acting styles have retarded progress. *Hamlet* and *Henry V* had the usual Guthrie eccentricities of pomp and bustle, with emphasis on the staging. *Death of a Salesman* was a desultory revival, but offset by an excellent production of *The Three Sisters*. Douglas Campbell's *Saint Joan* in 1964 was less a virtuoso exhibition of a director's skill than a brilliant adherence to the central theme and dramatic power of Shaw's play.

The season has now been extended to almost the full year, student performances have been added, and association with the University of Minnesota solidified, and though it is too early to judge, the theatre gives every indication of becoming a significant addition to the country's theatres. Douglas Campbell, an actor and director of considerable talent and definite ideas, formerly with Tyrone Guthrie at Stratford, Ontario, has been named artistic director. He faces the task of going beyond commendable productions of well-established plays.

The most recent addition to repertory is the Seattle Center Playhouse, operating in a building left over from the 1962 World's Fair. Civic leaders raised the funds, aroused popular support, enlisted subscriptions, and invited Stuart Vaughan, formerly with the Phoenix Theatre and the New York Shakespeare Festival, to direct the organization. The first season included *King Lear*, Max Frisch's broad satire *The Firebugs*, Christopher Fry's *The Lady's Not for Burning*, Chekhov's *The Sea Gull*, Robert Ardrey's *Shadow of Heroes*, and Miller's *Death of a Salesman*. The company, rigorously selected, fully professional but with no name stars, will play a nine-month season, offering all the plays in rotation. The program, especially for a fledgling organization still to be tested, is overambitious and too eclectic, with obvious obeisance to what Stuart Vaughan calls "classic and near-classic" works. Few veteran organizations could cope with so strenuous a program, but the audiences are enthusiastic, the performers willing, and Vaughan optimistic that repertory, by taxing the maximum artistic resources of everyone, can exceed normal expectations.

In sharp contrast is the San Francisco Actors Workshop, which for more than ten years has played in lofts, reconditioned churches, or any available convenient home in an effort to root itself in the community. Jules Irving and Herbert Blau, its founders and directors, have refreshingly adhered to nonconventional patterns. Although they do present established works, they have assiduously sought new or unusual plays, preferably by lesser-known writers, which elicit commitment and preserve discovery. Harold Pinter's *Birthday Party* was given its first American production at the Workshop and ran for three years. Works of Bertolt Brecht and García Lorca, as well as Samuel Beckett, are frequently seen. Unlike the Living Theatre, the Actors Workshop has avoided the pitfalls of preciosity and cultism. A pioneering theatre, however, has difficulty in attracting mass audiences, though it develops a loyal and dedicated minority following. The Actors Workshop needs a permanent home, yet when Stanford University offered both directors a faculty appointment and a haven on the Palo Alto campus, they declined, preferring their independence and an uncertain future.

The Association for Producing Artists, a company of dedicated actors under the leadership of Ellis Rabb, has fought job insecurity by touring colleges and community theatres for several years. In addition to its engagement as the resident company at the University of Michigan, the APA will now have a New York base. It is the only truly repertory company now functioning. The first season at the Phoenix Theatre introduced competent revivals of Pirandello, Gorki, and Molière and of George M. Cohan's *The Tavern*, an old American favorite. New plays, mostly by European playwrights, may be incorporated into the repertory. Scheduled is Erwin Piscator's adaptation of *War and Peace*, which has been highly acclaimed in Berlin. The organization is smooth-working, performs ably, but is uninspired. It lacks the fire that a common awareness of making a unique contribution can supply.

The National Repertory Company, with Eva LeGallienne as its attraction and with the support of ANTA and the State Department, has performed a valuable service by touring every state of the Union with such plays as *The Sea Gull, The Crucible*, and Anouilh's *Ring Round the Moon*. Bringing professional productions to small communities and colleges is an essential element in the development of new audiences, but National Repertory, like the Association of Producing Artists, are conventional producers, not crusaders. Their concern has not been with achievement of style, but with employing actors in a worthy undertaking.

The repertory movement includes many of the Shakespeare festivals which dot the land every summer. Of considerable importance in the development of the American theatre are the New York Shakespeare Festival and the American Shakespeare Festival at Stratford, Connecticut. The New York achievement is the personal triumph of Joseph Papp, whose organizational genius and undaunted spirit have overcome the most formidable obstacles to establish a theatre in Central Park which does not charge admission. The activities have been broadened to include a mobile unit that tours depressed areas of the city; a semi-resident company also visits the city schools with an abbreviated version of a Shakespearean play. For the regular season, three plays run for one month each, with a different cast, eliminating repertory or ensemble work.

The quality of the productions has been uniformly high, despite the difficulties of voice projection in an outdoor arena, but Papp's contribution lies in different directions. Others fight the tyranny of the box office; he has eliminated it completely and made the theatre a community need. The city and private donors underwrite all expenses. He has proved that catering to so-called popular taste is a producer's fiction. The Delacorte Theatre in Central Park is crowded to capacity for every performance, even for Sophocles' *Electra*, the only non-Shakespearean play added to the program. People other than those able to afford excessive Broadway prices have been made part of the theatre.

The American Shakespeare Festival in Connecticut has likewise grown to more than a summer activity. The additional months have been added for student performances. An all-year-round academy provides continuous actor preparation and study. The theatre is similar to the one in Canada, using a permanent thrust stage and unit set with emphasis on props and costumes. The elaborately staged productions are occasionally brilliant. Morris Carnovsky's *King Lear* was a highlight of the most successful season, which also included a bubbling *Comedy of Errors* and a stirring *Henry V*. The company suffers from lack of an overall artistic policy. A long-range plan with full responsibility rested in a capable director could aid in realizing the enormous potential of a well-endowed and fully equipped organization.

DECENTRALIZATION

In addition to repertory companies, the present decade has seen the remarkable growth of resident professional companies away from New York. Broadway's anemia has induced vitality in widely dispersed sectional theatres. Outstanding are Houston's Alley Theatre, founded in 1947 by Nina Vance; the Arena Stage in Washington, D.C., ably guided by Zelda Fichandler; the reorganized Fred Miller Theatre in Milwaukee, now under the direction of John McQuiggan; the Memphis Front Street Theatre still operated by its founder, George Touliatos; the forward-looking Oklahoma City Mummers Theatre under Mack Scism; the Dallas Theatre Center with Paul Baker as its moving spirit; and the long-established Barter Theatre in Virginia with Robert Potterfield in charge. These communities need not depend solely on the visits of tired road companies packaged on Broadway, but can boast of high-level productions by an indigenous group.

Actors today are willing to accept lower salaries in exchange for continuous work and broader artistic opportunities. They no longer dread isolation in a decentralized theatre. Torn to bits and boiled in the cauldron of Broadway, the theatre springs full-blown in the provinces.

Four professional companies are now operating in connection with the theatre arts departments of universities. The Theatre Group at UCLA was initiated by the Hollywood producer, John Houseman, whose long association with the stage goes back to the Mercury Theatre in the thirties. The wealth of talent in the motion picture colony is available for productions. Princeton University's McCarter Theatre has a 25-member group offering a living library of well-known plays. The Tyrone Guthrie Minneapolis Theatre works in co-operation with the University of Minnesota, and the APA is in residence for twenty weeks at the University of Michigan.

What will eventually result from this declaration of independence from Broadway is uncertain. Communities which once resented association with art and preferred the free-enterprise methods of Broadway are frantically engaged in constructing multimillion-dollar cultural centers. Resistance to subsidy has vanished. The fight is no longer to initiate such theatres, but to insure their continuance. Survival depends on money and programming and the apparently indispensable ingredient of a strong-willed director with a sense of purpose, a personal style, and full responsibility.

The discovery of worthwhile new plays or the development of new techniques, the proudest boast of any theatre, has not been a frequent phenomenon. The new permanent theatres have up to now leaned too heavily on the tired and the outworn. The playwright still offers his work first to New York. The grass-roots theatre gets the rejects, a practice which results eventually in a reliance on Shaw and Shakespeare.

Great promise attends the formation of the American Playwrights Theatre, a joint enterprise of ANTA, the AETA, and Ohio State University. Conceived by Jerome Lawrence and Robert E. Lee, it aims "to get the theatre out of the capsule of Manhattan Island," and give the colleges an opportunity to produce an original play by a well-known writer. The plan calls for at least 100 college theatres to guarantee production and pay advance royalties equal to what an established playwright would earn in New York. *Banners of Steel* by Barrie Stavis and *Forest in the Night* by Arnold Sundgaard were chosen for the 1964–65 season by a committee made up of Alan Schneider, Harold Clurman, and John Gassner. Both playwrights will be available for consultation and will work in residence during rehearsals. Should the project prosper, it could well mean the next formidable challenge to Broadway's imperialism. The concept is not to supplant New York but to complement it. Successful plays could find their way to Times Square, but in the meantime the writer would have at least fifty workshops available and the college would see something beside carbon copies of Broadway shows.

University science departments vie for new research discoveries, but the humanities departments remain content with transmission of the past. Leaders at university theatres profess disdain for Broadway but slavishly adhere to its model. Moral prejudices, strong with college boards of trustees, enhance fear of the untried. It is doubtful if *A Streetcar Named Desire* would have been given its first performance on a college campus, but once acclaimed in New York, a play has the seal of approval. This colonial mentality will be eliminated when willingness to use the theatre as an expression of our age and a search for meaning replaces the compulsion to use it merely as a tame production center. Standards different from those of Broadway take time to develop. The American Playwrights Theatre, with its selections endorsed by professional men of high reputation, may be able to insure acceptance of new plays. The first step has been taken. The rest depends on the vision and courage of audiences everywhere.

NEW THEMES

A changing society provides the playwright with ever-new material. Old themes persist, but new ones arise. It was inevitable that the theatre would reflect the social tensions created by the struggle for civil rights. Repeatedly represented in the past as the faithful Uncle Tom, the minstrel blackface comedian, or the butt of racial jokes in the manner of Harrigan and Hoyt, the Negro is today accepted as worthy of dramatic stature.

Eugene O'Neill in 1919 wrote a one-act play, *The Dreamy Kid*, about a Negro gangster and his dying mother. The parts were played by Negro actors. *All God's Chillun* followed, with Paul Robeson playing the part of a Negro lawyer who marries a white girl. *The Emperor Jones* saw Charles Gilpin portraying a Negro caught in the lust for power, betrayed by atavistic superstition. Paul Green, a southerner, in 1926 won a Pulitzer Prize with *In Abraham's Bosom*, a story of a Negro's drive to educate himself. The thirties, more socially conscious, witnessed many working-class dramas, like *Stevedore* (1934) by Paul Peters and George Sklar, in which Negro and white join in open revolt against class tyranny. In the forties, Richard Wright's *Native Son*, adapted for the stage, depicted the fear and agony of Bigger Thomas, misfit and murderer. Lillian Smith's *Strange Fruit* (1945) and Maxine Wood's *On Whitman Avenue* dealt with Negro middle-class suffering. There were a host of others.

What is new in the plays of today is that they grow out of the Negro's demand for freedom now and the laws of the federal government giving him the legal right to assume it. Lorraine Hansberry's *A Raisin in the Sun* (1958), the Drama Critics' Award-winning play, set the tone for the treatment of the Negro as a human being faced with the same problems of survival as the white man, but with these problems intensified by the pressures of discrimination. With Sidney Poitier playing the rebellious son, the work attracted considerable attention. It is in the tradition of the realistic family drama of the thirties. (Odets wrote far more effectively about the Jewish middle class.) The power of Lorraine Hansberry's play lies in its subject matter; it is a social document aimed at "cracking the metaphor," as James Baldwin has said.

Ossie Davis, the actor, presented *Purlie Victorious* (1961), a broad and witty satire which ridiculed the white man's stereotypes, humbly accepted by the fearful few and scorned by the Negro majority. The clever melodrama piled together all the clichés of history. *Fly Blackbird* (1962), the James Hatch–C. Jackson musical, mocked in song and dance the popular notion of gradual integration. But the decisive change occurred in the 1963–64 season—thirteen plays dealing with race problems were presented, most of them written by Negro playwrights. They ranged from gospel-singing exhortations to James Baldwin's fiery denunciation in *Blues for Mr. Charlie.*

Ballad for Bimshire was Loften Mitchell's sentimental book set to Irving Burgie's music, with the Bahamas as background. *Trumpets of the Lord* was an adaptation of James Weldon Johnson's *God's Trombones* (called "sermons in verse"). *Jerico-Jim Crow*, rich with the poetry of Langston Hughes, was put on for special performances in a small church in Greenwich Village, a stirring choral evocation of the Negro rise from slavery. From South Africa came Alan Paton's imperfect but deeply moving *Sponono*, set in a reform school for delinquents. It is filled with new rhythms and haunting chants.

First plays by Negro writers indicate a literary awakening and a source of untapped talent. Edward Albee, a co-producer of Theatre 64, sponsored *Funnyhouse of a Negro* by Adrienne Kennedy, a long one-act play of the hallucinations that torment a Negro girl who resents the burden of being black and is too proud to accept the token comforts offered grudgingly by a white world. As she lies in bed in a rented room, the figments of her imagination, varying specters of her own self, come to life to haunt her final moments. Her light-skinned mother becomes Queen Victoria and the Duchess of Hapsburg in a series of animated obsessions that include Jesus and Patrice Lumumba. Less a play than a visualized nightmare, *Funnyhouse of a Negro* portrays honestly the girl's longing to be white, carried to self-destruction.

The well-received one-act play *Dutchman*, by LeRoi Jones, poet and novelist, was also presented by Theatre 64. A well-dressed Negro intellectual is accosted by a white girl on a subway train. When her advances are politely rejected, she lashes out in fury at the Negro's pretense. "What right have you to wear a tie and a neatly buttoned suit? Your grandfather was a slave." When he can take no more, the young man flails back at her with a scathing verbal attack. The girl takes out a switchblade and kills him. As his body is removed, she advances to another Negro who has just entered the subway train. LeRoi Jones writes with powerful imagery and savage intensity, but the play is weakened by faulty structure. The first half is a long speech by the white girl, the second a long reply by the Negro, like a neatly divided debate. Long-winded speeches and searing metaphors are not theatre. The play is an apostrophe to hate, reviling those who pretend friendship only to serve as executioner, and castigating the white for dragging the Negro down to the animal level, but LeRoi Jones's personal catharsis lacks dramatic form.

Blues for Mr. Charlie, James Baldwin's first play, was presented by the Actors Studio. It burns with a white heat, rising to uncontrollable fury, the language fierce and penetrating. Like *The Deputy* by Rolf Hochhuth, presented earlier in the season, which condemned the Pope for failure to speak out against Hitler's extermination of the Jews, this is a crudely fashioned play that cries aloud to the conscience of man. The plot is concerned with the conventional murder of a young Negro who returns to his home in the South, and the acquittal of the white man whose guilt is obvious. Baldwin uses a series of vignettes moving back and forth in time. When scenes with white folks are enacted downstage, the black folk are huddled in the background. When the Negroes act out their scenes, the whites form ominous tableaux on varying levels. The two groups represent Whitetown and Blacktown in Plaguetown, U.S.A., where "the plague is race, the plague is our concept of Christianity." The Negroes are alive, filled with congealed hate; the whites are cardboard stereotypes, including Parnell, the friend of the Negroes, who betrays them at the moment of decision. The play is memorable for its unrelieved passion, but is weakened by the repeated hammer blows that pound out the same theme—that the white man cannot be free as long as his black brother is in chains. Baldwin assumes the role of Christian prophet, drawing the limit beyond which submission will not go and shouting aloud the shame of our "spiritual darkness." Message dominates art. One scene approached magnificence. Juanita (played by Diana Sands) stands alone, the spotlight focused on her, silhouettes of the members of the court behind her, as she relives the moments spent with her murdered lover. From hushed whispers and brooding fear, she rises to exultation as she cries aloud to be pregnant, to be able to carry within her a life that can grow to the fullness of a man.

Only the Negro can give expression to the search and the agonized life of a stranger in a white man's world. The material is new, but it has to be fashioned into dramatic power. The human and social implications, however, belong to the white writer as well. *Blood Knot* (1964), written by Atholl Fugard, a white author from South Africa, depicts the suspicion, tenderness, and violence that separate two brothers, one white, the other black. The historical excerpts that make up Martin Duberman's *In White America* show, more startlingly than fiction, the humiliation and indignity visited upon the Negro.

The Negro actor is in greater demand. Frederic O'Neal, a Negro, has been elected president of Actors Equity. Sidney Poitier, Harry Belafonte, and Sammy Davis, Jr., have become national celebrities. The problem, however, is not the use of the Negro where he logically fits into a role, but the use of fully integrated casts. Joseph Papp of the New York Shakespeare Festival has pioneered in casting Negroes without regard to their color. Musical plays today have mixed dance and chorus lines. There is no doubt that once economic and social equality have been achieved, once mental blocks have been removed, audiences will accept the absence of discrimination in casting.

Indiscriminate integration, however, runs full tilt against the requirements of meaning and history. *Dutchman* can be performed only by a white girl and a Negro man, whereas Genet's *The Blacks* is designed for an all-Negro cast. In *The Ballad of the Sad Cafe*, Albee used Roscoe Lee Browne, a Negro, as narrator in a play that deals with whites in a southern community, and introduced overtones of race relations foreign to the essence of the conflict.

The few opportunities for Negro actors are sometimes offset by revising plays to conform to the present social tensions. The theme of *Home of the Brave* was transformed from prejudice against the Jew to prejudice against the Negro. Clifford Odets' *Golden Boy* became a musical with Sammy Davis, Jr., playing the part originally created by John Garfield.

Despite many efforts, no writer has yet caught on stage the drama and majesty of a revolution in human relations. Most such plays, like *Blues for Mr. Charlie*, have been polemics rather than drama, expressions of hate and channels for emotional release. They have been unduly praised and given credit for dramatic power they did not possess. Audiences, anxious to applaud, brought to the theatre the drama of the day's headlines.

The old fight with Mrs. Grundy and Puritanism has also undergone qualitative change in the present decade. Language taboos are gone and four-letter words freely used. Richness of imagery and subtle suggestions have given way to abusiveness and vulgarity. At the end of the last century, Alfred Jarry's *Ubu Roi*, that wild fantasy of cruelty and corruption, opened the gates to a complete breakdown of language restrictions. Many young American writers exploit this freedom to shock rather than communicate. The motion picture of Jack Gelber's *The Connection* won a court fight permitting language that only a few years ago was unthinkable on the screen.

Sex, too, has come in for fewer restrictions. From Aristophanes to Anouilh, the theatre has not shied away from frank revelation of sexual adventure, but not until the present decade has adultery been considered therapeutic. With *Any Wednesday*, the mistress became tax-deductible. Adultery committed in the presence of the husband, and with his open connivance, is used as a weapon for psychological destruction in *Who's Afraid of Virginia Woolf?* In *Silent Night, Lonely Night*, a man and woman fence all evening before eventual capitulation, which will return them more safely to their respective mates. *The Heroine* has a wife employ an attractive young girl to seduce her husband in order to restore his confidence. In 1930, John Dos Passos was exultant that

> the good old days when a man could get sexually excited at the sight of a woman's ankle and a girl would faint if handed a pair of suspenders [were] gone never to return.

What a far cry from the situation today.

Significant, too, is the drastic change in the image of woman on stage. In the past, she was identified with purity, devotion, and sacrifice for her loved ones. As the giver of life, she was the symbol of the home, motherhood, and the continuity of the race. Today, in the few memorable female characters created by contemporary American playwrights, woman is pictured as self-seeking, possessive, domineering, the destroyer of man, and—in extreme cases—the incarnation of evil. Mom in Edward Albee's *The American Dream*, and Madam Rosepettle in *Oh, Dad, Poor Dad* are examples. In popular comedies and musical plays, innocence and love still triumph. In *Dear Me, the Sky Is Falling,*

Gertrude Berg, as the mother, wins out even over the psychiatrist, and in *Hello, Dolly!* Mrs. Levy gets the curmudgeon from Yonkers. The change dates back to Ibsen's Nora, who left her children and family for the unprecedented challenge of finding out who she was. In Arthur Miller's *After the Fall*, Louise, the first wife, follows her psychiatrist's advice on the path to self-discovery.

Strindberg had depicted marriage as a savage battle of the sexes. Martha and George in *Who's Afraid of Virginia Woolf?* are far more coldly calculating and totally devastating. In *Epiphany* by Carlino, man becomes a hen and lays an egg in the lap of his domineering wife. Many explanations—economic, psychological, social—have been offered for the emphasis on impotence and sterility, but the basic cause is philosophical. When the touch of a switch can destroy all civilization, when automation replaces man, when the individual self is lost in contemplation of the computer age, when language no longer communicates, new symbols arise to express the emptiness of the future. Woman, the giver of life, takes on the brunt of new symbols for non-life.

There are healthy indications today of a return to an affirmation of life and to the search for positive belief. Total negativism may have run its course. Works by Sartre, Brecht, *A Man for All Seasons*, *The Deputy*, are evidences of a return to the dignity of man and a reaching beyond personal despair. In the United States, the writer has feared social commitment. The civil rights movement may now have marked the turn. Young people are no longer a generation without a cause. *Blues for Mr. Charlie* is a plea for recognition of guilt, which can clear away the obstacles to the fraternity of man. *After the Fall* is a re-evaluation and a rejection of past claims to "a better way of life," but also an honest pursuit of new values and a discovery of hope in the willingness to begin anew. Lorraine Hansberry's eagerly awaited second play, *The Sign in Sidney Brustein's Window*, is an acid comment on intellectual pretense and a call for renewed faith in the idealist.

NEW FORMS

The one-act play has had a remarkable revival. The theatre of the absurd turned naturally to the form, for it lends itself to the development of a single conceit, as evidenced in the work of Ionesco, Beckett, and Pinter. Many younger writers first achieved recognition through one-act plays, which are easier to produce and are often combined on the same bill with works of more established writers. Broadway, traditionally hostile to one-act plays, discovered a hit with Peter Shaffer's beautifully written and highly ingenious *Private Ear* and *Public Eye*.

Plays with two or three characters have been much in evidence—more for financial reasons than aesthetic ones—not only in the one-act play but in the full-length form as well. *Kataki* by Shimon Wincelberg deals with an American and a Japanese soldier on an island in the Pacific; one character speaks no English and can only gesture. The size of the cast does not determine the merit of a play, but most few-character plays are limited to the repeated theme of non-communication, which has long since grown threadbare.

A more meaningful variation in form has been the dramatic anthology, or compilation of excerpts. *Brecht on Brecht*, a composite of scenes, sayings, and poems by the German playwright, led the way. Success with this device depends on the importance of what is said and on the director's ingenuity in building pace, rhythm, and power. Group readings, too, often are a substitute for doing a play. Lewis John Carlino's *Telemachus Clay*, a "collage for voices," was an exception. The concert reading conveyed the full scope of the text and challenged the imagination of the audience. *Spoon River*, a dramatization of the poems of Edgar Lee Masters, carefully prepared and brilliantly executed under the direction of Charles Aidman, was an outstanding contribution. Four actors play all the roles, with two folk singers for background music. As each in turn acts out a separate epitaph, an entire village comes to life. Characters rise from the graveyard to talk about themselves and their neighbors. The village becomes all of America and the people we know, as for a brief moment each has his say.

The dramatic anthology has employed historical vignettes also. Helen Hayes toured in A. E. Hotchner's *The White House*, a succession of scenes about Presidents and their first ladies, but the honors go to an off-Broadway triumph, *In White America*, by Martin B. Duberman of Princeton University. Duberman arranged historical documents in chronological order to depict the

Negro in America from the advent of slavery to the present day. A cast of six, three Negro and three white, read and perform on a bare stage. The material is authentic and startling, such as the lines from the diary of a doctor on a slave ship in 1738:

> The confined air soon produces fever and fluxes which carry off great numbers of them. The floor of their rooms can be so covered with blood and mucus in consequence of the flux that it resembles a slaughter house . . .

The program wisely indicated that, terrifying as the problem is, man does achieve progress.

These various non-plays have provided variety and the opportunity for experiments in staging. They are significant because they demonstrate the power of the theatre as education. But they are also indicative of the scarcity of good plays. The failure to develop original work is further evidenced by the excessive number of adaptations. Most such efforts do not succeed, for art forms have a habit of resisting conversion. Almost all of Henry James has been transferred to the theatre, but he still remains more convincing as a novelist. The Russians have done the same with Dostoyevsky, but the interior action and inner psychological struggles are lost in the process. Ruth and Augustus Goetz, professional adapters, turned from Henry James's *The Heiress* to André Gide's *The Immoralist*, and eliminated the core of the novel, the struggle between the flesh and the mind, transforming it into a study of homosexuality. Novels that are frankly melodramatic are more likely to survive adaptation, for the emphasis is on action, as in Joseph Hayes's *The Desperate Hours;* or those which have an outlandish character who can be utilized, as in *Auntie Mame*, which Lawrence and Lee rearranged from the novel by Patrick Dennis. Inner thoughts, moods, secret longings, are more difficult to dramatize. Millard Lampell's *The Wall* could not evoke the brooding prison of the Warsaw ghetto in John Hersey's novel. *Look Homeward, Angel* presented an impossible task for Ketti Frings, with the result that Thomas Woolf's personal story become that of the mother. Ken Kesey's novel of absolute conformity in a mad world became a case study in a mental institution in Dale Wasserman's adaptation, *One Flew Over the Cuckoo's Nest.*

More than a third of the new offerings in New York in 1963 were adaptations from other media or other playwrights. Sidney Michaels translated freely Billetdoux's *Tchin-Tchin* and was hailed as the author of a new play. Maurice Valency and Gore Vidal have both recarpentered works of Duerrenmatt and taken major credit for authorship. *The Visit* was softened for American audiences, and *Romulus the Great* was given a few current American wisecracks. Shakespeare and Brecht plagiarized unashamedly, but they imposed the stamp of their genius on the source material.

Finally, in recent years, there has been a decided movement away from the proscenium theatre and a preference for the thrust stage. Removal of the fourth wall and peephole observation have given way to a more theatrical theatre and, paradoxically, a closer relation with audiences. Clifford Odets, once a champion of naturalistic staging, said, "When you have a community of values in the theatre the proscenium arch disappears." The open stage may, to some extent, be responsible for the diminution of faith in "method" acting. The actor's "inner truth" has been overshadowed by a concern for social truth and fuller awareness of the theatre as an art which is not a substitute for life, but another form that life assumes.

REFERENCES

The sources of most quotations are given in the text. The following is a list of references which have not been specifically indicated:

p. 11   The opening quote by Arthur Miller is from "International Message," *World Premières Mondiales*, No. 34, March, 1963.

p. 12, l. 31   Arnold Toynbee, "One World or None," *The New York Times Magazine*, April 5, 1964.

pp. 15, 16   The opening quotation about "Mystery" and the one on p. 16, (l. 5) about "transfigured modern values" are from O'Neill's letter to A. H. Quinn. See Quinn's *A History of the American Drama* (London: Pitman and Sons Ltd., 1937).

p. 17, l. 32   John Gassner, *The Theatre in Our Times* (New York: Crown Publishers, Inc., 1954).

p. 18, l. 26   From a letter to George Jean Nathan, quoted in Joseph Krutch's introduction to *Nine Plays* by Eugene O'Neill (New York: Random House, Inc., 1932).

p. 36, l. 12   "The Salesman Has a Birthday," *The New York Times*, February 5, 1950.

p. 37, l. 31   Foreword to *After the Fall* by Arthur Miller, *Saturday Evening Post*, February 10, 1964.

p. 38, l. 15   Arthur Miller, *Show: Magazine of the Arts*, January, 1964.

p. 41, l. 37   Harold Clurman, "Arthur Miller: Theme and Variations," *Playbill*, March, 1964.

p. 42, l. 28   Michael Smith, in *The Village Voice*, January 30, 1964.

p. 46, l. 1   Arthur Miller, "The Playwright and the Atomic World," *Tulane Drama Review,* June, 1961.

p. 46, l. 26   This and the following quotations are from the author's introduction to *Arthur Miller's Collected Plays* (New York: The Viking Press, Inc., 1957).

p. 54, l. 1   This quotation is from "Prelude to Comedy" by Tennessee Williams, *The New York Times,* November 6, 1960, as is that in l. 22, this page.

p. 54, l. 14   "Cried the Fox," from Tennessee Williams, *Collected Poems* (New York: New Directions, 1963).

p. 57, l. 6   *Esquire,* December, 1960.

p. 67, l. 18   From *The New York Times,* November 6, 1961, as are the quotations on p. 68 and p. 75.

p. 77, l. 14   John Gassner, *Best American Plays: Fifth Series* (New York: Crown Publishers, Inc., 1963).

p. 78, l. 23   Preface to William Saroyan, *Three Plays* (New York: Harcourt, Brace and Company, 1939).

p. 86, l. 7   This and the following quotation are from Edward Albee's preface to *The American Dream* (New York: Coward McCann, Inc., 1960).

p. 94, l. 16   *The Village Voice,* July 11, 1963.

p. 101, l. 14   Lillian Hellman's preface to *Six Plays* (New York: Modern Library, Inc., 1960).

p. 112, l. 36   "Odets at Center Stage," *Theatre Arts,* No. 5 (1963).

p. 131, l. 18   New York *Herald Tribune,* March 5, 1964.

p. 133, l. 19   *The New York Times,* March 8, 1964.

p. 136, l. 37   *The New York Times,* November 23, 1958.

p. 147, l. 23   *Saturday Review,* February 22, 1964.

p. 159, l. 22   *Theatre Arts,* January, 1962.

p. 164   The opening quote is from an interview with Ronald Alexander in *The New York Times,* March 15, 1964. The second quote, by Kenneth Tynan, is from *The New York Times Magazine,* December 1, 1963.

p. 172, l. 5   *The New York Times,* August 8, 1963.

p. 179, l. 40   *The New York Times,* December 8, 1963.

p. 187, l. 10   *The New York Times Book Review,* May 31, 1964.

p. 189, l. 6   *The New York Times,* March 15, 1964.

p. 196, l. 12   R. G. Collingwood is quoted by Harold Taylor in "Education by Theatre," *Educational Theatre Journal,* December, 1963.

p. 196, l. 19   *The New York Times Book Review,* January 14, 1962.

p. 213, l. 12   Alan Jay Lerner, *The New York Times,* August 25, 1963.

p. 214, l. 5   Gian-Carlo Menotti quotations are from *The New York Times,* January 19, 1964.

p. 221, l. 15   For this comment and comments by other composers, see "The American Theatre '64," *Saturday Review,* February 22, 1964.

p. 227   The opening comment by Eva LeGalliene is quoted in *The Off-Broadway Theatre* by Julia S. Price (New York: Scarecrow Press, Inc., 1962).

p. 236, l. 1   Price, *op cit.*

p. 239, l. 8   *The New York Times Magazine,* January 26, 1964.

p. 240   The comment by Robert W. Corrigan is from the introduction to *The New Theatre of Europe* (New York: Dell Publishing Co., Inc., 1962). Elia Kazan's statement is quoted in *Time,* February 14, 1964.

p. 256, l. 25   John Dos Passos, introduction to *Three Plays* (New York: Harcourt, Brace and Company, 1934).

INDEX